Microsoft®

Outlook®

Version 2002 Microsoft Office XP Application

Microsoft

Sambamurthy
19745 Northampton Dr.
Saratoga, CA 95070

plain & simple

Your fast-answers, no-jargon
guide to Outlook 2002!

Jim Boyce

PUBLISHED BY
Microsoft Press
A Division of Microsoft Corporation
One Microsoft Way
Redmond, Washington 98052-6399

Library of Congress Cataloging-in-Publication Data
Boyce, Jim, 1958–
  Microsoft Outlook Version 2002 Plain & Simple / Jim Boyce.
    p. cm.
  Includes index.
  ISBN 0-7356-1452-0
  1. Microsoft Outlook.   2. Business--Computer programs.   3. Time management--Computer programs.   4. Personal information
management--Computer programs.   I. Title.

HF5548.4.M5255 B693 2001
005.369--dc21   2001044259

Printed and bound in the United States of America.

1 2 3 4 5 6 7 8 9   QWT   6 5 4 3 2 1

Distributed in Canada by Penguin Books Canada Limited.

A CIP catalogue record for this book is available from the British Library.

Microsoft Press books are available through booksellers and distributors worldwide. For further information about international editions, contact your local Microsoft Corporation office or contact Microsoft Press International directly at fax (425) 706-7329. Visit our Web site at www.microsoft.com/mspress. Send comments to *mspinput@microsoft.com*.

Acquisitions Editor: Kong Cheung
Project Editor: Mark Diller
Technical Editor: David Robinson

Body Part No. X08-24316

Contents

4 Receiving and Reading E-Mail — 47

5 Using Instant Messaging — 69

6 Browsing Newsgroups — 83

13 Managing Your Outlook Files 205

14 Customizing Outlook 219

15 Using Office Tools with Outlook 235

i Index 247

Acknowledgments

I want to thank the people at Microsoft Press for another opportunity to work with a terrific acquisitions and editorial team. First, thanks go to Kong Cheung, acquisitions editor, for bringing the project to me. Thanks also go to David Fugate, my agent at Waterside Productions, for talking me into taking on the project instead of going on vacation!

Special thanks go to Mark Diller, the project editor, for fine-tuning the content and improving the finished product. I also offer my thanks to David Robinson for his meticulous technical editing, Becky Wendling and Holly Viola for their careful proofreading and copyediting, and Katherine Erickson, Carl Diltz, and Joel Panchot for laying out the book and tackling the formidable task of making so many graphics and labels work so well together. I would also like to thank Kari Kells for developing the index.

Last, but not least, big thanks go to Rob Tidrow for taking on a large portion of the book so we could reach our deadlines. Rob did his usual fine job of authoring and matching the voice and style needed.

About This Book

If you want to get the most from your computer and your software with the least amount of time and effort—and who doesn't?—this book is for you. You'll find *Microsoft Outlook Version 2002 Plain & Simple* to be a straightforward, easy-to-read reference tool. With the premise that your computer should work for you, not you for it, this book's purpose is to help you get your work done quickly and efficiently so that you can get away from the computer and live your life.

No Computerese!

Let's face it—when there's a task you don't know how to do but need to get done in a hurry, or when you're stuck in the middle of a task and can't figure out what to do next, there's nothing more frustrating than having to read page after page of technical background material. You want the information you need—nothing more, nothing less—and you want it now! *And* it should be easy to find and understand.

That's what this book is all about. It's written in plain English—no technical jargon and no computerese. There's no single task in the book that takes more than two pages. Just look the task up in the index or the table of contents, turn to the page, and there's the information you need, laid out in an illustrated step-by-step format. You don't get bogged down by the whys and wherefores: just follow the steps and get your work done with a minimum of hassle.

Occasionally you might have to turn to another page if the procedure you're working on is accompanied by a "See Also." That's because there's a lot of overlap among tasks, and we didn't want to keep repeating ourselves. We've scattered some useful Tips here and there, and thrown in a "Try This" or a "Caution" once in a while, but by and large we've tried to remain true to the heart and soul of the book, which is that the information you need should be available to you at a glance.

Useful Tasks...

Whether you use Outlook at home or on the road, we've tried to pack this book with procedures for everything we could think of that you might want to do, from the simplest tasks to some of the more esoteric ones.

...And the Easiest Way to Do Them

Another thing we've tried to do in this book is find and document the easiest way to accomplish a task. Outlook often provides a multitude of methods to accomplish a single end result—which can be daunting or delightful, depending on the way you like to work. If you tend to stick with one favorite and familiar approach, we think the methods described in this book are the way to go. If you like trying out alternative techniques, go ahead! The intuitiveness of Outlook invites exploration, and you're likely to discover ways of doing things that you think are easier or that you like better than ours. If you do, that's great! It's exactly what the developers of Outlook had in mind when they provided so many alternatives.

A Quick Overview

Your computer probably came with Outlook preinstalled, but if you do have to install it yourself, the Setup Wizard makes installation so simple that you won't need our help anyway. So, unlike many computer books, this one doesn't start with installation instructions and a list of system requirements.

Next you don't have to read this book in any particular order. It's designed so that you can jump in, get the information you need, and then close the book and keep it near your computer until the next time you need to know how to get something done. But that doesn't mean we scattered the information about with wild abandon. We've organized the book so that the tasks you want to accomplish are arranged in two levels—you'll find the overall type of task you're looking for under a main section title such as "Working with Distribution Lists," "Setting Up E-mail Accounts," "Communicating with Contacts," and so on. Then, in each of those sections, the smaller tasks are arranged in a loose progression from the simplest to the more complex.

Section 2 introduces Outlook, explaining how to start and exit the program, work with the Outlook program window, and use Outlook's standard set of folders. You'll also learn how to set up e-mail accounts, import data into Outlook from other programs, and work with items such as e-mail messages, contacts, and appointments. Information about how to get help and troubleshoot problems rounds out the section.

Sections 3 and 4 explain how to work with e-mail messages in Outlook, including addressing messages, using the address book, and working with distribution lists. The section also teaches you how to change and format message text to add emphasis or highlight information. You'll also learn how to add stationery to messages to give them a custom look. Section 3 finishes with a look at how to send files with messages, review messages you've already sent, and keep messages in the Drafts folder until you're ready to send them. Section 4 covers several topics about receiving and reading e-mail and will help you manage, filter, and follow up on messages.

In Section 5 you'll learn about the Instant Messenger program included with Outlook that lets you chat in real time with others across the Internet. You'll learn how to turn on Instant Messaging, find your friends and family on line, and send and receive messages.

Section 6 will get you started using Internet newsgroups—public servers on the Internet that host electronic message boards that allow you to communicate and share files with others around the world. The section explains how to use Outlook Express—a program separate from Outlook—to add a newsgroup account, view messages, and post your own messages.

Keeping track of your contacts' addresses, phone numbers, and other information is one of the main uses for Outlook, and Section 7 brings you up to speed on using the Contacts folder. You'll learn how to add new contacts, view and change contacts, and find a particular person. The section also explains how to organize contacts, schedule meetings for a contact, and communicate with people through the Contacts folder. The section rounds out with a look at how to share contacts with others, keep track of phone calls, and associate contacts with items such as tasks.

Section 8 covers the Calendar folder and how to view your schedule, add appointments and meetings, associate files or other items with schedule items, and work with reminders. You'll also learn how to share your calendar, print calendars, and use the Task Pad to keep track of your tasks without leaving the Calendar folder.

Section 9 expands on Section 8's coverage of tasks and explains how to use the Tasks folder. You can assign tasks to yourself or to others, associate contacts and other items with tasks, and mark tasks as complete.

Section 10 covers the Notes folder, which you can use to create electronic notes to replace those sticky notes littering your monitor and desk. The section explains how to create and edit notes, customize notes and the Notes folder, share notes with others, and print and copy notes.

Section 11 takes a look at ways you can manage your items in Outlook. The section explains how to assign categories to items, use folders to organize your information, delete items, and clean up folders. The section finishes with a look at how to keep and view a journal, which lets you keep track of phone calls, the time you spent on documents, and other information.

You're not limited to working only with Outlook items in Outlook, and Section 12 explains how to open drives and folders in Outlook, manage existing files, and create new folders and files. Section 13 will help you perform similar tasks with your Outlook folders, creating new data files, importing and exporting items in Outlook, and backing up and restoring your Outlook data file. You'll also learn how to use Outlook when you're not connected to your e-mail server, how to archive old items, and how to use the more common of Outlook's security features.

Outlook offers a wealth of options you can use to change the way the program looks and works, and Section 14 will show you how to set options for each of the Outlook folders and item types. The section also explains how to customize the Outlook Bar, toolbars, and menus.

After you're comfortable using Outlook, turn to Section 15 to learn how to use the most common Office tools with Outlook. You can check your spelling, customize how the spelling checker works, copy and cut data between Outlook and other Office programs, and use alternate input such as speech recognition and handwriting recognition.

A Few Assumptions

We had to make a few educated guesses about you, our audience, when we started writing this book. Perhaps your computer is solely for personal use—e-mail, surfing the Internet, playing games, and so on. Perhaps your work allows you to telecommute. Or maybe you run a small home-based business. Taking all these possibilities into account, we assumed that you'd either be using a stand-alone home computer or that you'd have two or more computers connected so that you could share files, a printer, and so on. We also assumed that you'd have an Internet connection.

Another assumption we made is that—initially, anyway—you'd use Outlook just as it came, meaning that you'd use the standard views and standard menus rather than custom ones, and that you'd use your little friend the mouse in the traditional way: that is, point and click to select an item, and then double-click to open it. If you'd prefer using the mouse as if you were working on a Web page—pointing to an item to select it and then opening it with a single click—you can easily do so. To switch between single-click and double-click, open My Computer and choose Options from the Tools menu. Use the Click Items As Follows controls to choose the method you prefer. However, because our working style is somewhat traditional, and because Outlook is set up to work in the traditional style, that's what we've described in the procedures and graphics throughout this book.

A Final Word (or Two)

We had three goals in writing this book:

- Whatever you want to do, we want the book to help you get it done.

- We want the book to help you discover how to do things you *didn't* know you wanted to do.

- And, finally, if we've achieved the first two goals, we'll be well on the way to the third, which is for our book to help you *enjoy* using Outlook. We think that's the best gift we could give you to thank you for buying our book.

We hope you'll have as much fun using *Microsoft Outlook Version 2002 Plain & Simple* as we've had writing it. The best way to learn is by *doing,* and that's how we hope you'll use this book. Jump right in!

2 Getting Started

Microsoft Outlook is designed to help you manage almost every aspect of your day. With it you can send and receive e-mail messages, chat with others using instant messaging, and manage your schedule, complete with reminders to keep you on track and on time. Outlook also lets you store and search addresses, phone numbers, and other contact information through its Contacts folder. You can create tasks for yourself or assign them to others, using Outlook to organize those tasks electronically. You can also keep notes with Outlook, eliminating the need to keep sticky notes on your monitor or scraps of paper littering your desk. The Journal lets you keep track of phone calls, time spent on documents, and other tasks and events.

Even with all of the features it contains, Outlook is easy to use. The program provides simple forms for creating and viewing messages, meetings, tasks, and other items. You have several options for viewing your information in Outlook, and the program offers the ability to customize the existing views and create new ones to give you exactly the view of your data that you need. With this book in hand, you'll be up to speed with Outlook in just a few hours.

This section of the book offers a quick overview of Outlook and how to start using it. You'll learn how to open Outlook and how to move through the various folders it uses to store your data. You'll also learn how to work with Outlook items (such as messages, meetings, and contacts), import e-mail accounts and messages from other programs, and get help when you need more information on a particular feature or task.

Outlook 2002 at a Glance

Although Outlook is easy to use, the Outlook program window can seem overwhelming to new users because it contains so much information. Once you understand how Outlook organizes and presents that information, however, you'll have no trouble moving from folder to folder to view and manage your information. The main program window organizes all of your Outlook folders for easy access, and individual windows help you work with the different types of Outlook item.

Overview of Outlook Program Window

Outlook provides several folders and ways to view the contents of those folders. The default view is the Outlook Today view, which combines several types of data in one view.

Select commands from the menu bar.

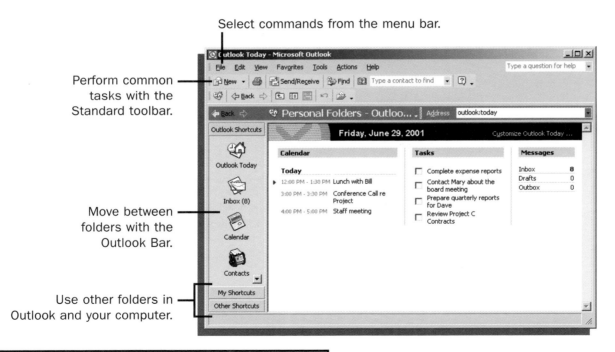

Perform common tasks with the Standard toolbar.

Move between folders with the Outlook Bar.

Use other folders in Outlook and your computer.

> **TIP:** If you need more space to display your schedule or other data, you can turn off the Outlook Bar and use the Personal Folder's drop-down list to select the folder you need to use.

> **SEE ALSO:** Outlook Today is Outlook's default view, but you can choose a different view as your default view. See "Set the Startup View" on page 19 for details.

Overview of an Outlook Item Window

Each Outlook folder uses a different type of form to let you view, create, and work with items. Simply double-click an item to open its form, or click the small arrow beside the New command on the Standard toolbar and choose the type of item you want to create.

SEE ALSO: For information on customizing the Outlook Bar to add or remove icons, see "Customizing the Outlook Bar" on page 230.

Click the arrow beside the New button to select the type of item you want to create.

Double-click an item to open the item for viewing and editing.

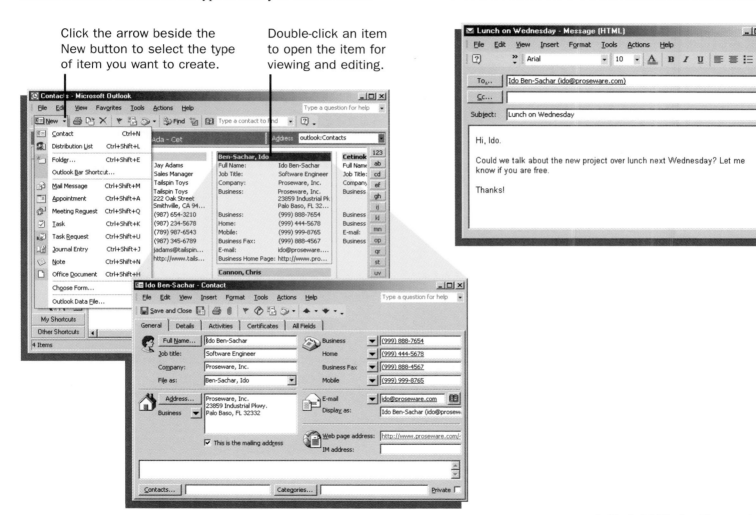

Starting and Exiting Outlook

Before you can work with your Outlook items you need to open Outlook. The program works much like any other Windows program when it comes to starting, working in, or exiting the program.

TRY THIS! Drag the Outlook icon from the desktop to the Quick Start toolbar just to the right of the Start menu to give you an easy way to open Outlook from the taskbar. Then just click the icon to start Outlook.

Start Outlook

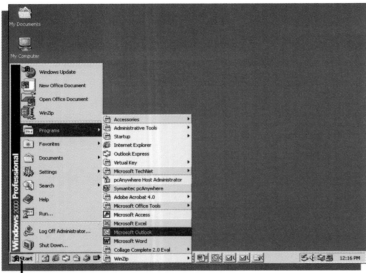

1 Click Start, Programs, Microsoft Outlook.

TIP: If you work with Outlook much of the day or every time you work on your computer, drag the Outlook icon from the Windows desktop to the Programs/Startup folder on the Start menu to create a shortcut there for Outlook. Outlook will then start when you log on to your computer.

Exit Outlook

1 Choose Exit from the file menu; or

2 Click the Close button.

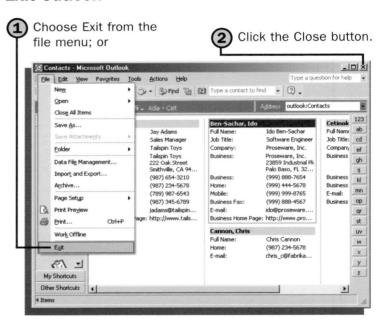

TIP: You can press Alt+F4 to close whichever program is currently active.

Exploring Outlook's Folders

Outlook includes several folders that contain different types of data. Incoming messages are placed in the Inbox and outgoing messages are placed in the Outbox, while the Drafts folder holds messages that you are working on, and the Sent Items folder keeps a copy of messages you send. You can use the Contacts folder to store contact information and the Calendar folder to store your schedule. The Outlook Bar and the Folder list give you quick access to your folders.

Use the Outlook Bar

1 Click the Inbox icon to open the Inbox folder.

2 Click the Outlook Today icon to open your Outlook Today folder.

3 Click Other Shortcuts to change the list of icons shown in the Outlook Bar.

4 Click My Documents to open your document folder.

> **SEE ALSO:** For information on customizing the Outlook Bar to add or remove icons, see "Customizing the Outlook Bar" on page 230.

Use the Folder List

② Click the push-pin icon to keep the folder list open.

① Click the folder name drop-down button.

③ Click a plus sign to expand a folder's listing.

④ Click a minus sign to collapse a folder's listing.

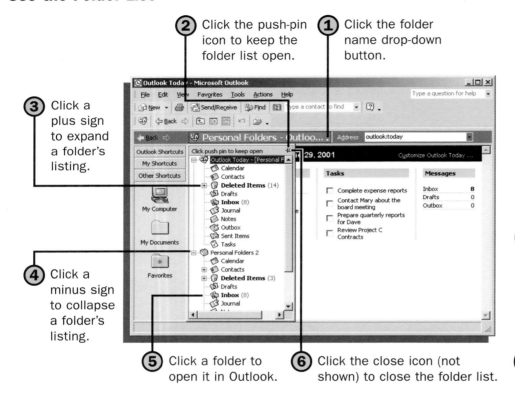

⑤ Click a folder to open it in Outlook.

⑥ Click the close icon (not shown) to close the folder list.

> SEE ALSO: For more information on setting up e-mail accounts for Hotmail and other e-mail services, see "Setting Up E-Mail Accounts" on page 12.

> TIP: You can use more than one set of personal folders at a time, and Outlook shows them all in the folder list. For example, if you have a Hotmail account, you'll see a set of Hotmail folders in addition to your Exchange Server mailbox or personal folders.

Working with Outlook Items

Outlook offers several types of items you can use to store information and send messages. These items include messages, contacts, journal entries, tasks, appointments, meetings, and notes. Outlook stores each type in a particular folder and presents the information in a way that makes the most sense for that type of data. In many situations you can retrieve the information you need simply by opening the folder, without actually opening the item.

> TIP: The preview pane appears below the folder pane and displays the contents of an item when you click it. To turn the preview pane on or off, choose Preview Pane from the View menu.

> TIP: Outlook provides an Auto-Preview option for list views such as the default Inbox, Tasks, and Notes folder views. When Auto-Preview is turned on, Outlook displays the first few lines of the item below the item's header. To turn AutoPreview on or off, choose AutoPreview from the View menu.

Review Items in a Folder

(1) In the Outlook Bar, click the folder whose contents you want to view.

(2) Use the scroll bar to view additional items.

(3) View the item either directly in the folder pane or in the preview pane.

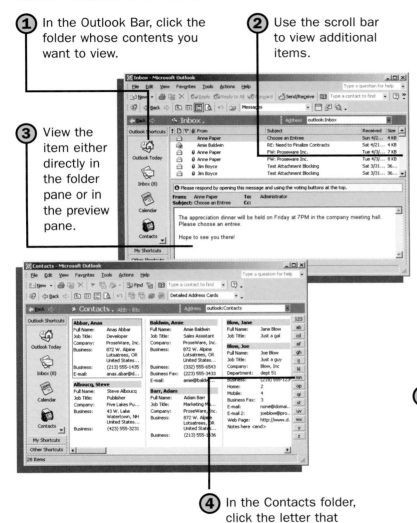

(4) In the Contacts folder, click the letter that corresponds to the first initial of other names you want to view.

Open an Item

(1) In the Outlook Bar, click the folder containing the item you want to open.

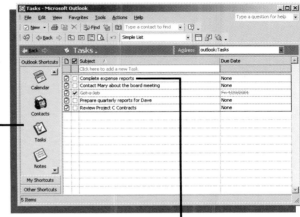

(2) Locate the item in the folder pane, and double-click it.

(3) View the item in its form, or make changes as necessary.

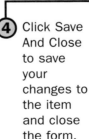

(4) Click Save And Close to save your changes to the item and close the form.

Setting Up E-Mail Accounts

You can use Outlook to send and receive messages for several different types of e-mail accounts. Outlook supports Microsoft Exchange Server, POP3 services such as CompuServe Classic, IMAP services such as CompuServe 2000, and HTTP-based e-mail services such as Hotmail. You can easily add a new account, or import e-mail account settings from Microsoft Outlook Express, Eudora, Netscape Mail and Messenger, and Microsoft Internet Mail.

Import E-Mail Account Settings

(1) Open Outlook, and choose Import And Export from the File menu.

(2) Select Import Internet Mail Account Settings, and click Next.

> **TIP:** Most Internet providers include POP3 e-mail accounts when you sign up for Internet service. Your Internet provider can give you details on the type of e-mail account you have and what settings to use in Outlook for that account.

(3) Select the program from which you're importing accounts, and click Next.

(5) Verify or change your name in the account, and click Next.

(4) Select the account you want to import, and click Next.

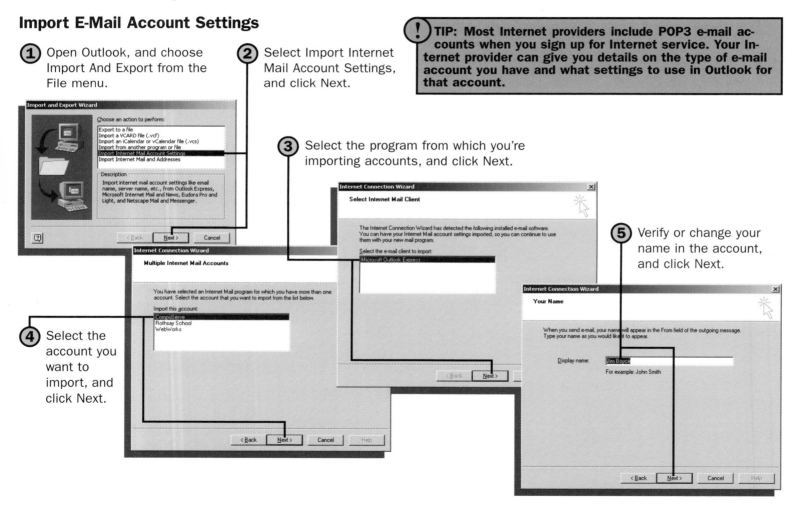

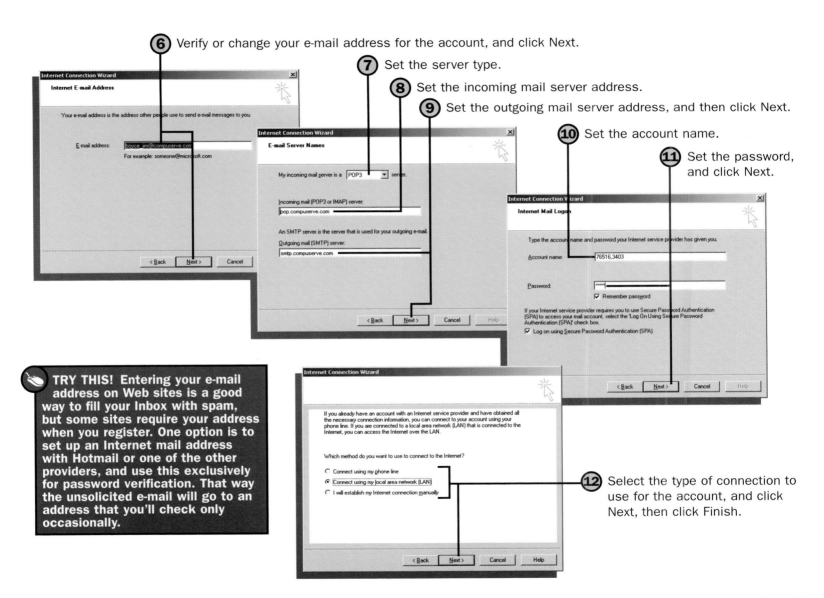

⑥ Verify or change your e-mail address for the account, and click Next.

⑦ Set the server type.

⑧ Set the incoming mail server address.

⑨ Set the outgoing mail server address, and then click Next.

⑩ Set the account name.

⑪ Set the password, and click Next.

Internet Connection Wizard

Internet E-mail Address

Your e-mail address is the address other people use to send e-mail messages to you.

E-mail address: boyce_jim@compuserve.com

For example: someone@microsoft.com

< Back | Next > | Cancel

Internet Connection Wizard

E-mail Server Names

My incoming mail server is a POP3 server.

Incoming mail (POP3 or IMAP) server:

pop.compuserve.com

An SMTP server is the server that is used for your outgoing e-mail.

Outgoing mail (SMTP) server:

smtp.compuserve.com

< Back | Next > | Cancel | Help

Internet Connection Wizard

Internet Mail Logon

Type the account name and password your Internet service provider has given you.

Account name: 76516,3403

Password: *****

☑ Remember password

If your Internet service provider requires you to use Secure Password Authentication (SPA) to access your mail account, select the 'Log On Using Secure Password Authentication (SPA)' check box.

☑ Log on using Secure Password Authentication (SPA)

< Back | Next > | Cancel | Help

TRY THIS! Entering your e-mail address on Web sites is a good way to fill your Inbox with spam, but some sites require your address when you register. One option is to set up an Internet mail address with Hotmail or one of the other providers, and use this exclusively for password verification. That way the unsolicited e-mail will go to an address that you'll check only occasionally.

Internet Connection Wizard

If you already have an account with an Internet service provider and have obtained all the necessary connection information, you can connect to your account using your phone line. If you are connected to a local area network (LAN) that is connected to the Internet, you can access the Internet over the LAN.

Which method do you want to use to connect to the Internet?

○ Connect using my phone line

● Connect using my local area network (LAN)

○ I will establish my Internet connection manually

< Back | Next > | Cancel | Help

⑫ Select the type of connection to use for the account, and click Next, then click Finish.

Add an E-Mail Account

① Open Outlook, and choose E-Mail Accounts from the Tools menu.

② Select Add A New E-Mail Account, and click Next.

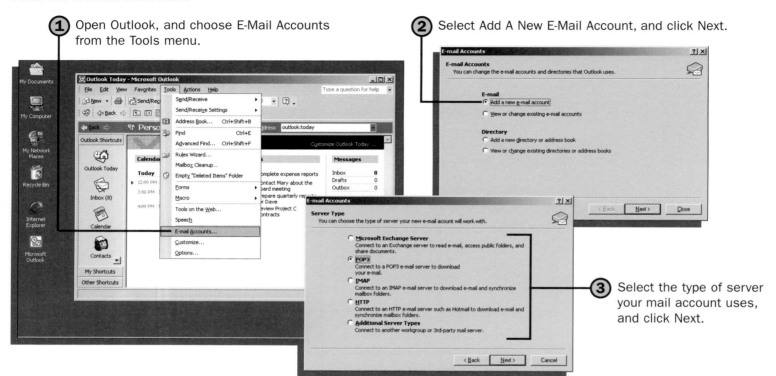

③ Select the type of server your mail account uses, and click Next.

🖱 **TRY THIS! Outlook stores your account and address book settings in an Outlook** *profile*. **Although you can use a single profile for all of your e-mail accounts, you might prefer to use separate profiles in some situations. For example, you might use one profile for your business e-mail accounts and a second for your personal accounts. Open the Mail icon in the Control Panel, and click Show Profiles to open a dialog box you can use to add, copy, and remove Outlook profiles.**

❗ **TIP: You can add, change, and remove Outlook e-mail accounts, personal folders, address books, and directory services through the Mail icon in the Control Panel.**

🔗 **SEE ALSO: For information on keeping messages from different accounts separated from one another, see "Working with the Rules Wizard" on page 62.**

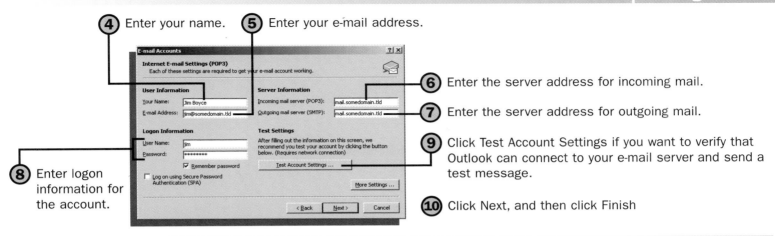

④ Enter your name.

⑤ Enter your e-mail address.

⑥ Enter the server address for incoming mail.

⑦ Enter the server address for outgoing mail.

⑨ Click Test Account Settings if you want to verify that Outlook can connect to your e-mail server and send a test message.

⑧ Enter logon information for the account.

⑩ Click Next, and then click Finish

Importing Data from Another Program

If you're switching to Outlook from another program, you might want to import your existing messages and contacts so that you can continue working with them. Importing messages, addresses, and data into Outlook saves the time you'd need to recreate them manually. You can import mail and addresses from Microsoft Internet Mail and News, Outlook Express, Eudora, and Netscape Mail and Messenger.

Retrieve Internet Mail and Addresses

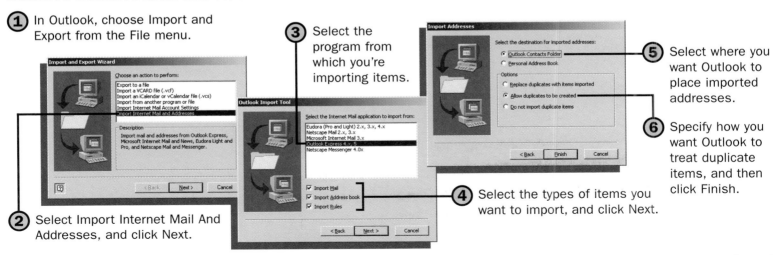

① In Outlook, choose Import and Export from the File menu.

② Select Import Internet Mail And Addresses, and click Next.

③ Select the program from which you're importing items.

④ Select the types of items you want to import, and click Next.

⑤ Select where you want Outlook to place imported addresses.

⑥ Specify how you want Outlook to treat duplicate items, and then click Finish.

Retrieve Data from Another Program

(1) In Outlook choose Import and Export from the File menu.

(2) Select Import From Another Program Or File, and click Next.

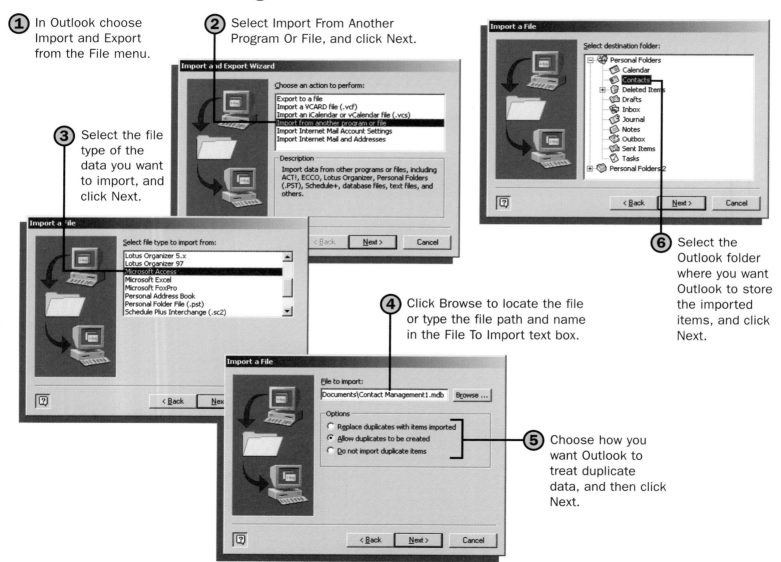

(3) Select the file type of the data you want to import, and click Next.

(4) Click Browse to locate the file or type the file path and name in the File To Import text box.

(5) Choose how you want Outlook to treat duplicate data, and then click Next.

(6) Select the Outlook folder where you want Outlook to store the imported items, and click Next.

(7) Place a check beside the item(s) you want to import. If the Map Custom Fields dialog box doesn't open, click Map Custom Fields.

Import a File

The following actions will be performed:

☐ Import "Calls" into folder: Contacts
☐ Import "Contact Types" into folder: Contacts
☑ Import "Contacts" into folder: Contacts
☐ Import "Switchboard Items" into folder: Contacts

Map Custom Fields ...

Change Destination ...

This may take a few minutes and cannot be canceled.

[?]   < Back   Finish   Cance

(8) Click and drag an item from the From list to the To list and drop it on the Outlook field where you want the item copied. This tells Outlook where to place the incoming data. Repeat for all items to be imported, and then click OK.

Map Custom Fields   [x]

Drag the values from the source file on the left, and drop them on the appropriate destination field on the right. Drag the item from the right to the left to remove it from the field mapping.

From:
Microsoft Access
Contacts

Value
StateOrProvince
PostalCode
Region
Country/Region
CompanyName
Title
WorkPhone

To:
Microsoft Outlook
Contacts

Field	Mapped from
First Name	First Name
Middle Name	
Last Name	Last Name
Suffix	
Company	CompanyName
Department	
Job Title	

< Previous   Next >   Clear Map   Default Map

OK   Cancel

> **! TIP:** When you import data from certain programs you might need to perform some additional steps before bringing the data into Outlook. For example, you must name one or more ranges in Excel before you can import spreadsheet data into Outlook.

(9) Click Finish when you're ready to import the data.

Viewing Items and Folders

Outlook offers several different views depending on the folder you open. You can use the default views to work with the data in the folder or change the view to tailor it to your needs. The Outlook Today view gives you a single place to view your pending appoint- ments, tasks, and messages, giving you a summary of your workday or workweek. You can also use the View menu to switch easily between the available views for a particular Outlook folder.

Use the Outlook Today View

(1) In Outlook, click the Outlook Today icon in the Outlook Bar.

(2) To open an appointment, click the appointment in the Calendar list.

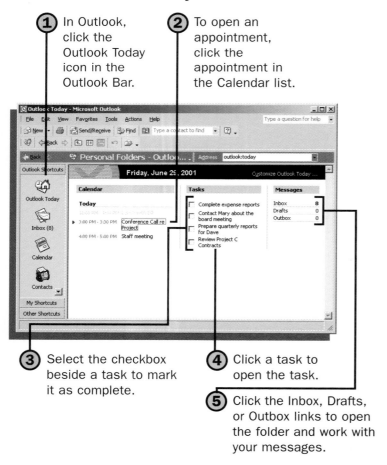

(3) Select the checkbox beside a task to mark it as complete.

(4) Click a task to open the task.

(5) Click the Inbox, Drafts, or Outbox links to open the folder and work with your messages.

Use the Current View Menu

(1) In Outlook, select the folder you want to view.

(2) Choose Current View from the View menu.

(3) Choose the view you want to use from the Current View submenu.

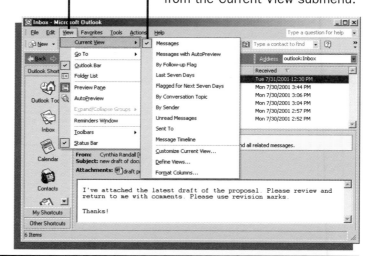

TRY THIS! Open the Contacts folder and click New in the Standard toolbar to create a new contact. Fill in the fields on the General tab, and click Save and Close to save the contact. With the Contacts folder open, choose Current View on the View menu, then select Detailed Address Cards. Outlook will display more information in the Contacts folder. Choose Current View on the View menu, then select Phone List to change to a view that is handy for quickly locating phone numbers.

Set the Startup View

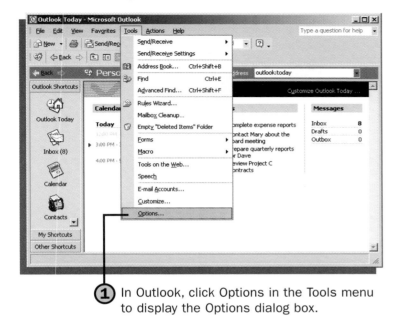

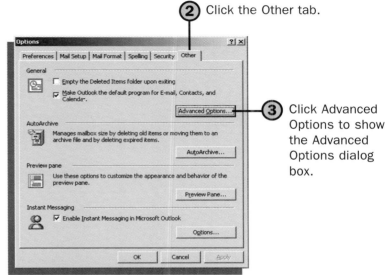

② Click the Other tab.

③ Click Advanced Options to show the Advanced Options dialog box.

① In Outlook, click Options in the Tools menu to display the Options dialog box.

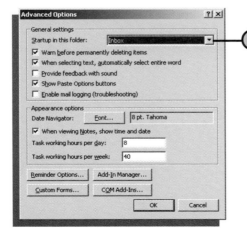

④ From the Startup In This Folder drop-down list, choose the folder you want Outlook to display when you first start the program.

Getting Help in Outlook 2002

Every new program has a learning curve. Getting up to speed with Outlook can take some time because of the sheer number of features it offers. Even after you become comfortable using Outlook on a day-to-day basis, you'll still run into situations where you need some help with features you've never used before or those you seldom use. Outlook provides two primary ways to get additional information about the program: the Office Assistant and Online Help.

Use the Office Assistant

① If the Office Assistant isn't showing, choose Show The Office Assistant on the Help menu.

! TIP: You can choose from several Office Assistants included with Outlook. To do so, right-click the Office Assistant and click Choose Assistant. In the Office Assistant dialog box, use the Back and Next buttons to browse through the available Office Assistants.

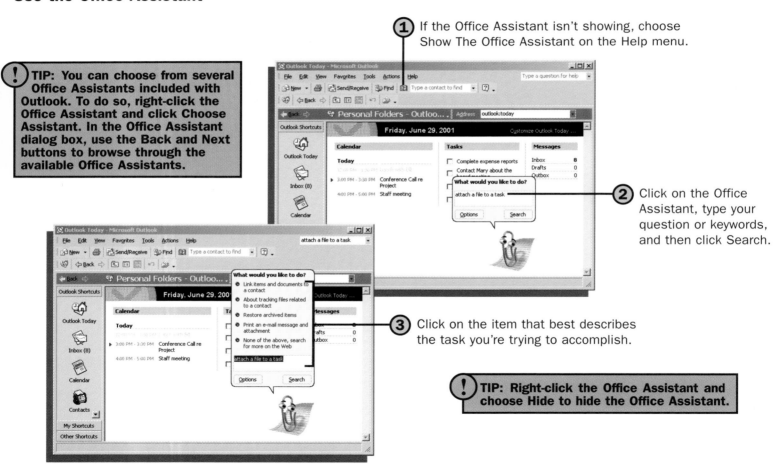

② Click on the Office Assistant, type your question or keywords, and then click Search.

③ Click on the item that best describes the task you're trying to accomplish.

! TIP: Right-click the Office Assistant and choose Hide to hide the Office Assistant.

Ask a Quick Question

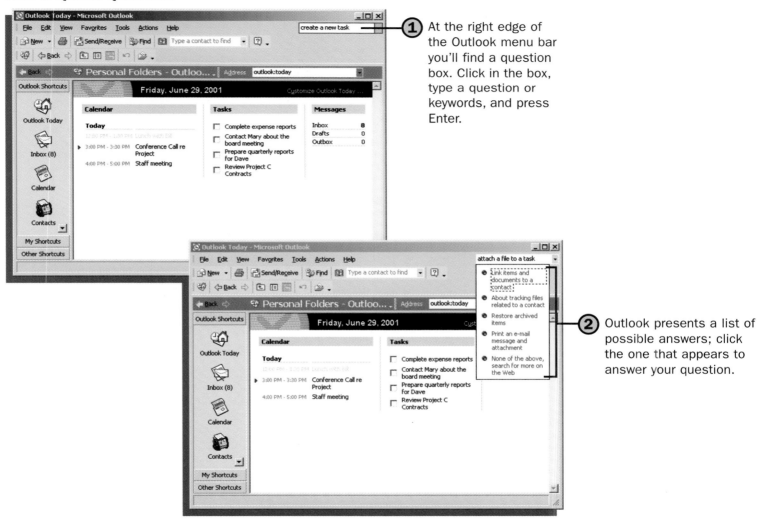

① At the right edge of the Outlook menu bar you'll find a question box. Click in the box, type a question or keywords, and press Enter.

② Outlook presents a list of possible answers; click the one that appears to answer your question.

Use Outlook's Online Help

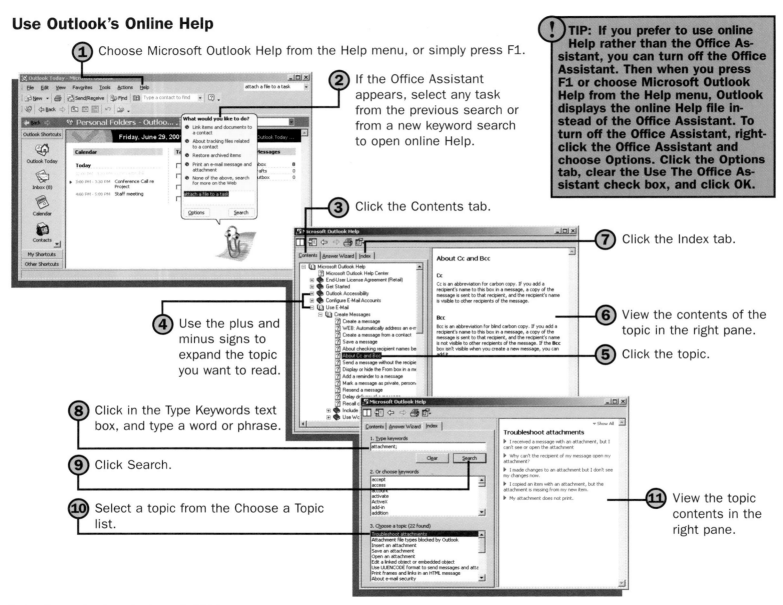

1. Choose Microsoft Outlook Help from the Help menu, or simply press F1.

2. If the Office Assistant appears, select any task from the previous search or from a new keyword search to open online Help.

3. Click the Contents tab.

4. Use the plus and minus signs to expand the topic you want to read.

5. Click the topic.

6. View the contents of the topic in the right pane.

7. Click the Index tab.

8. Click in the Type Keywords text box, and type a word or phrase.

9. Click Search.

10. Select a topic from the Choose a Topic list.

11. View the topic contents in the right pane.

Troubleshooting Problems

Sometimes the online Help file and the Office Assistant can't solve your problem. Fortunately, Microsoft has a wealth of information about Office and Outlook available online through its Web site. If you're looking for additional information about specific features or just want to learn more about Outlook, try the Outlook Web page. For troubleshooting problems, try the Microsoft Knowledge Base.

Get Online Help

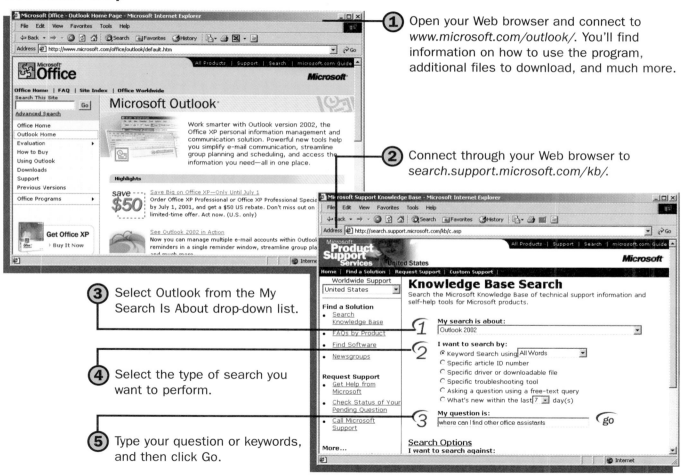

1 Open your Web browser and connect to *www.microsoft.com/outlook/*. You'll find information on how to use the program, additional files to download, and much more.

2 Connect through your Web browser to *search.support.microsoft.com/kb/*.

3 Select Outlook from the My Search Is About drop-down list.

4 Select the type of search you want to perform.

5 Type your question or keywords, and then click Go.

Writing and Sending E-Mail

Microsoft Outlook handles many daily tasks for you, such as keeping your calendar, collecting notes, and saving your contacts. But the main feature of Outlook is its electronic mail (e-mail) features. Outlook is often referred to as a universal inbox—it can send, receive, and store messages from a number of different e-mail sources. These sources can include internal networks, Internet e-mail accounts, and other sources.

Outlook's e-mail features enable you to create e-mail messages and send them to other users. With the help of the Outlook Address Book, you can quickly access a recipient's e-mail address when you are ready to address your new e-mail message. Outlook also provides ways to send one message to multiple users using distribution lists, format e-mail message text to contain rich content (such as hypertext format), use signatures at the bottom of all your outgoing messages, and create HTML stationery.

In this section, you learn how to write and modify e-mail messages, send messages, and review messages you've already sent. In addition, you learn how to use the Address Book to select recipient names, create and use distribution lists, format your messages, use signatures, send attached files, and work with HTML stationery.

Writing an E-Mail Message

When you write new messages in Outlook, you use the Message window. This window has a line for recipients (called the To line), a line for "carbon copied" recipients (the Cc line), a Subject line, and an area for the text of the message. Every new message must have at least one recipient. If you want, you can leave the Cc and Subject lines blank, but it's a good idea to give your messages a subject.

Address an E-Mail Message

1 In Outlook, click New on the Standard toolbar to display a new Message window.

2 To open the Select Names dialog box, click To.

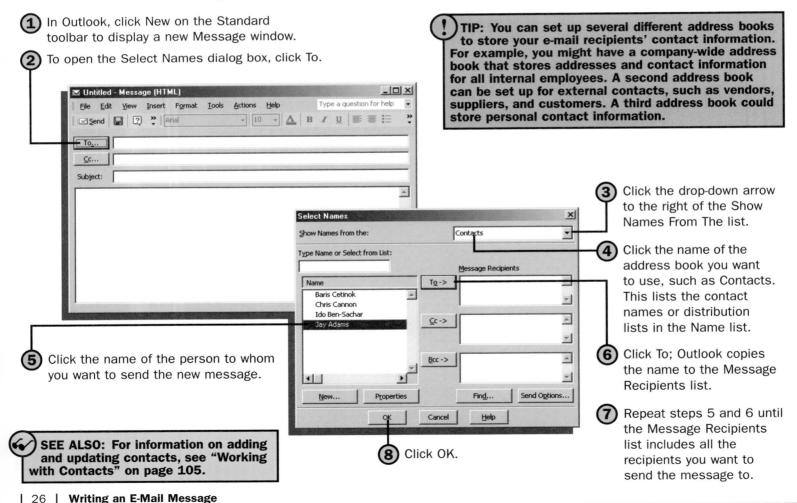

! **TIP:** You can set up several different address books to store your e-mail recipients' contact information. For example, you might have a company-wide address book that stores addresses and contact information for all internal employees. A second address book can be set up for external contacts, such as vendors, suppliers, and customers. A third address book could store personal contact information.

3 Click the drop-down arrow to the right of the Show Names From The list.

4 Click the name of the address book you want to use, such as Contacts. This lists the contact names or distribution lists in the Name list.

5 Click the name of the person to whom you want to send the new message.

6 Click To; Outlook copies the name to the Message Recipients list.

7 Repeat steps 5 and 6 until the Message Recipients list includes all the recipients you want to send the message to.

8 Click OK.

SEE ALSO: For information on adding and updating contacts, see "Working with Contacts" on page 105.

Enter Your Message Subject and Text

(1) In the New Message window, enter a subject for the new message in the Subject field.

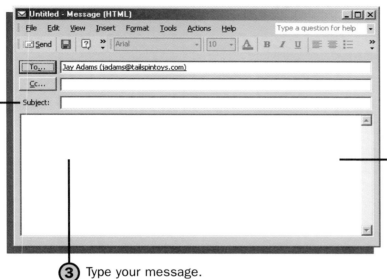

(3) Type your message.

(2) Press Tab or click in the message body area.

> **!** **TIP:** As you write your message, you do not have to press Enter at the end of each line. Keep typing and Outlook wraps the text to the next line. To create a new paragraph, press Enter. If you want each paragraph to be separated by two spaces, press Enter twice at the end of each paragraph. This will make your messages easier to read than single-spaced messages.

> **SEE ALSO:** After you type your message, you can send it. Sending messages is discussed later in "Sending Messages" on page 42.

> **CAUTION:** You can apply special formatting to your message (see "Formatting Message Text" on page 34), but you might not want to. If you're sending mail to people who use a different e-mail program, they might not see the formatting that you intended. When in doubt, it's usually a good policy to keep your messages simple so nothing gets lost in the translation.

Working with the Address Book

You can use the Outlook Address Book to search for and select names, e-mail addresses, and distribution lists. When you type a recipient name, Outlook searches the Address Book for a match. The Address Book is actually a compilation of several address books, including information from the Contact folder, Microsoft Exchange Server, and Internet directory services. Depending on the way you have Outlook set up, you may have information from only one of these sources, or you may have contact information from all three types.

Open the Address Book

(1) In Outlook, choose Address Book from the Tools menu.

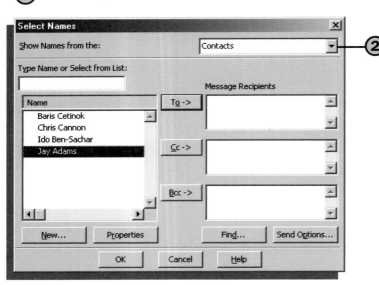

 SEE ALSO: For more on working with your contact information, see "Working with Contacts" on page 105.

(2) Click the selection arrow on the Show Names From The drop-down list.

(3) Click the address book from which you want to view addresses.

! TIP: If your version of Outlook is not set up for other address books, such as an Exchange Server Global Address List, the only address book you can select from the Show Names From The drop-down list is the Outlook Contacts folder.

Find a Name in the Address Book

1 In the Address Book dialog box, click in the Type Name Or Select From List field.

2 Type the name of the contact you are searching for.

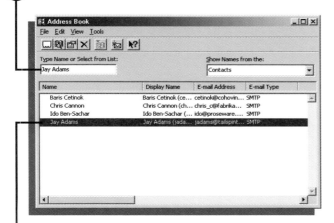

3 The first contact that matches is highlighted in the list of names.

TRY THIS! Assume you want to find a contact whose name is Dave. You are not sure if you listed him as "Dave" or "David" in your Contacts folder. To find him, choose Find from the Tools menu, type dav, and press Enter. Outlook displays all names containing "dav", such as "Dave", "Davey", "David", and so on.

TIP: If you want to redisplay your entire address book, select an address book from the Show Names From The drop-down list. Notice that Outlook now lists search results as a selection in case you want to return to your latest search results.

E-Mail a Name in the Address Book

1 In the Address Book dialog box, click a contact to whom you want to send an e-mail message.

2 Choose New Message from the File menu.

3 Type a subject. **4** Type your message text in the message body area.

SEE ALSO: For more information on sending your message, see "Sending Messages" on page 42.

TIP: When you're finished with the Address Book, close it by choosing Close from the File menu.

Working with Distribution Lists

A distribution list is a group of contacts who are related in some way. For example, you could create a distribution list that includes contacts working on the same project. Then when you need to send messages to the entire project team, you would simply select the distribution list for that project; Outlook sends the message to all the contacts in the list. Distribution lists are stored in the Contacts folder by default.

Create a Distribution List

① In Outlook, choose New from the File menu.

② Choose Distribution List from the New submenu.

③ Click in the Name field and type a name for the new distribution list.

④ Click Select Members to open the Select Members dialog box.

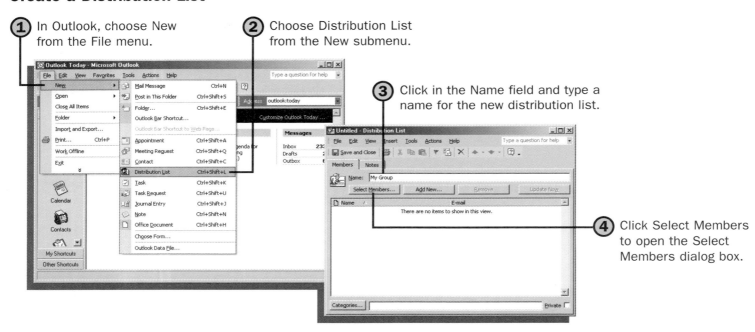

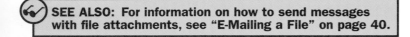

SEE ALSO: For information on how to send messages with file attachments, see "E-Mailing a File" on page 40.

TIP: You can share a distribution list with other users. To do so, open a new message and choose Item from the Insert menu. In the Look In list, select the folder, such as Contacts, that includes your distribution list. In the Items list, select the distribution list you want to send. Click OK to attach the list to your new message.

6 Click in the Type Name Or Select From List field and type a name you want to add to the distribution list, or choose a name from the list that appears in the Name field.

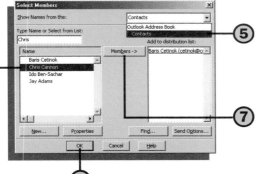

5 From the Show Names From The drop-down list, select the address book that contains the names you want to add to the distribution list.

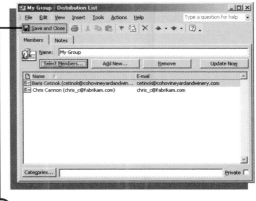

7 Click Members to copy the name to the Add To Distribution List field.

9 Click Save And Close.

8 Click OK when your list is complete.

Use a Distribution List

1 In Outlook, click New from the Standard toolbar.

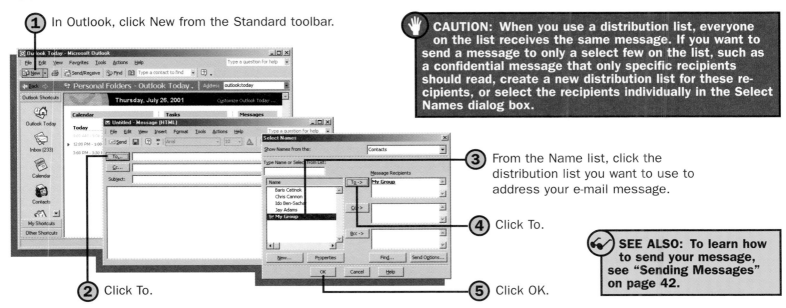

2 Click To.

3 From the Name list, click the distribution list you want to use to address your e-mail message.

4 Click To.

5 Click OK.

CAUTION: When you use a distribution list, everyone on the list receives the same message. If you want to send a message to only a select few on the list, such as a confidential message that only specific recipients should read, create a new distribution list for these recipients, or select the recipients individually in the Select Names dialog box.

SEE ALSO: To learn how to send your message, see "Sending Messages" on page 42.

Changing Message Text

After you create a message and before you send it, you should proofread it for errors or omissions. If you discover a typo or other error, you can edit it the same as you would a word processing document. You can use familiar commands like Copy and Paste or operations like drag and drop to edit your text.

SEE ALSO: If you need to modify a contact's information, such as her e-mail address or name, you can do so in the Contacts folder. See "Updating an Existing Contact" on page 115.

Edit Your Message

(1) In Outlook, create a new mail message with recipients, a subject, and message text.

(2) To change the recipient, click To.

(3) In the Select Names dialog box, click a name to remove from the Message Recipients list. Press Delete or Backspace to remove that person from the list.

(4) Continue adding or deleting recipients until your recipient list includes all those you want to send the message to.

(5) Click OK.

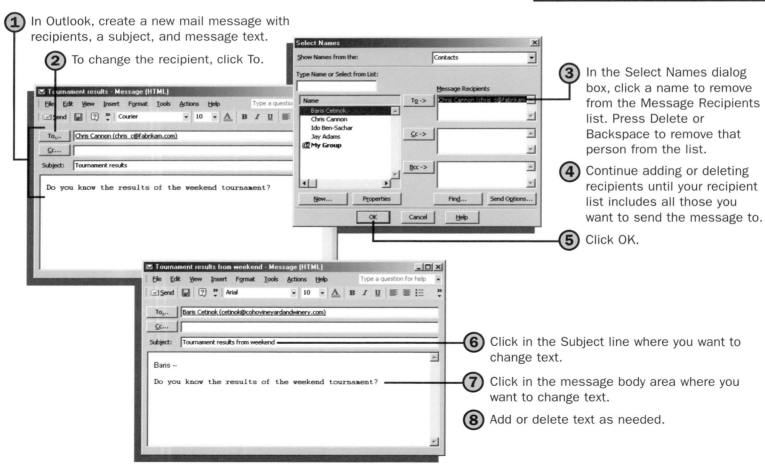

(6) Click in the Subject line where you want to change text.

(7) Click in the message body area where you want to change text.

(8) Add or delete text as needed.

Move and Copy Message Text

1 Display the message containing the text you want to move or copy.

2 Select the text you want to move or copy.

3 Drag the text to a new location. Or, to copy the text, hold down Ctrl as you drag the text.

4 Drop the text.

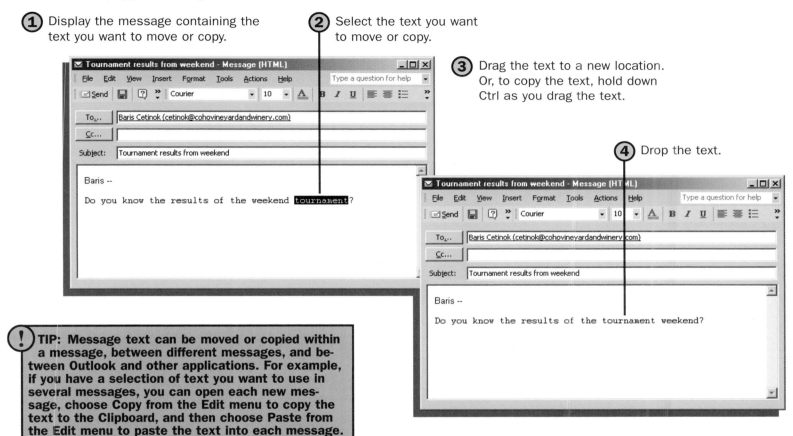

! TIP: Message text can be moved or copied within a message, between different messages, and between Outlook and other applications. For example, if you have a selection of text you want to use in several messages, you can open each new message, choose Copy from the Edit menu to copy the text to the Clipboard, and then choose Paste from the Edit menu to paste the text into each message.

TRY THIS! You can drag text from one message to another. Open both messages and position them so you can see both windows. Select the text you want to move and drag it to the other message window. Release the mouse button.

Formatting Message Text

Outlook lets you format text so that it looks more attractive to you and your recipients. For example, you can apply bold, italic, underline, colors, and other rich formatting to your messages. You also can add HTML formatting to your messages, including tables, hyperlinks, heading levels, and more.

Use a Rich Text or HTML Message Format

(1) Create a new message, and add some text.

(2) Click on the Format menu.

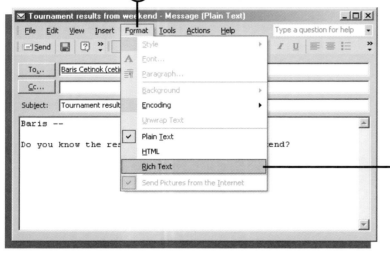

(3) To change from Plain Text, choose Rich Text or HTML from the Format menu.

TIP: To add a hyperlink to an e-mail message, type the hyperlink in your message and Outlook converts it to a live link that your recipient can click. For example, you can add a hyperlink to the Microsoft Web site by typing *www.microsoft.com.*

CAUTION: If you add a hyperlink to a message, your recipient will need access to that site or document. For example, if the document you specify in the hyperlink is on the Internet, your recipient must have Internet access. Likewise, if your link is to a document you have stored locally on your hard drive, your recipient must have share privileges to that document.

CAUTION: Some recipients may not be able to handle rich-formatted text. In these cases, the formatted text you see in your message window will appear to your recipients as plain text or be converted to unrecognizable characters.

TIP: If you want to compose your e-mail messages in Word, choose Options from the Tools menu and, in the Options dialog box, click the Mail Format tab. Select Use Microsoft Word To Edit E-Mail Message. Click OK.

Add Formatting to a Message

1 Select the text you want to format.

2 Click Bold to bold the text.

3 Click Italic to italicize the text.

4 Click Underline to underline the text.

5 Select a value from the Font drop-down list to change the text font.

7 Select a color from the Font Color drop-down list to change the text font color.

6 Select a value from the Font Size drop-down list to change the text font size.

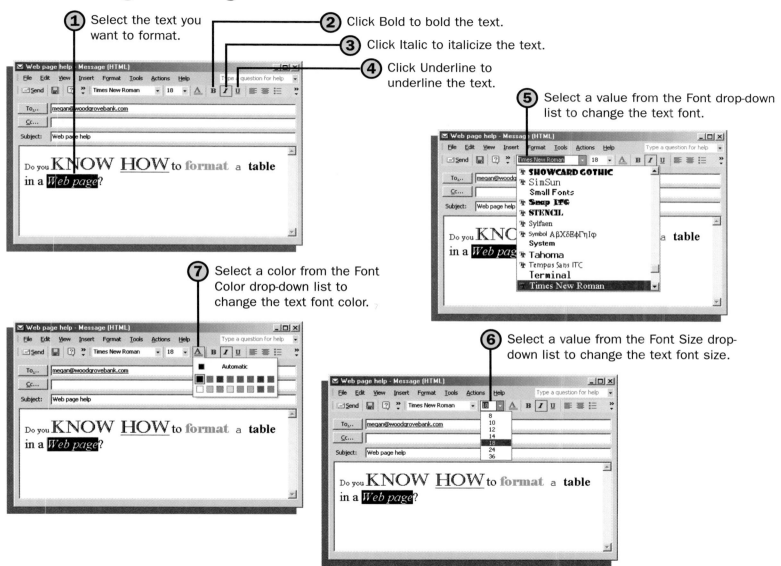

Using Signatures

A signature is boilerplate text or a file that is attached to any new messages you compose. The signature appears at the bottom of your messages, like the signature that you would write on paper documents.

Create a Signature

(1) In Outlook, choose Options from the Tools menu.

(2) In the Options dialog box, click the Mail Format tab.

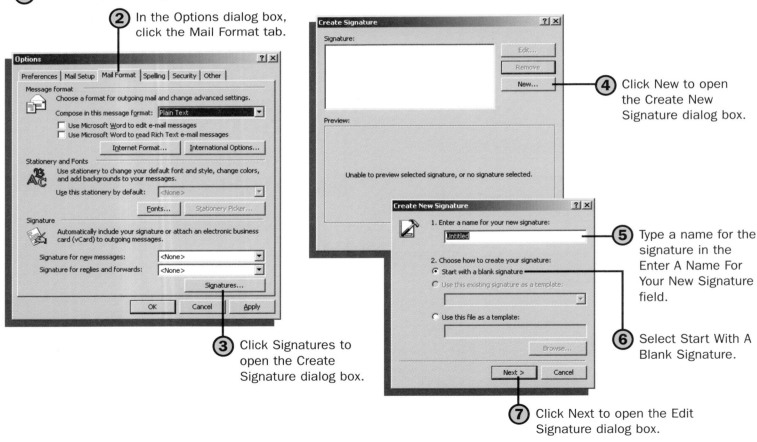

(4) Click New to open the Create New Signature dialog box.

(3) Click Signatures to open the Create Signature dialog box.

(5) Type a name for the signature in the Enter A Name For Your New Signature field.

(6) Select Start With A Blank Signature.

(7) Click Next to open the Edit Signature dialog box.

(!) TIP: A common signature includes your name, title, company name, address, phone number, and e-mail address.

(8) In the Signature Text field, type the text you want to appear in your signature.

(9) Click Finish. Click OK twice to save your signature.

(!) TIP: You can create custom signatures for the type of e-mail message you create. For instance, you can create a friendly signature for messages intended for family or friends.

Tell Outlook to Use Your Signature

(1) In Outlook, choose Options from the Tools menu.

(2) Click the Mail Format tab.

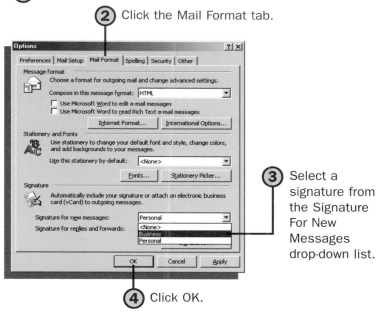

(3) Select a signature from the Signature For New Messages drop-down list.

(4) Click OK.

(!) TIP: If you want your signature to appear in messages you reply to or forward, select the appropriate signature from the Signature For Replies And Forwards drop-down list.

(✓) SEE ALSO: For information on replying to and forwarding messages, see "Replying to and Forwarding E-Mail" on page 57.

Working with HTML Stationery

Outlook includes a set of predefined designs and color schemes you can add to your rich-formatted messages. These are known as HTML stationery. You can use or modify the stationery Outlook provides, create your own, or download new stationery from the Web. When you create a message, you can specify which stationery is used or set Outlook to use a default stationery pattern each time you create a new message. You can also specify the background image or color for an individual message.

Select Stationery

(1) In Outlook, choose New Mail Message Using from the Actions menu.

(2) Choose More Stationery from the submenu.

TIP: If you want more stationery, connect to the Internet and then, in Outlook, click Get More Stationery in the Select A Stationery dialog box. This launches your Web browser and connects you to the Microsoft Office Download Center. Select the Add-Ins And Extras check box and click Update List. The bottom of the Web page lists available stationery for Outlook.

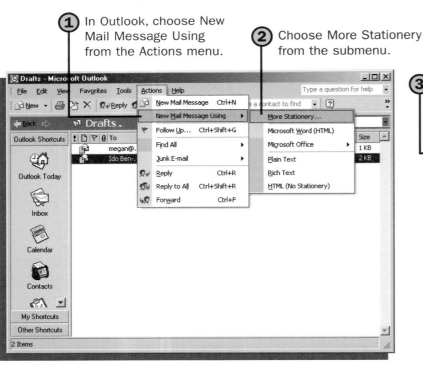

(3) Choose the stationery you want for your new message from the Select A Stationery dialog box.

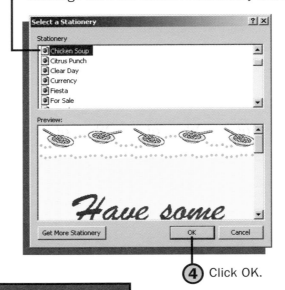

(4) Click OK.

CAUTION: To use HTML stationery, your message must be in HTML format. Your recipients' e-mail program must be able to read this type of formatting or they will not be able to see the stationery or any other formatting on your page.

Edit Stationery

(1) Choose Options from the Tools menu.

(2) Click the Mail Format tab.

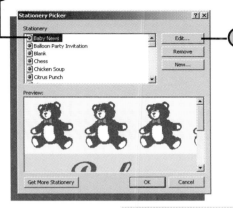

(3) Select HTML from the Compose In This Message Format drop-down list.

(4) Click Stationery Picker to open the Stationery Picker dialog box.

(5) Choose the stationery you want to edit.

(6) Click Edit to open the Edit Stationery dialog box.

(7) Choose the options you want to modify:

- Click Change Font to select a font to be used in the stationery.

- Select Picture, and then click Browse to select a different picture.

- Select Color, and then choose a new color from the Color drop-down list.

- Select Do Not Include A Background In This Stationery if you do not want a background image.

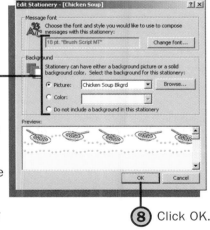

(8) Click OK.

> **SEE ALSO: To learn how to change to HTML formatting, see "Use a Rich Text or HTML Message Format" on page 34.**

> **TRY THIS!** Some stationery uses only a picture or color. If you'd like to try editing one that uses both elements, edit the Citrus Punch stationery so it has a different background color.

E-Mailing a File

Sometimes when you create an e-mail message, you will want to send along a binary file as well. Files sent with e-mail are called message attachments. When you send the message, the file goes along with the message so the recipient can open it on his or her computer. Outlook also allows you to insert a picture into your e-mail messages.

Insert a Picture

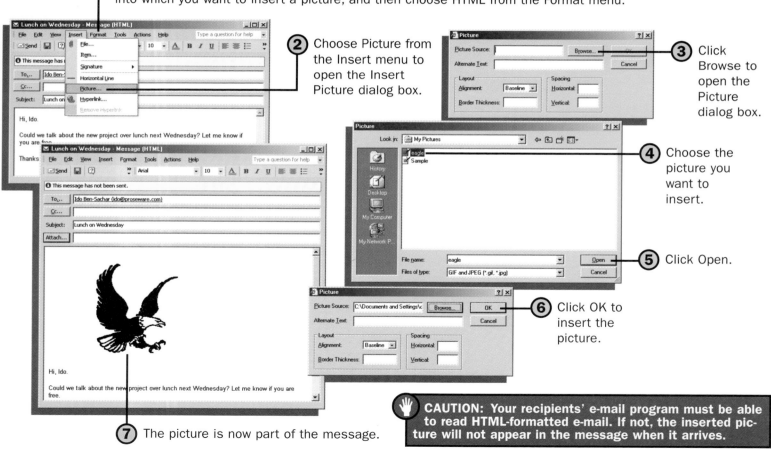

① To insert a picture in a message, you must have HTML formatting turned on. Open the message into which you want to insert a picture, and then choose HTML from the Format menu.

② Choose Picture from the Insert menu to open the Insert Picture dialog box.

③ Click Browse to open the Picture dialog box.

④ Choose the picture you want to insert.

⑤ Click Open.

⑥ Click OK to insert the picture.

⑦ The picture is now part of the message.

✋ **CAUTION: Your recipients' e-mail program must be able to read HTML-formatted e-mail. If not, the inserted picture will not appear in the message when it arrives.**

Insert a File

(1) Open a new message, and choose File from the Insert menu.

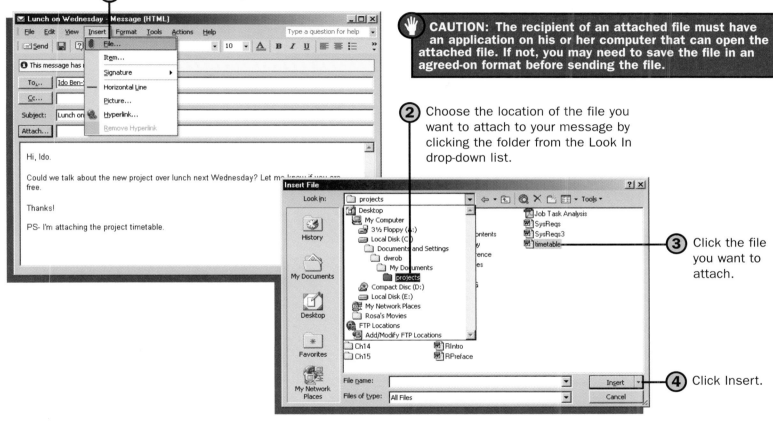

CAUTION: The recipient of an attached file must have an application on his or her computer that can open the attached file. If not, you may need to save the file in an agreed-on format before sending the file.

(2) Choose the location of the file you want to attach to your message by clicking the folder from the Look In drop-down list.

(3) Click the file you want to attach.

(4) Click Insert.

SEE ALSO: For information on saving and opening file attachments you receive from other people, see "Working with Attachments" on page 55.

Sending Messages

When you send a message, it travels across the local area network or the Internet to the person you specify as the recipient. If you specify more than one recipient, Outlook sends a copy of the message to every one you specify. By default, Outlook sends messages automatically when you click the Send button on the Outlook standard toolbar. You also can configure Outlook to hold your messages in the Outbox until you're ready to send them.

Transmit E-Mail Messages Automatically

(1) Create a new message.

(2) Click the Send button on the standard toolbar.

> **!** TIP: When your reply to or forward a message, you send it the same way you would send a new mail message. For more information, see "Replying to and Forwarding E-Mail" on page 57.

> **✋** CAUTION: If Outlook is set up to send your messages as soon as you click the Send button, you will not have a chance to change anything in your message before it's routed to your recipients. Even if your message was incomplete or contained confidential information, you won't be able to recall the message.

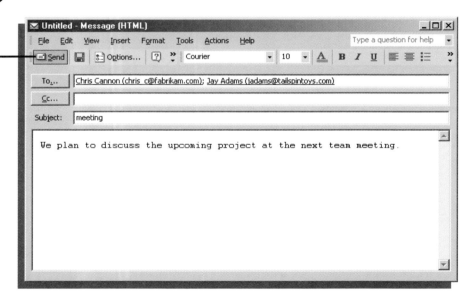

Transmit E-Mail Messages Manually

(1) In Outlook, choose Options from the Tools menu.

(2) Click the Mail Setup tab

(4) Create a new message.

(5) Click Send to send the message to the Outbox folder.

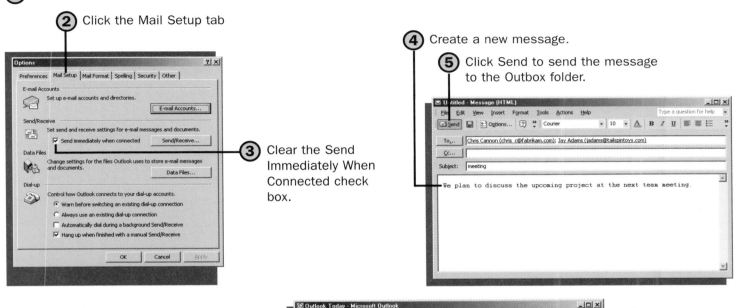

(3) Clear the Send Immediately When Connected check box.

(8) To send the message, click Send/Receive on the standard toolbar.

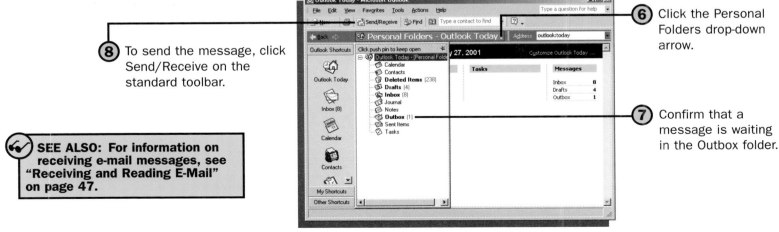

(6) Click the Personal Folders drop-down arrow.

(7) Confirm that a message is waiting in the Outbox folder.

SEE ALSO: For information on receiving e-mail messages, see "Receiving and Reading E-Mail" on page 47.

Reviewing Sent Messages and Drafts

When you send a message, Outlook stores a copy of it in the Sent Items folder. This folder enables you to keep track of all the messages you've sent to recipients. You can open this folder and review messages you've sent other users. Outlook also includes a Drafts folder that stores new messages you are working on but are not ready to send.

Open the Sent Items Folder

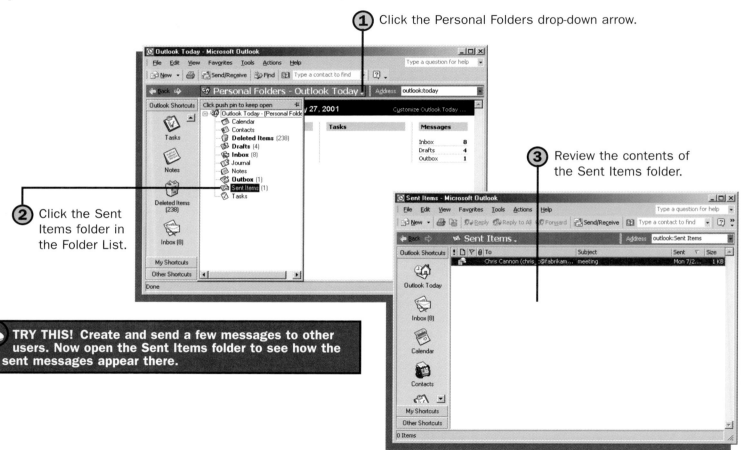

(1) Click the Personal Folders drop-down arrow.

(2) Click the Sent Items folder in the Folder List.

(3) Review the contents of the Sent Items folder.

TRY THIS! Create and send a few messages to other users. Now open the Sent Items folder to see how the sent messages appear there.

Open the Drafts Folder

1 Create a new message and add a recipient, subject line, and message text.

2 Choose Save from the File menu.

3 Click the Close box to close the message window.

4 Click the Drafts folder in the Folder List. Your saved message is displayed.

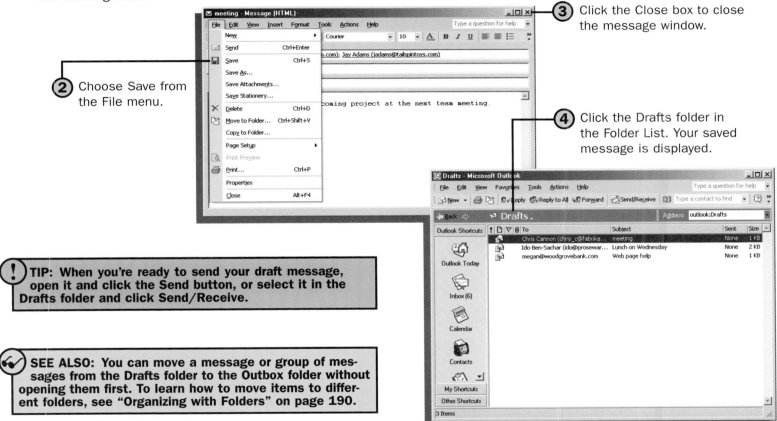

> **TIP:** When you're ready to send your draft message, open it and click the Send button, or select it in the Drafts folder and click Send/Receive.

> **SEE ALSO:** You can move a message or group of messages from the Drafts folder to the Outbox folder without opening them first. To learn how to move items to different folders, see "Organizing with Folders" on page 190.

4

Receiving and Reading E-Mail

To receive e-mail messages that have been sent to you, Outlook connects to an e-mail server on which messages are stored (such as servers located on a local area network or the Internet) and downloads the message to your Inbox folder. From there you can read a message, reply, forward it to someone, flag it for later, and open file attachments. In most cases, messages that you have downloaded are then deleted from the server.

Outlook can also filter out junk e-mail by blocking mail that arrives from certain addresses. You can adjust these filters to block mail from unwanted senders and let through the mail that you want to read. You also can set up Outlook Rules, which help you manage your messages by moving them to designated folders, flagging them, or otherwise processing the message in accordance with rules that you define.

This section shows you how to receive, read, reply to, follow up, and forward messages in Outlook. You'll learn how to manage your Inbox by deleting, saving, and printing messages. Finally, you'll learn how to handle junk mail, set up rules that personalize your e-mail experience, and work with e-mail attachments.

Receiving E-Mail

Outlook makes it easy for you to receive your incoming messages. You can schedule Outlook to download your new messages, or you can manually download new messages when you want.

Retrieve E-Mail Automatically

(1) Choose Options from the Tools menu, and click the Mail Setup tab.

(2) Click Send/Receive.

(3) Using the checkbox, choose the option to Schedule An Automatic Send/Receive Every *X* Minutes.

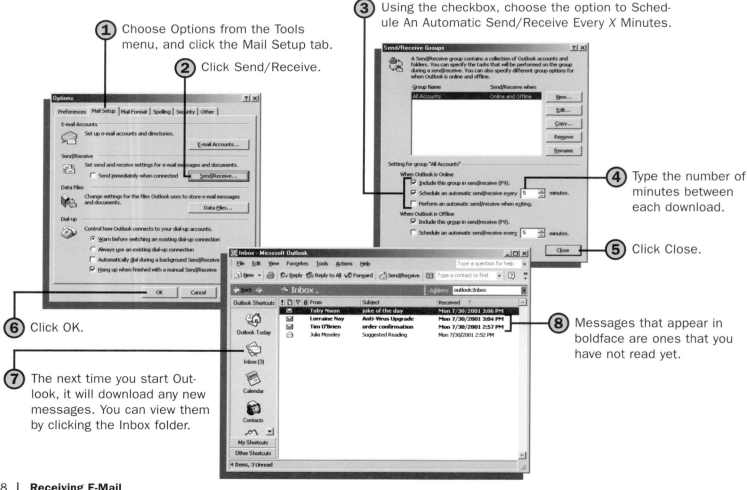

(4) Type the number of minutes between each download.

(5) Click Close.

(6) Click OK.

(7) The next time you start Outlook, it will download any new messages. You can view them by clicking the Inbox folder.

(8) Messages that appear in boldface are ones that you have not read yet.

Retrieve E-Mail Manually

(1) Click Send/Receive on the Standard toolbar.

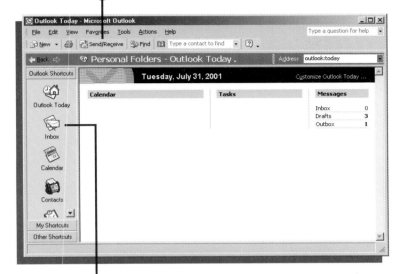

> **!** **TIP:** If you have Outlook configured for several e-mail message services, such as a Microsoft Exchange service and an Internet e-mail service, clicking Send/Receive downloads new messages from all these services. If you want to download messages from only one service, choose Send/Receive from the Tools menu and then select a service from the Send and Receive submenu.

> **!** **TIP:** The number of e-mail messages you have received in your Inbox folder appears on the status bar, and the number of unread messages appears next to the Inbox icon and on the status bar.

(2) Click the Inbox icon on the Outlook bar to see your new messages.

Reading E-Mail

After you receive a message in your Inbox folder, you can preview it or read its content. The Inbox folder displays the sender's name, the message subject, the date the message was received, the size of the message, and whether the message has an attachment.

! TIP: To find a message from a specific sender, click the From column. This sorts messages alphanumerically based on the sender's name.

Locate New Messages

① Click the Inbox icon on the Outlook Bar to display your new messages.

② Click the Received column to sort your new messages by the date you received them. Messages you have not read appear in boldface.

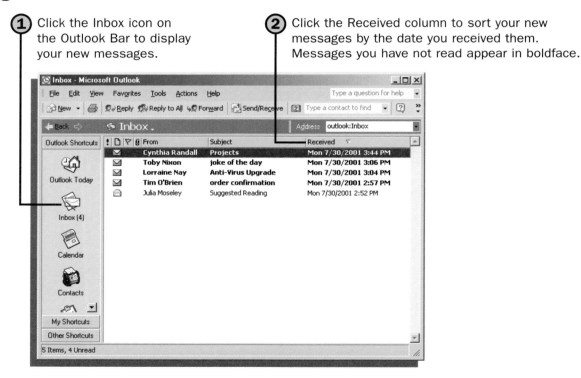

TRY THIS! Click the Received column once. If the most current date is at the top of the list, then you are sorting from the most current date received to the earliest date received. Click the Received column again to reverse the order of sorting, from the earliest date to the most current.

Open Message Items

1 Click the Inbox icon on the Outlook Bar to display your new messages.

2 Click on Preview Pane in the View menu.

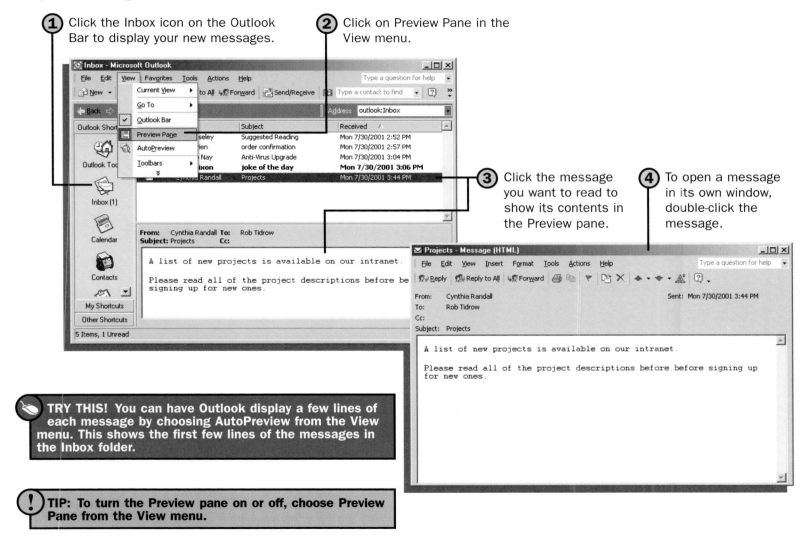

3 Click the message you want to read to show its contents in the Preview pane.

4 To open a message in its own window, double-click the message.

> **TRY THIS!** You can have Outlook display a few lines of each message by choosing AutoPreview from the View menu. This shows the first few lines of the messages in the Inbox folder.

> **TIP:** To turn the Preview pane on or off, choose Preview Pane from the View menu.

Managing the Inbox Folder

Over time, your Inbox folder can quickly get jumbled with hundreds of messages. This makes finding messages more difficult and takes up hard disk space. You can reduce these problems by managing your Inbox folder. Some of the administrative tasks you can perform include deleting unneeded messages, saving important messages, and printing a copy of a message to read or store in hard copy format.

Delete Unneeded Messages

(1) Click the Inbox icon on the Outlook Bar to display messages in your Inbox folder.

(2) Select the message you want to delete.

(3) Click Delete on the Standard toolbar.

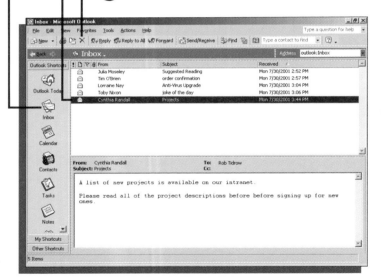

CAUTION: Outlook does not ask if you are sure you want to delete a message. Make sure that you want to delete the message before you press Delete or choose the Delete command.

SEE ALSO: To learn more about managing items and folders, see "Managing Items and Folders" on page 187.

TIP: Deleted messages are moved to the Deleted Items folder and can be moved back to your Inbox folder if necessary. If you delete messages from the Deleted Items folder, that item is gone for good (unless you've copied it to another folder).

Save Important Messages

(1) Click the Inbox icon on the Outlook Bar to display messages in your Inbox folder.

(3) Choose Save As from the File menu.

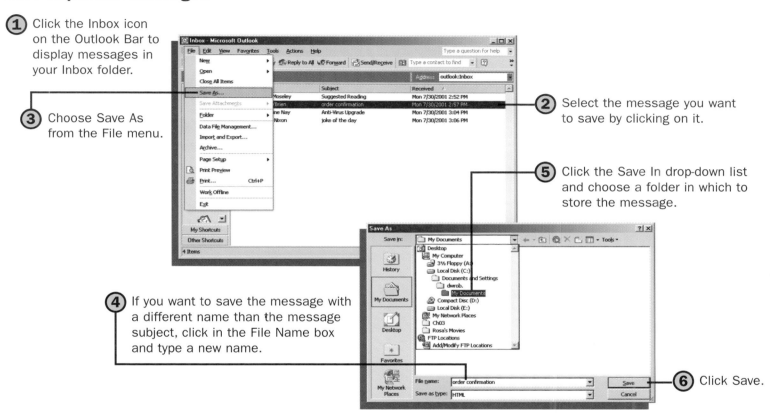

(2) Select the message you want to save by clicking on it.

(5) Click the Save In drop-down list and choose a folder in which to store the message.

(4) If you want to save the message with a different name than the message subject, click in the File Name box and type a new name.

(6) Click Save.

TIP: To save the message in a format other than message format (.msg), click the Save As Type drop-down list and choose the format type. You can save messages in text, HTML, Outlook template, and message format. This makes it handy when you want to open the message in another application, such as a word processor or Internet Web browser.

CAUTION: When you save a message in a format other than .msg, the formatting of the message itself may change. If this is the case, you may find it difficult to read the message without modifying it.

Print a Copy of a Message

① Display or select a message in your Inbox folder.

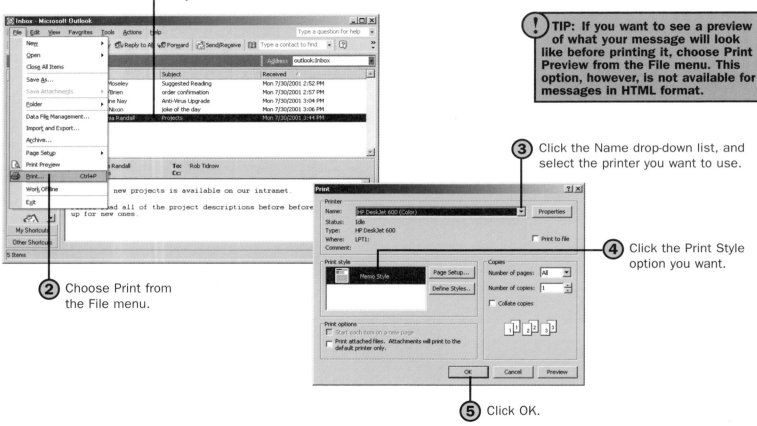

② Choose Print from the File menu.

TIP: If you want to see a preview of what your message will look like before printing it, choose Print Preview from the File menu. This option, however, is not available for messages in HTML format.

③ Click the Name drop-down list, and select the printer you want to use.

④ Click the Print Style option you want.

⑤ Click OK.

TIP: Clicking Print on the Standard toolbar sends the message to the default printer using the default settings.

Working with Attachments

When you receive an e-mail attachment, you can open it directly from the message, save it to your hard disk and open it from there, or print it straight from the message to a printer. Messages that have attachments display a paper clip icon to the left of the message author's name.

> **! TIP:** To open an attachment, you must have an application that supports the attached file. For instance, if you receive a PowerPoint file (.ppt), you must have Power-Point, the PowerPoint Viewer, or some similar application installed on your system to view the file.

Open an Attachment

(1) Click the Inbox icon on the Outlook Bar to display messages in your Inbox folder.

(2) Open the message with the attachment.

(3) Double-click the attachment in the Attachments field.

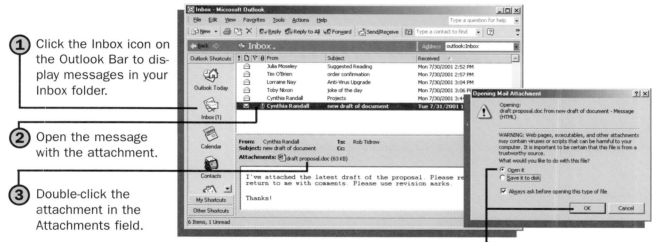

(4) If asked if you want to open or save the attachment, select Open It and then click OK.

> **✋ CAUTION:** Some files, such as programs, Web pages, and script files, that you receive from another user can be infected with a computer virus. You should save all executable files to your system and run an antivirus program that checks the file for a virus before you open it. If you receive an attachment from someone you do not know (as happens a lot with junk e-mail), you should *never* open it. Just delete the message.

> **SEE ALSO:** For information on attaching files to messages you send, see "E-Mailing a File" on page 40.

Save an Attachment

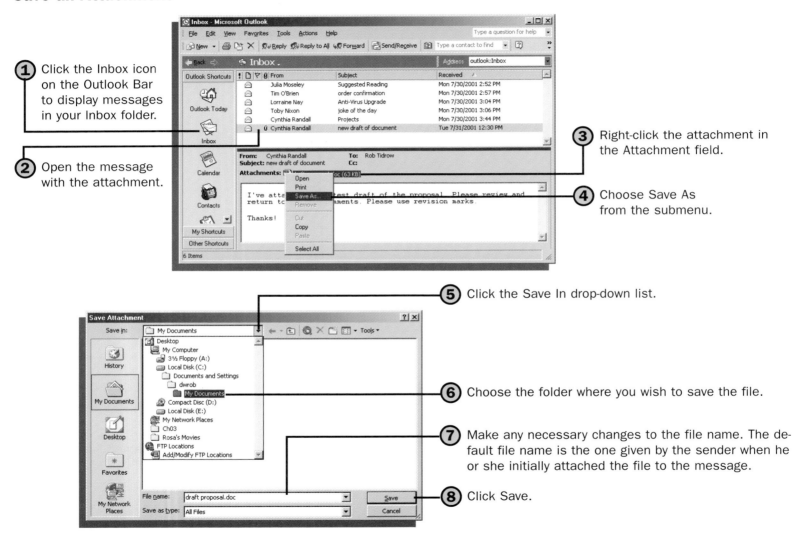

① Click the Inbox icon on the Outlook Bar to display messages in your Inbox folder.

② Open the message with the attachment.

③ Right-click the attachment in the Attachment field.

④ Choose Save As from the submenu.

⑤ Click the Save In drop-down list.

⑥ Choose the folder where you wish to save the file.

⑦ Make any necessary changes to the file name. The default file name is the one given by the sender when he or she initially attached the file to the message.

⑧ Click Save.

Replying to and Forwarding E-Mail

When you receive a message, you can reply directly back to the sender. You also have the option of forwarding the message or sending a response to everyone who received the message. When you reply to a message, Outlook keeps the original message text and lets you add your new text above the original text. The sender's name becomes the recipient name, and the subject line begins with "RE:" to denote that the message is a reply.

Reply to an E-Mail Message

1 Click the Inbox icon on the Outlook Bar to display messages in your Inbox folder.

2 Click the message you want to reply to.

3 Click Reply on the Standard toolbar.

4 Click in the space above the Original Message line, and type your reply.

5 Click the Send button.

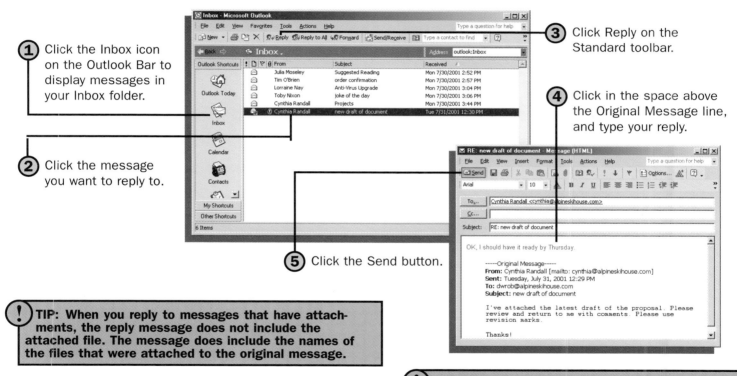

(!) TIP: When you reply to messages that have attachments, the reply message does not include the attached file. The message does include the names of the files that were attached to the original message.

(!) TIP: To reply to all recipients of a message, click Reply To All on the Standard toolbar.

Forward an E-Mail Message

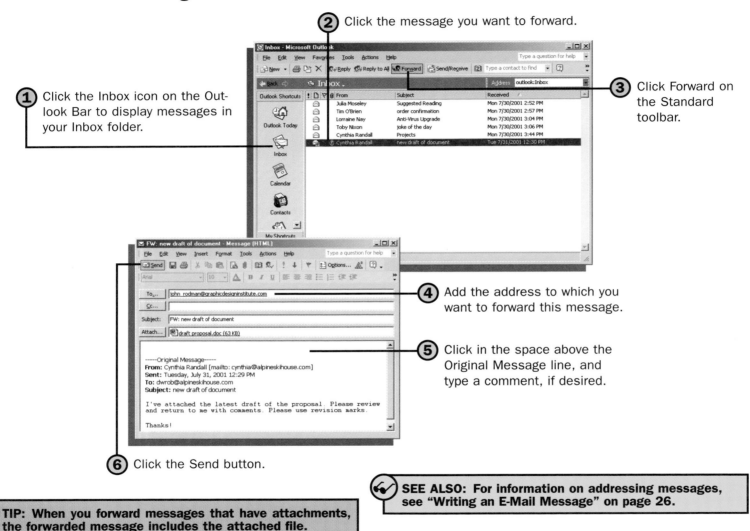

② Click the message you want to forward.

① Click the Inbox icon on the Outlook Bar to display messages in your Inbox folder.

③ Click Forward on the Standard toolbar.

④ Add the address to which you want to forward this message.

⑤ Click in the space above the Original Message line, and type a comment, if desired.

⑥ Click the Send button.

> ⊙ SEE ALSO: For information on addressing messages, see "Writing an E-Mail Message" on page 26.

> ❗ TIP: When you forward messages that have attachments, the forwarded message includes the attached file.

Handling Junk Mail

Just like the junk mail that you receive in your regular mailbox, you'll probably get too many junk e-mail messages (also known as *spam*) inside your Outlook Inbox. Outlook makes it easy to set up mail filters that can sort your incoming mail so that junk mail is moved to its own folder, flagged, or deleted. Outlook also allows you to turn on mail filters so only specific messages are displayed in the Inbox.

Turn on Mail Filters

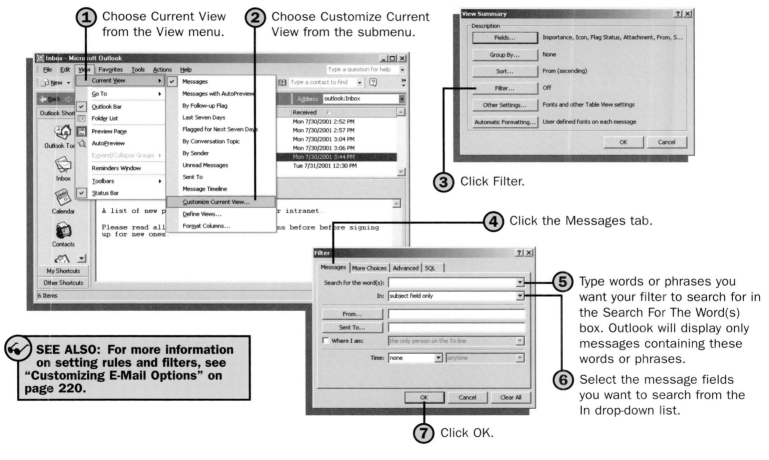

(1) Choose Current View from the View menu.

(2) Choose Customize Current View from the submenu.

(3) Click Filter.

(4) Click the Messages tab.

(5) Type words or phrases you want your filter to search for in the Search For The Word(s) box. Outlook will display only messages containing these words or phrases.

(6) Select the message fields you want to search from the In drop-down list.

(7) Click OK.

> **SEE ALSO:** For more information on setting rules and filters, see "Customizing E-Mail Options" on page 220.

Add to the Junk Mail Senders List

(1) In the Inbox folder, click a message from a person who you want to add to the junk mail senders list.

(2) Select Junk E-Mail on the Actions menu.

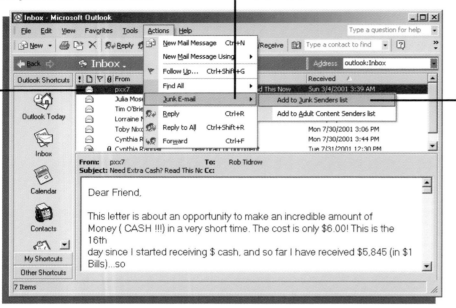

(3) Choose Add To Junk Senders List. A message box may appear, telling you that the sender has been added to the junk e-mail list. Click OK.

CAUTION: If you add a sender to the junk e-mail list by accident, all messages from this sender may be deleted as soon as they are received by Outlook. If you think a legitimate sender is on your junk mail filter, see the next procedure for removing him or her from the list.

TIP: One way you get on a junk mail list is by filling out surveys and other online forms on Web sites. Usually these forms ask for your e-mail address to process the form. To reduce the amount of junk e-mail you get, limit the number of Web site surveys you fill out.

Fine-tune the Junk Mail Filter

(1) With the Inbox showing, select Organize from the Tools menu.

(2) Click the Junk E-mail link.

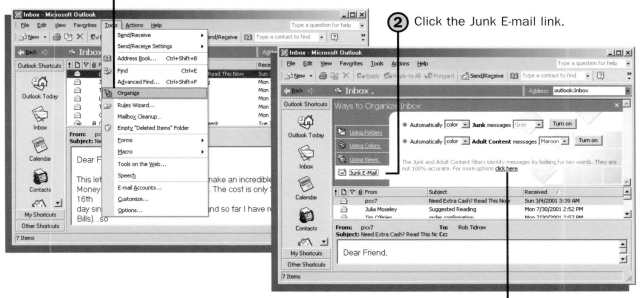

(4) To remove a sender from the Junk Mail list, select a name and click Delete.

(5) To add a sender to the Junk Mail list, click Add.

(3) At the bottom of the Ways To Organize Inbox pane, click on the link that allows you to see more options. On the list of options that comes up, click the Edit Junk Senders link.

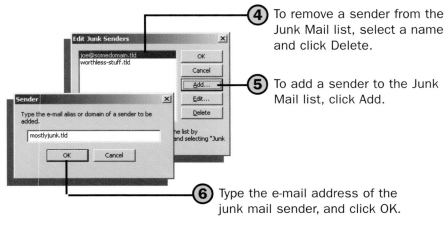

> **For more information on setting rules, see "Customizing E-Mail Options" on page 220.**

(6) Type the e-mail address of the junk mail sender, and click OK.

Working with the Rules Wizard

Outlook makes it easy to manage your e-mail by using rules. Rules are actions that Outlook performs on your messages to organize them. Once you have Outlook rules set, many management tasks are taken care of automatically when your new messages arrive. To make setting up rules painless, Outlook includes a Rules Wizard that walks you though the process of creating a rule by referring to a message you have already received. You can also create a rule from scratch.

Create a Rule Based on a Message

(1) In the Inbox folder, right-click the message on which you want to base the new rule.

(2) Click Create Rule on the shortcut menu to display the Rules Wizard.

(3) In the first wizard screen, select the condition(s) under which you want the rule applied, and then click Next.

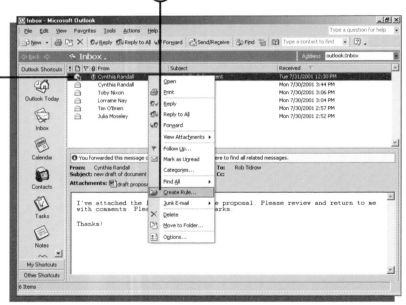

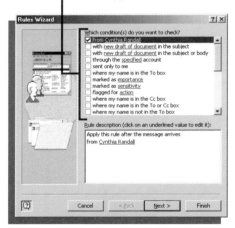

> **!** **TIP:** You can select multiple conditions under which your new rule is applied. When you do this, however, the rule will not be applied unless *all* the conditions are met.

(!) TIP: For some of the conditions and actions (that is, what you want Outlook to do with a message), you must identify something specific. This is done by clicking the blue hyperlink text in the condition or action item. For example, if you select the Move It To The Specified Folder action, you must click the "Specified" link in that option, select a folder to which you want the message moved, and click OK.

(4) In the second screen, select what you want done with the message, and then click Next.

(5) In the third screen, select exceptions to the rule, and then click Next.

(6) In the final screen, type a name for your rule.

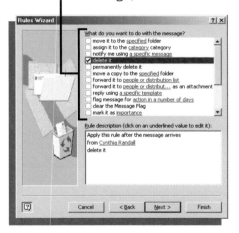

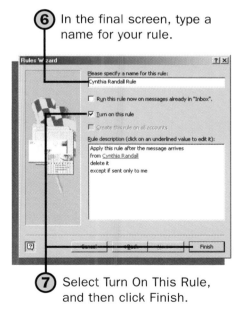

(7) Select Turn On This Rule, and then click Finish.

Create a Rule from Scratch

(1) With the Inbox folder displayed, choose Rules Wizard from the Tools menu.

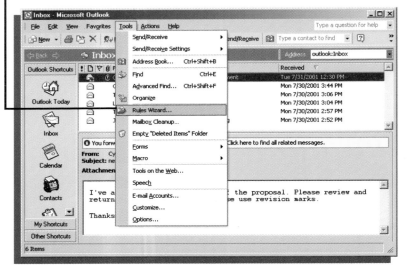

SEE ALSO: For more information on setting rules in Outlook, see "Customizing E-Mail Options" on page 220.

TRY THIS! To run rules manually, click Run Now on the Rules Wizard dialog box. Select the rules you want to run, and click Run Now again.

(2) In the Apply Changes To This Folder drop-down list, select the folder to which you want the new rule applied.

(3) Click New.

(4) In the next screen, select Start From A Blank Rule, and then click Next.

⑤ Select the condition(s) under which you want the rule applied, and then click Next.

⑥ Select what you want done with the message, and then click Next.

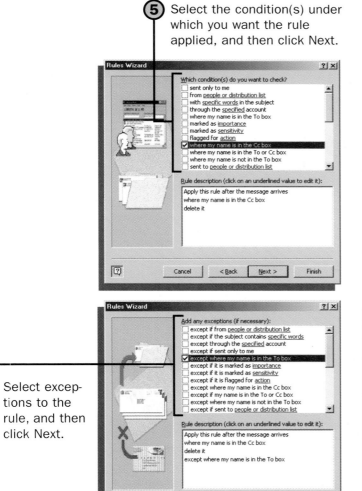

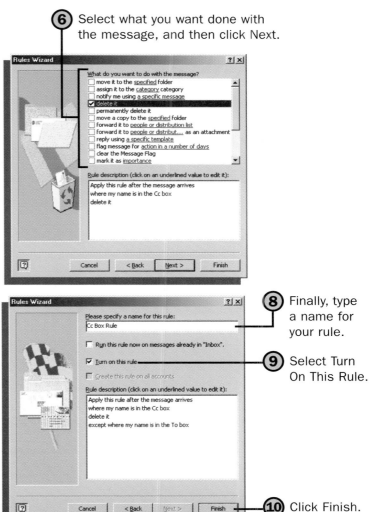

⑦ Select exceptions to the rule, and then click Next.

⑧ Finally, type a name for your rule.

⑨ Select Turn On This Rule.

⑩ Click Finish.

Following Up on a Message

When you receive a message, you may not have time or the information you need to reply to it. In such cases, you can flag a message to remind yourself to follow up on it later. You can designate different types of follow-up, including reminders to reply by e-mail, forward the message to a third party, or reply by telephone.

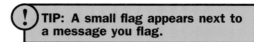

⚠️ **TIP: A small flag appears next to a message you flag.**

Flag a Message for Follow-Up

1 In the Inbox pane, right-click the message you want to flag and choose Follow Up from the submenu.

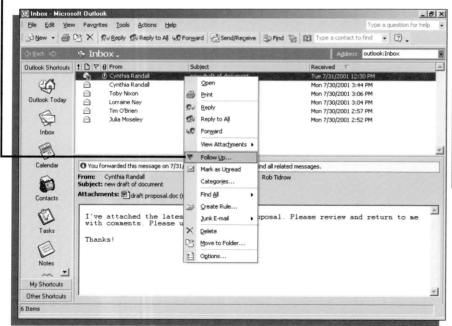

2 Select a type of follow-up.

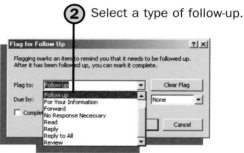

3 If necessary, select a due date and time, then click OK.

🖱️ **TRY THIS! In the Flag For Follow Up dialog box, set a flag that is due today at 30 minutes from the current time. When the time expires, Outlook will display a message prompting you to follow up on the message.**

Clear a Follow Up Flag

(1) In the Inbox pane, right-click the message that includes a follow-up flag.

(2) Choose Flag Complete from the submenu.

TIP: When you clear a follow-up flag, a clear flag appears next the message subject. If you later determine that you want to set the flag again, right-click the message, choose Follow Up from the submenu, deselect the Completed option, and click OK.

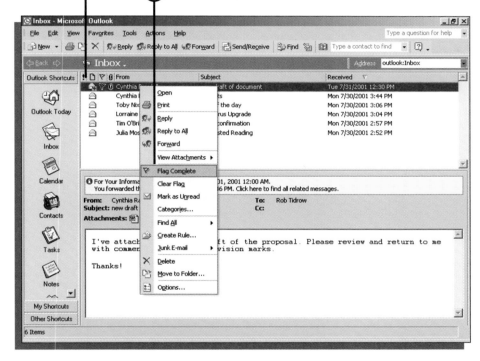

SEE ALSO: For information on replying to e-mail messages, see "Replying To and Forwarding E-Mail" on page 57.

5) Using Instant Messaging

In this section

Turning On Instant Messaging

Configuring Instant Messaging

Finding Friends

Writing and Reading Instant Messages

When the Internet first became popular, most people communicated only using e-mail. Over time, chat rooms became more and more popular as people realized they could chat with others in real time instead of sending a message and waiting—sometimes a long time—for a reply. Now you can type a message, send it, and the person at the other end of the conversation receives it immediately and can send a response.

This section covers the Instant Messenger software that Microsoft integrated into Outlook. The MSN Messenger Service software isn't included with Outlook, but after you download the software and set it up, you can work with it from Outlook. Microsoft provides a Web site where you can download the program, and the Microsoft Exchange 2000 Server CD-ROM also includes the MSN Messenger Service software.

You can use the MSN Messenger Service software to find out when friends or coworkers are online and chat with them. The program includes a contact list that you can use to quickly and easily start a chat session. Best of all, with the contact list you can tell at a glance whether a particular person is online.

Turning On Instant Messaging

Outlook isn't set up right away to use the MSN Messenger software. The first task you need to accomplish before you can use Messenger is to obtain a Microsoft Passport. The Passport is a type of electronic ID that you associate with your e-mail address. When other people want to contact you through Messenger, they can use your e-mail address as your instant messaging address. You also need to download the software and set it up. All of these tasks are easy to accomplish, given a little direction.

Get a Passport

(1) Open your Web browser, and connect to *www.passport.com*.

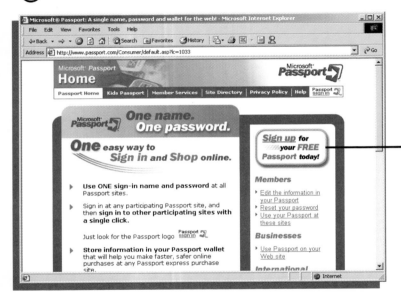

> **TIP:** If you already have a Hotmail account, you should already have a Microsoft Passport. You can configure your Passport settings through the Hotmail Web site at **www.hotmail.com**.

(2) Click the Sign Up link.

> **TIP:** After you sign up, Microsoft stores your connection information on its instant messaging server—there is nothing to download or store on your computer.

> **TRY THIS!** Many Web sites let you use your Microsoft Passport to log in. To view a list of these sites, open your Web browser and point it to *www.passport.com*. Click the link titled Use Your Passport At These Sites to open a page listing sites that use Microsoft Passport for login and for express purchasing.

③ Enter the e-mail address that you want to use as your instant messaging address.

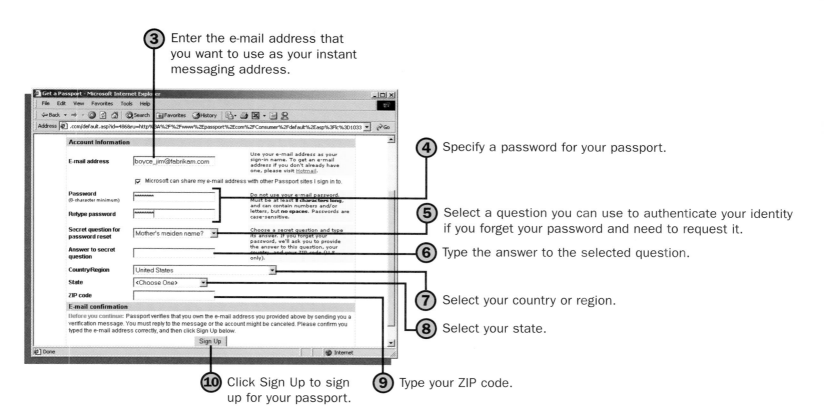

④ Specify a password for your passport.

⑤ Select a question you can use to authenticate your identity if you forget your password and need to request it.

⑥ Type the answer to the selected question.

⑦ Select your country or region.

⑧ Select your state.

⑩ Click Sign Up to sign up for your passport.

⑨ Type your ZIP code.

Download MSN Messenger

(1) Open Outlook, and choose Options on the Tools menu to open the Options dialog box.

(2) Click the Other tab.

Options ?|x|

Preferences | Mail Setup | Mail Format | Spelling | Security | Other |

General

☐ Empty the Deleted Items folder upon exiting

☑ Make Outlook the default program for E-mail, Contacts, and Calendar.

[Advanced Options...]

AutoArchive

Manages mailbox size by deleting old items or moving them to an archive file and by deleting expired items.

[AutoArchive...]

Preview pane

Use these options to customize the appearance and behavior of the preview pane.

[Preview Pane...]

Instant Messaging

☑ Enable Instant Messaging in Microsoft Outlook

[Options...]

[OK] [Cancel] [Apply]

> **! TIP: Most chat programs don't work with other chat programs. So you won't be able to use the MSN Messenger Service program to chat with people who use other chat programs.**

Install MSN Messenger? x|

⚠ This feature requires MSN Messenger 3.5 or later. Do you want Outlook to open the MSN Messenger download web page?
After you install MSN Messenger, the changes will be visible after you shut down and restart Outlook.

[Yes] [No] [Cancel]

(3) Select Enable Instant Messaging In Microsoft Outlook.

(4) Click Yes when prompted by Outlook to download the MSN Messenger software.

(5) Designate your region, operating system, and desired language, and then start the download. When prompted, select Run This Program From Its Current Location.

> **! TIP: If you prefer that Outlook not attempt to determine the online status of people who send you messages, you can disable instant messaging in Outlook but still use the MSN Messenger Service software.**

6 Step through the wizard, entering your Passport sign-in name (the e-mail address you used to sign up for your Microsoft Passport) and your password.

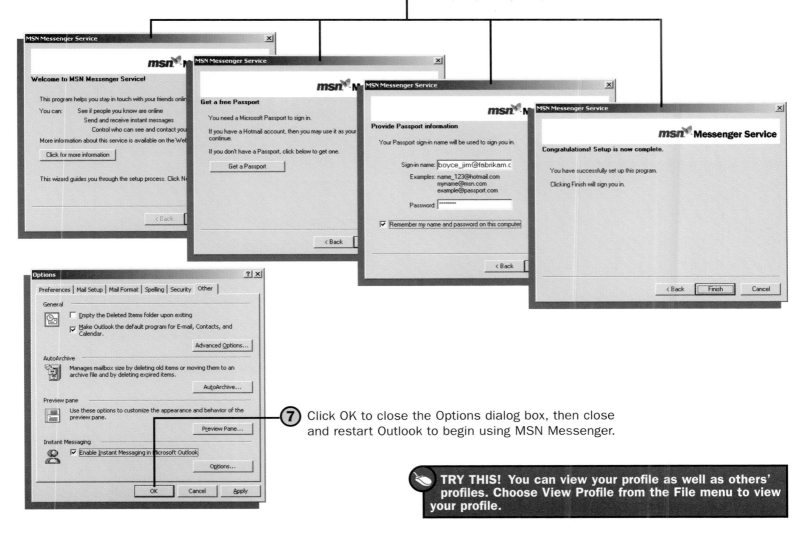

7 Click OK to close the Options dialog box, then close and restart Outlook to begin using MSN Messenger.

TRY THIS! You can view your profile as well as others' profiles. Choose View Profile from the File menu to view your profile.

Configuring Instant Messaging

Although you can start using MSN Messenger right after you install the software, you will probably want to configure some of the settings. One of the first steps is to set up your personal information in the program. You can specify the name that others will see online and other information items that make up your *personal profile*—information about you that others can see online. You can also specify settings that protect your privacy, and set the font used by the program when you send and receive messages.

Provide Personal Information

(1) While connected to the Internet, right-click the MSN Messenger Service icon on the tray and choose Open.

(2) In MSN Messenger, choose Options from the Tools menu to open the Options dialog box.

(3) On the Personal tab, double-click in the My Display Name text box and type the name that you want others to see when you are online. By default this field shows your Microsoft Passport logon name (your e-mail address.)

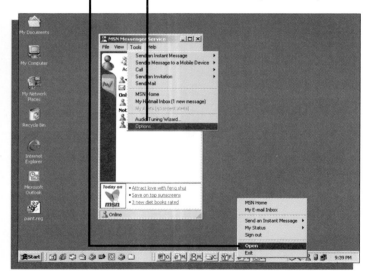

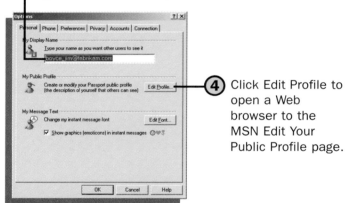

(4) Click Edit Profile to open a Web browser to the MSN Edit Your Public Profile page.

✋ CAUTION: Your profile can include information such as name, gender, location, marital status, occupation, and other personal data. When you create your profile you can completely control the information that is included. However, you should be careful not to include personal information—such as your address or phone number—that you don't want others to see. Remember, your public profile is visible to anyone who adds you to their contacts list.

(5) Fill in whatever options you wish, and click Save near the bottom of the page.

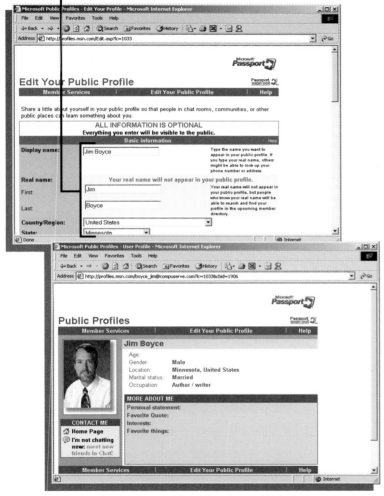

(6) After you save the changes the MSN site displays your profile.

Format Instant Message Text

(1) Open the MSN Messenger Service software, and choose Options from the Tools menu.

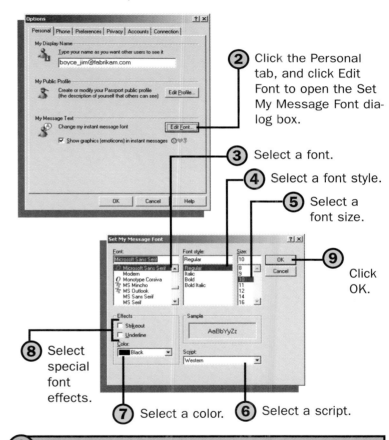

(2) Click the Personal tab, and click Edit Font to open the Set My Message Font dialog box.

(3) Select a font.

(4) Select a font style.

(5) Select a font size.

(9) Click OK.

(8) Select special font effects.

(7) Select a color.

(6) Select a script.

! TIP: Unfortunately you can't change the font used by the other person—you can only change your own. If you have trouble reading their font, choose Text Size from the View menu in the chat window and choose a larger size font. Or send a message to the other person asking him or her to change fonts.

Finding Friends ⊕ NEW FEATURE

When you use MSN Messenger, you no doubt will want to be able to see if your friends or coworkers are online. The Messenger software shows the online status of people you have added to your contact list. Likewise, your online status shows for those who have added your instant messaging address to their contact lists.

See Who is Online

(1) Connect to the Internet, and then open the MSN Messenger Service program.

(2) Choose Add A Contact from the File menu to start the Add A Contact Wizard.

(3) Select By E-mail Address Or Sign-In Name.

(5) Enter the other person's e-mail address.

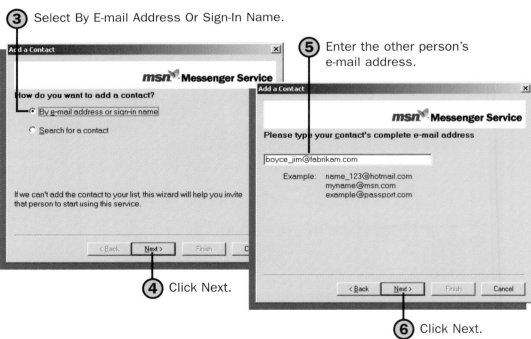

(4) Click Next.

(6) Click Next.

TRY THIS! If a friend or coworker isn't using MSN Messenger Service, you can send an e-mail containing instructions on how to download and use the software. In the MSN Messenger Service program, choose Add A Contact from the File menu. Select By E-Mail Address Or Sign-In Name, and click Next. Enter the e-mail address, and click Next. Click Send Mail, edit the message, and click Finish to send the message.

(7) To allow the contact to know when you are online, choose Allow This Person To See When You Are Online And Contact You.

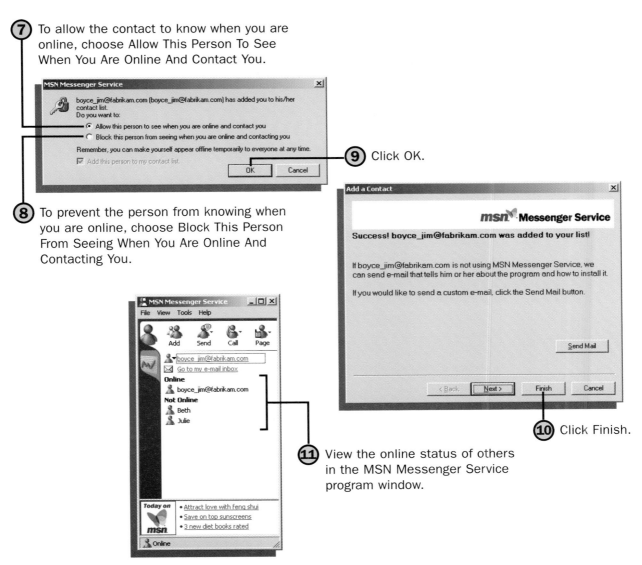

(9) Click OK.

(8) To prevent the person from knowing when you are online, choose Block This Person From Seeing When You Are Online And Contacting You.

(10) Click Finish.

(11) View the online status of others in the MSN Messenger Service program window.

Specify Who Can Contact You

(1) Open the MSN Messenger Service window, and choose Options from the Tools menu.

(2) Click the Privacy tab.

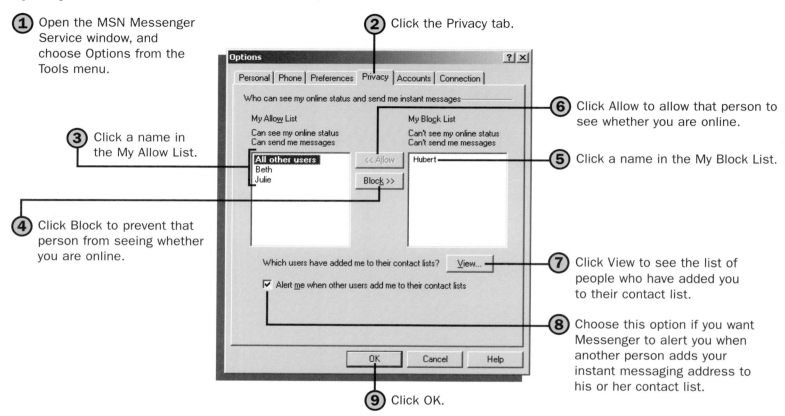

(3) Click a name in the My Allow List.

(4) Click Block to prevent that person from seeing whether you are online.

(6) Click Allow to allow that person to see whether you are online.

(5) Click a name in the My Block List.

(7) Click View to see the list of people who have added you to their contact list.

(8) Choose this option if you want Messenger to alert you when another person adds your instant messaging address to his or her contact list.

(9) Click OK.

> **!** **TIP: Blocking someone not only prevents them from seeing your online status but also blocks them from sending you messages.**

Writing and Reading Instant Messages

Writing and reading instant messages is easy with the MSN Messenger Service software. After you connect to the Internet you can simply open the program, click on a person's name if he or she is online and begin a chat session. Because the MSN Messenger Service software starts when your system starts, it waits in the background, listening for chat requests from others and starting sessions for you when someone tries to contact you.

Send an Instant Message

1 Double-click the MSN Messenger Service program icon on the tray to open the program.

3 Locate the person with whom you want to chat in the online list, and double-click the person's name.

2 If you haven't signed in, click the Click Here To Sign In link.

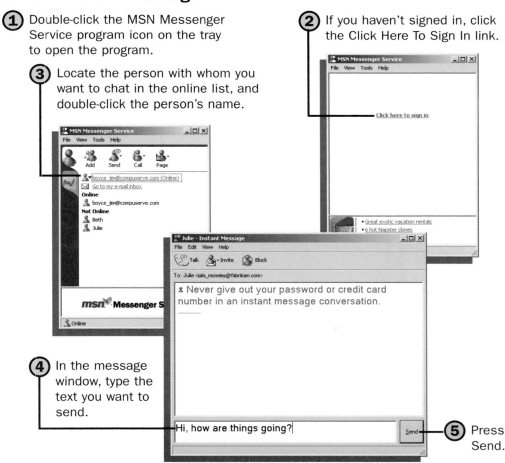

4 In the message window, type the text you want to send.

5 Press Send.

> **TIP:** You can also start a chat session from within Outlook. When you click on a message in the Inbox, Outlook checks the on-line status of the sender, and if the sender is online, displays a message to that effect in the preview pane's InfoBar. You can then click on the InfoBar message to quickly start a chat session.

> **TRY THIS!** You can't send a chat message to someone if he or she is offline, but you can send an e-mail message to him. Double-click on the person's name in the Not Online section of the MSN Messenger Service program window. Click Yes when asked if you want to send a message. Outlook will open a new message form with the recipient's address in the To field.

Receive an Instant Message

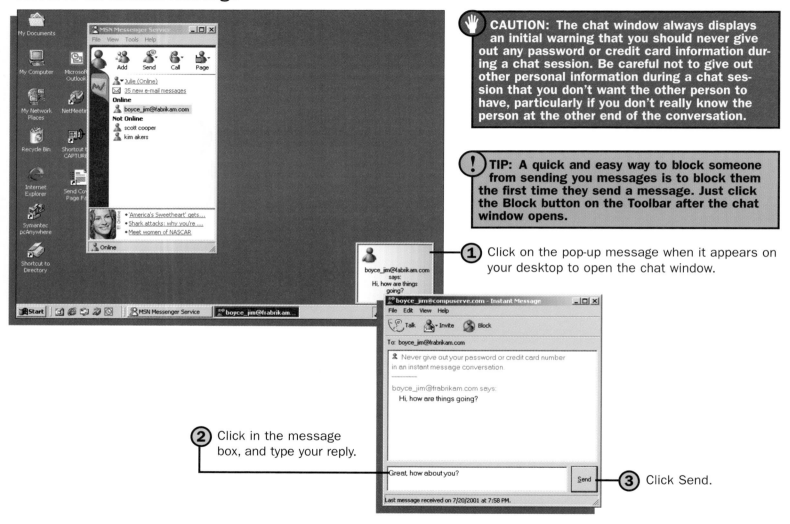

CAUTION: The chat window always displays an initial warning that you should never give out any password or credit card information during a chat session. Be careful not to give out other personal information during a chat session that you don't want the other person to have, particularly if you don't really know the person at the other end of the conversation.

TIP: A quick and easy way to block someone from sending you messages is to block them the first time they send a message. Just click the Block button on the Toolbar after the chat window opens.

① Click on the pop-up message when it appears on your desktop to open the chat window.

② Click in the message box, and type your reply.

③ Click Send.

Set Your Online Status

(1) Open the MSN Messenger Service program window.

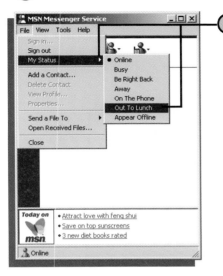

 Choose My Status from the File menu, then select the status you want others to see for you.

TRY THIS! You can set your online status through the Messenger icon on the system tray. Right-click the icon and choose My Status, then choose the desired status from the menu.

TIP: The Messenger software sets your status to Away if there is no keyboard or mouse activity on your computer for five minutes.

TIP: You can appear offline even though you are still connected to the Internet. Choose the Appear Offline option from the status options any time you want to remain online but not receive chat messages.

6 Browsing Newsgroups

Internet newsgroups are like electronic bulletin boards: users can connect to them and post messages about a topic and other users can read and reply to those messages. While many messages on news servers consist only of text, you can attach files to news messages as a means of sharing graphics, sound, and other types of files. Newsgroups are a popular means of sharing files.

There are thousands of newsgroups on a number of different subjects. In fact most Internet newsgroup servers host over 40,000 public newsgroups. Many companies also host their own newsgroup servers to provide information about their company, products, and services to their customers. For example, Microsoft hosts many different newsgroups to provide technical support for users of its products. You can find several groups devoted to Microsoft Office programs on *news.microsoft.com*.

To join and participate in newsgroups, you must have a newsreader program. A newsreader allows you to connect to a news server, view the message categories (newsgroups) hosted on the server, read messages, and post your own messages. Microsoft Outlook uses the Outlook Newsreader to handle newsgroup tasks. Outlook Newsreader is actually a subset of Outlook Express, which is included with Windows. If you have your own newsreader, you can start it from within Outlook and use it rather than Outlook Express.

Setting Up a Newsgroup Account

Before you can participate in newsgroups, you need to set up a newsgroup account. Usually your Internet Service Provider (ISP) gives you access to newsgroups. You need to ask your ISP what their news server is. For example, if your ISP is named adatum.com, the news server would be something like "nntp.adatum.com" or "news.adatum.com". After you set up your newsgroup account, you connect to the Internet and download a list of all the available newsgroups. From this list, you can pick those to which you want to subscribe.

Add an Internet Newsgroup Account

(1) Start Outlook.

(2) Choose Go To from the View menu.

(3) Choose News from the Go To submenu to start Outlook Newsreader.

(4) If the Internet Connection Wizard does not open, click Set Up A Newsgroups Account in the right-hand pane.

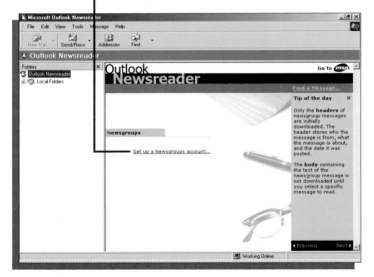

CAUTION: If you do not fill out the news server information correctly, you will not be able to access the newsgroups. Be sure to ask your ISP what the correct setting is for your account. If you are part of a local area network at work, ask your system administrator for help.

TIP: If your news server requires you to log on before you can browse newsgroups, select My News Server Requires Me To Log On in the Internet Connection Wizard. Click Next, and then fill in username and password information. Click Next to see the final screen.

(5) Step through the screens in the wizard, entering your name, email address, and your ISP's news (NNTP) server name in the appropriate fields.

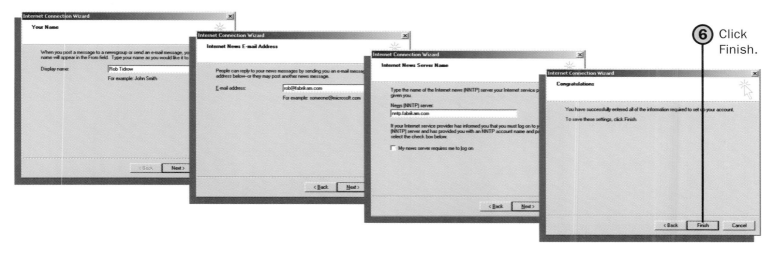

(6) Click Finish.

Retrieve the List of Newsgroups

(1) After you add a newsgroup account, Outlook Newsreader asks if you want to download the newsgroup list for the server. Click Yes when asked if you would like to download newsgroups.

(2) Wait while the newsgroups download.

! TIP: When you are prompted to download newsgroups, you are actually downloading a list of newsgroup names. You are not downloading newsgroup messages.

! TIP: Not all ISPs allow access to all newsgroups. This is to decrease the amount of traffic your ISP's servers have to handle. If you know of a particular newsgroup that your ISP does not carry, send them an e-mail asking if they will subscribe to it.

✋ CAUTION: At last count, there were over 40,000 newsgroups available. When you download the list of newsgroups, it will take a while if you are connected by a standard modem. You may want to perform this task during a lunch break or start it before attending a staff meeting.

Subscribing and Unsubscribing to Newsgroups

After you download the list of available newsgroups on your news server, you can review the list and select the groups you want to subscribe to. Most newsgroups are freely available, so subscribing just means you want to download messages from the newsgroup and have the ability to send your own messages to the newsgroup for others to see. If you grow tired of a newsgroup, you can unsubscribe from it by deleting it from your list of subscribed newsgroups.

Review the Newsgroups List

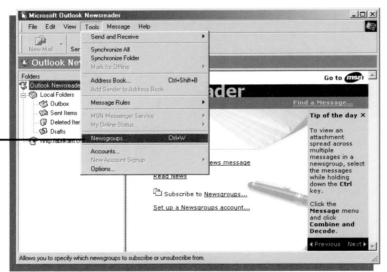

① If the Newsgroup Subscriptions dialog box is not open, choose Newsgroups from the Tools menu in Outlook Newsreader.

! TIP: When you use the Display Newsgroups Which Contain box, you can display all the newsgroups that are of a given topic. For example, if you type "music," you will see newsgroups that are related to the music industry, musical instruments, and so on. Outlook Newsreader displays all newsgroups on the server that contain "music" in the newsgroup name.

TRY THIS! Some newsgroups do not have much activity—fewer than 10 messages a day—while others may have thousands of postings a day. Before subscribing to a newsgroup, review it to see if it meets your expectations.

② Click the server with the newsgroups you want to review.

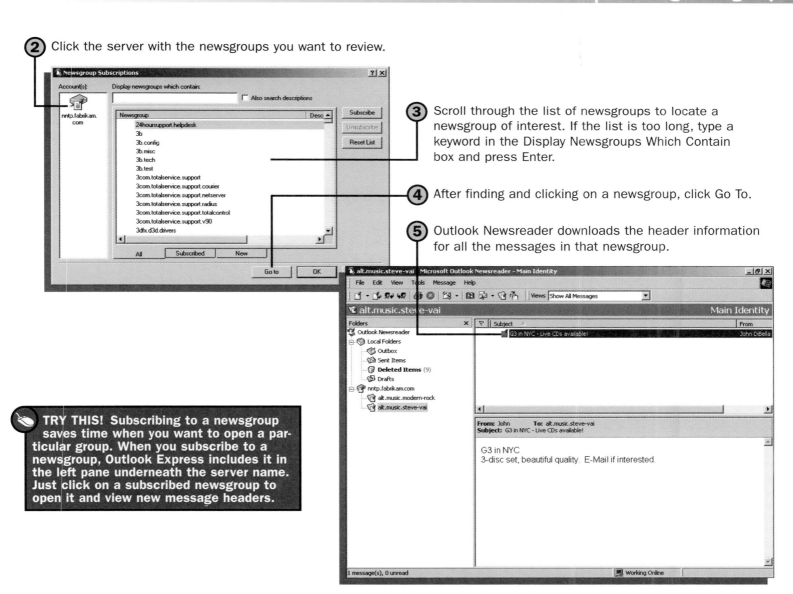

③ Scroll through the list of newsgroups to locate a newsgroup of interest. If the list is too long, type a keyword in the Display Newsgroups Which Contain box and press Enter.

④ After finding and clicking on a newsgroup, click Go To.

⑤ Outlook Newsreader downloads the header information for all the messages in that newsgroup.

TRY THIS! Subscribing to a newsgroup saves time when you want to open a particular group. When you subscribe to a newsgroup, Outlook Express includes it in the left pane underneath the server name. Just click on a subscribed newsgroup to open it and view new message headers.

Subscribe to Newsgroups

① Open Outlook Newsreader, and select a news server.

② Click Newsgroups to open the Newsgroup Subscriptions dialog box.

③ Select a newsgroup from the list, and click Subscribe.

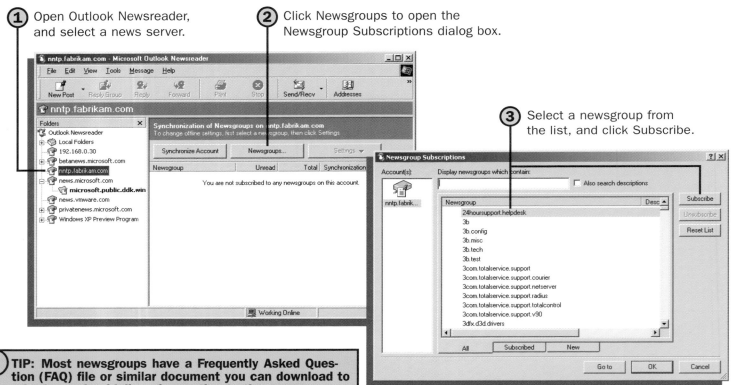

> **! TIP:** Most newsgroups have a Frequently Asked Question (FAQ) file or similar document you can download to read rules and guidelines for posting to the newsgroup. For instance, some newsgroups are moderated, meaning a person combs through each message to ensure it meets the basic requirements for the newsgroups. The FAQ will cover this type of information and other beginning-level material.

> **✋ CAUTION:** Some newsgroups have questionable content in them and should not be accessed by young children.

Unsubscribe to a Newsgroup

1 Open the Newsgroups Subscriptions dialog box.

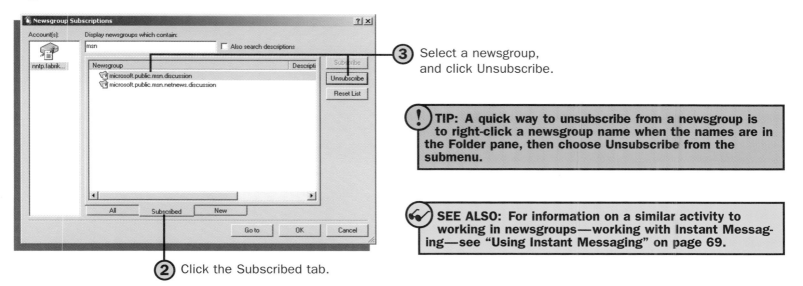

3 Select a newsgroup,
and click Unsubscribe.

> **!** **TIP:** A quick way to unsubscribe from a newsgroup is to right-click a newsgroup name when the names are in the Folder pane, then choose Unsubscribe from the submenu.

> **SEE ALSO:** For information on a similar activity to working in newsgroups—working with Instant Messaging—see "Using Instant Messaging" on page 69.

2 Click the Subscribed tab.

> **!** **TIP:** Subscribing to a newsgroup does not mean that your privacy is compromised. Outlook Express stores the subscription on your local computer but does not upload any information about your subscriptions to the news server. So no one else on the Internet knows to which newsgroups you subscribe.

> **TRY THIS!** Occasionally you might want to get rid of old messages, maybe to free up some disk space. Choose Options from the Tools menu, click the Maintenance tab, and then click Clean Up Now. Click Browse to select the newsgroup, and then click Delete. When the process finishes, click Close, and then click OK to close the Options dialog box.

Viewing Newsgroup Posts

After subscribing to a newsgroup, your next task is to download newsgroup posts. A newsgroup post is just like an e-mail message, except it is sent to a newsgroup rather than to an individual. You can read the post, reply to it, save it to your disk, or ignore it. Prior to downloading the actual message part of a post, however, you download the message headers, which are the messages' subject lines. You can use Outlook Newsreader to search for a message based on keywords and other criteria.

Download Message Headers

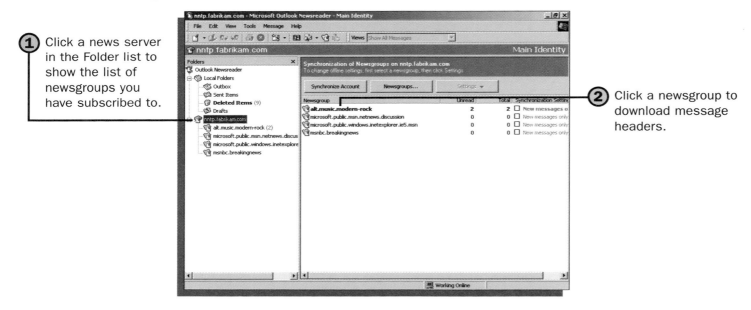

1 Click a news server in the Folder list to show the list of newsgroups you have subscribed to.

2 Click a newsgroup to download message headers.

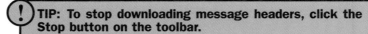

> **!** **TIP:** Depending on the number of messages in a newsgroup and your connection speed to the Internet, the time it takes to download all the message headers will vary. If there are only a few headers, the time is a matter of moments. However, if you have a slow Internet connection and there are 500 or more headers, it may take several minutes to download the headers alone.

> **!** **TIP:** To stop downloading message headers, click the Stop button on the toolbar.

Sort Newsgroup Messages

1 Click the Subject column to sort message headers by their subject.

2 Click the From column to sort message headers by the author of the message.

3 Click the Size column to sort message headers by their size.

4 Click the Sent column to sort message headers by the date the message was posted to the newsgroup.

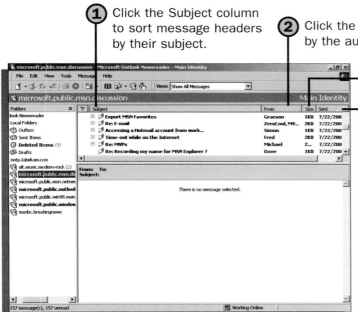

! **TIP: As you participate in a particular newsgroup, you'll start noticing which users provide the best posts. This is one reason to sort newsgroups by name.**

! **TIP: The size column shows the size of the message and any attachments the message may have. Most messages are small—1 kilobyte (KB) to 10 KB in size. However, if they have attached files, they can grow as large as 600 KB or larger. Keep this in mind as you start to download messages.**

Customize the Message List

1 In Outlook Newsreader, Choose Columns from the View menu.

2 To remove a column from the message list, clear the check box next to the column name. To show a column, select the check box next to the column name.

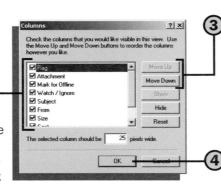

3 To reorder the columns, click a column and click the Move Up and Move Down buttons accordingly.

4 Click OK.

TRY THIS! To show the message list with the Name column first, click it in the Columns dialog box and click Move Up until it is at the top of the list. Now the Name column appears at the far left of the message list.

! **TIP: To set the message list back to its original order, click the Reset button.**

Find a Message

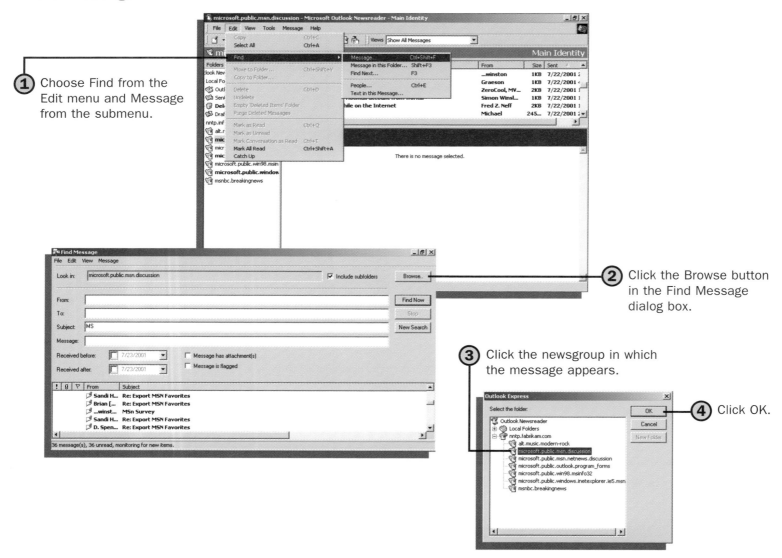

① Choose Find from the Edit menu and Message from the submenu.

② Click the Browse button in the Find Message dialog box.

③ Click the newsgroup in which the message appears.

④ Click OK.

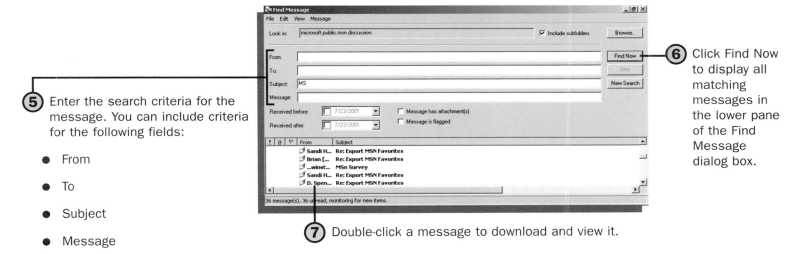

(5) Enter the search criteria for the message. You can include criteria for the following fields:

- From
- To
- Subject
- Message
- Received Before
- Received After
- Message Has Attachment(s)
- Message Is Flagged

(6) Click Find Now to display all matching messages in the lower pane of the Find Message dialog box.

(7) Double-click a message to download and view it.

 SEE ALSO: For more information about attachments, see "Download a Binary Message" on page 95.

TIP: If you know the message has an attachment with it, open the Find Message dialog box as explained in this task and select Message Has Attachment(s). This causes Outlook Newsreader only to search for messages that contain attachments and that meet your other search criteria. Do not select this option if you are not sure if the message contains an attachment. If you select this option, Outlook Newsreader assumes the message has an attachment and may overlook the message you really want if it does not have an attachment.

Opening a Newsgroup Post

Now that you have the message headers downloaded to your system, you're ready to open and read newsgroup posts. Posts come in two basic types: text and binary. A text message is one that appears just like an e-mail message in the message body area. Binary messages are files, such as word processing files or graphics, that must be converted or opened by another application to be readable.

Download a Text Message

① With Outlook Newsreader open, download message headers for a newsgroup.

② Click the message header for a message you want to download.

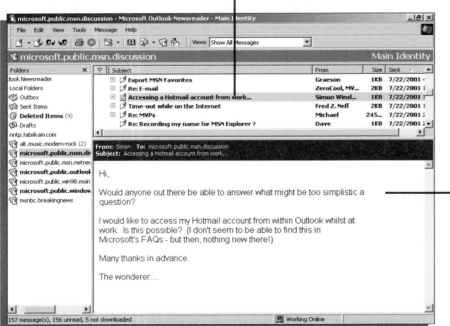

> **!** TIP: Messages with a torn icon next to them are ones that you have not downloaded yet. Messages with a full page icon are ones that you've downloaded. Messages in boldface are ones that have not been read.

> **!** TIP: Messages with a plus sign next to them are part of a *thread*. A thread is a group of messages relating to a single topic or conversation. A thread does not always stay on topic, but you can usually follow along in the conversation if you missed earlier posts about a topic.

③ Read the message text in the bottom pane.

Download a Binary Message

(1) With Outlook Newsreader open, download message headers for a newsgroup.

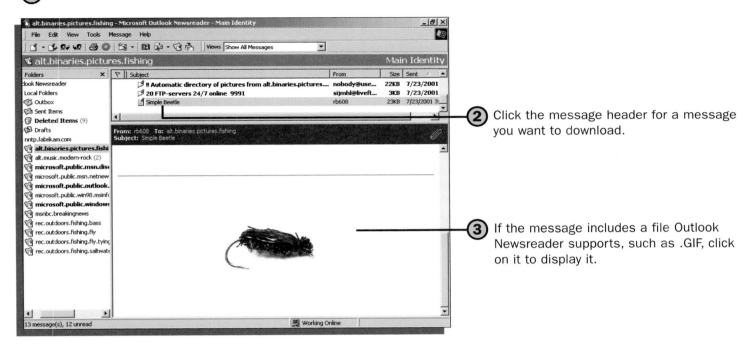

(2) Click the message header for a message you want to download.

(3) If the message includes a file Outlook Newsreader supports, such as .GIF, click on it to display it.

(!) TIP: Some binary files are too large to include in one message. These messages are broken into two or more files and posted in separate messages. Usually the sender names each part numerically and states the number of files, such as "Part 2 of 11". You must download each part and combine them by choosing **Combine And Decode** from the Message menu in Outlook Reader.

(✋) CAUTION: Any binary file you receive from a newsgroup has the potential of being a virus program. Viruses can damage your data and system. Be careful when you choose which files to download and run. You should always run virus checking software against any file you receive on the Internet before running the program on your computer.

Saving Newsgroup Posts

Outlook Newsreader allows you to save newsgroup posts to your hard drive for future reference. You can save a text message or binary message and print text messages much like you would an e-mail message.

Save a Text Message

① With a newsgroup's headers displayed, download a text message.

② Choose Save As from the File menu.

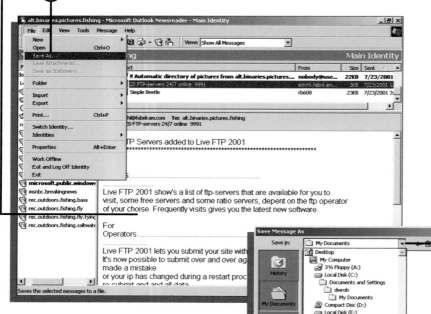

③ Select the Save In drop-down list.

④ Click a folder in which to store the message.

⑤ Enter a name for the message in the File Name box, and then click Save.

Print a Text Message

(1) With a newsgroup's headers displayed, download a text message.

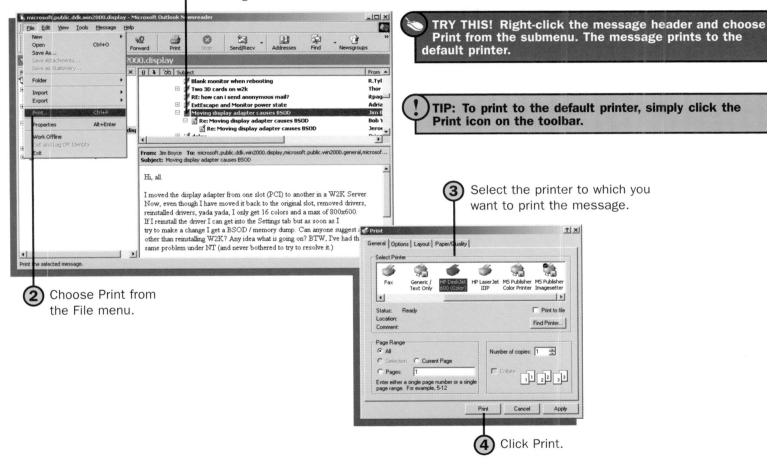

TRY THIS! Right-click the message header and choose Print from the submenu. The message prints to the default printer.

TIP: To print to the default printer, simply click the Print icon on the toolbar.

(3) Select the printer to which you want to print the message.

(2) Choose Print from the File menu.

(4) Click Print.

Save a Binary Message

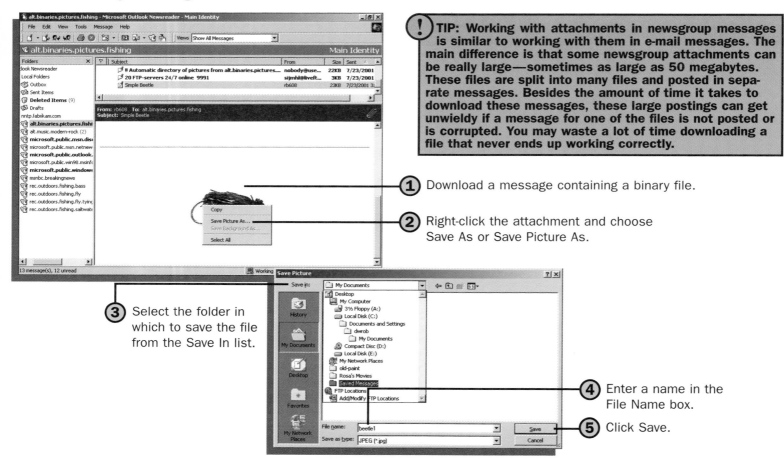

TIP: Working with attachments in newsgroup messages is similar to working with them in e-mail messages. The main difference is that some newsgroup attachments can be really large—sometimes as large as 50 megabytes. These files are split into many files and posted in separate messages. Besides the amount of time it takes to download these messages, these large postings can get unwieldy if a message for one of the files is not posted or is corrupted. You may waste a lot of time downloading a file that never ends up working correctly.

1 Download a message containing a binary file.

2 Right-click the attachment and choose Save As or Save Picture As.

3 Select the folder in which to save the file from the Save In list.

4 Enter a name in the File Name box.

5 Click Save.

SEE ALSO: For information on handling file attachments in e-mail messages, see "E-mail a File" on page 40.

Posting a Newsgroup Message

If you spend all your time reading messages on newsgroups and not responding to any or providing information to others, you're known as a "lurker." If you're interested in a topic and have something worthwhile to say, you should feel welcome to participate in any newsgroup. To do so, you need to learn how to create the message text and how to address the message to the correct newsgroup or set of newsgroups.

Address the Message

(1) With Outlook Newsreader open, choose New from the File menu.

(2) Choose News Message from the submenu.

> **TIP:** When you first join a newsgroup, it's best to get to know the type of posts that are welcomed there. If the topic covers expert level information, don't waste other people's time with trivial comments or questions. Conversely, if the newsgroup is devoted to beginning information, don't come in with a lot of high-end information about a topic.

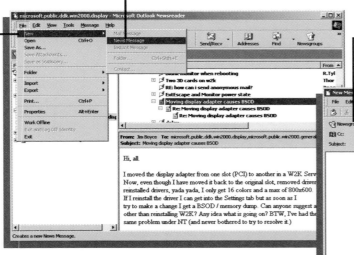

(3) Click the Newsgroups label to open the Pick Newsgroups dialog box.

(5) Click Add.

(6) Click OK.

(4) Select the newsgroups to which you want to post the message. You can pick one or more newsgroups to send the same message to.

> **TRY THIS!** If you're brand new to newsgroups, sometimes it's a good idea to reply to a post that you have some good insight on. This is better than posting a new message that may be off target or may not get any replies. To reply to a message, click Reply To Group on the toolbar, write your reply, and click Send.

Enter your Message Subject and Text

① With Outlook Newsreader open, create a news message and address it.

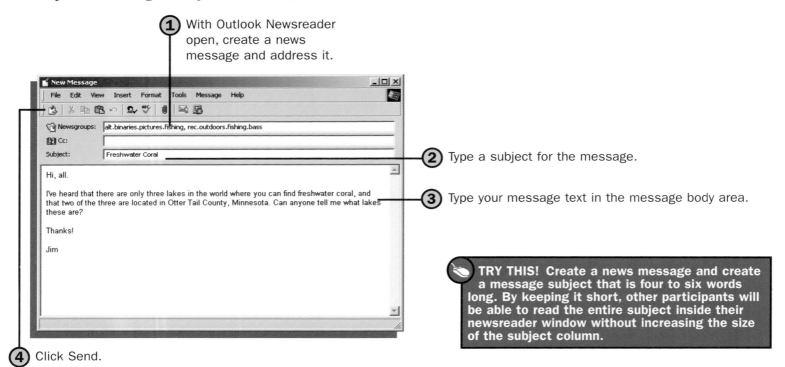

② Type a subject for the message.

③ Type your message text in the message body area.

> **TRY THIS!** Create a news message and create a message subject that is four to six words long. By keeping it short, other participants will be able to read the entire subject inside their newsreader window without increasing the size of the subject column.

④ Click Send.

> **CAUTION:** A common message subject is "Can you help?" Try to be more descriptive in your subjects so other subscribers will know what you are talking about just by reading the header.

Managing a Newsgroup Subscription

As you become more involved in newsgroups, your Outlook Newsreader will become loaded up with old messages and headers. You can remove downloaded messages, delete headers and messages, reset a newsgroup, and synchronize a newsgroup for offline reading.

Remove Downloaded Messages

(1) With Outlook Newsreader open, choose Options from the Tools menu.

TIP: If you do not want to delete every downloaded message, click No when asked if you want to delete all messages.

TIP: If you have a large number of downloaded messages, the deletion phase may take a few minutes to complete.

(2) Click the Maintenance tab.

(3) Click Clean Up Now.

(4) Click Remove Messages.

(5) Click Yes.

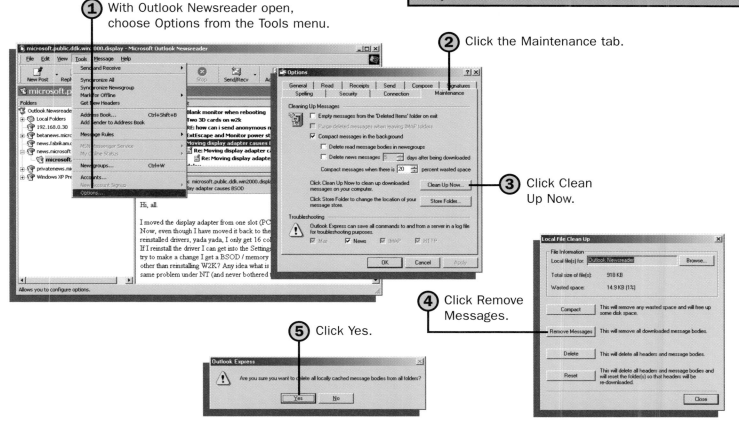

Delete Headers and Messages

(1) With Outlook Newsreader open, choose Options from the Tools menu.

TRY THIS! Get in the habit of deleting message headers and messages every few weeks. You'll notice a performance improvement in Outlook Newsreader because you will not have all those extra files slowing it down.

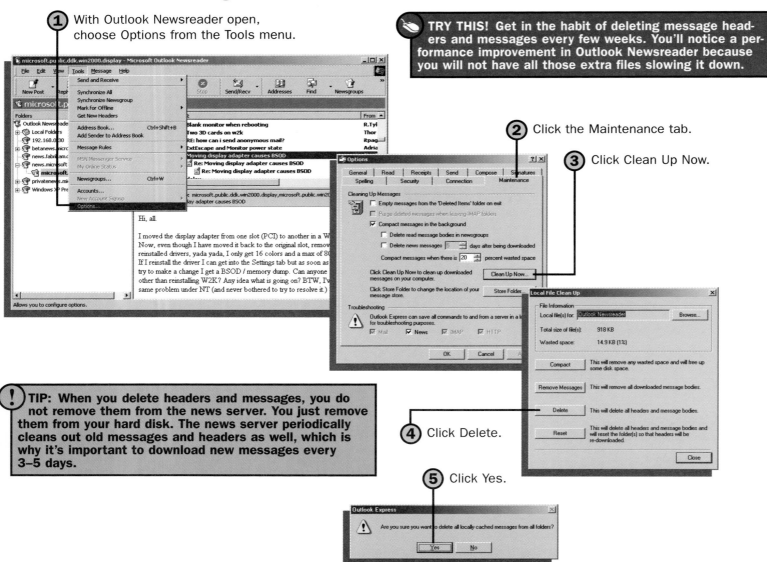

(2) Click the Maintenance tab.

(3) Click Clean Up Now.

TIP: When you delete headers and messages, you do not remove them from the news server. You just remove them from your hard disk. The news server periodically cleans out old messages and headers as well, which is why it's important to download new messages every 3–5 days.

(4) Click Delete.

(5) Click Yes.

Reset a Newsgroup

(1) With Outlook Newsreader open, choose Options from the Tools menu.

CAUTION: When you reset a newsgroup, all messages and headers are deleted and all headers are downloaded again.

(2) Click the Maintenance tab.

(3) Click Clean Up Now.

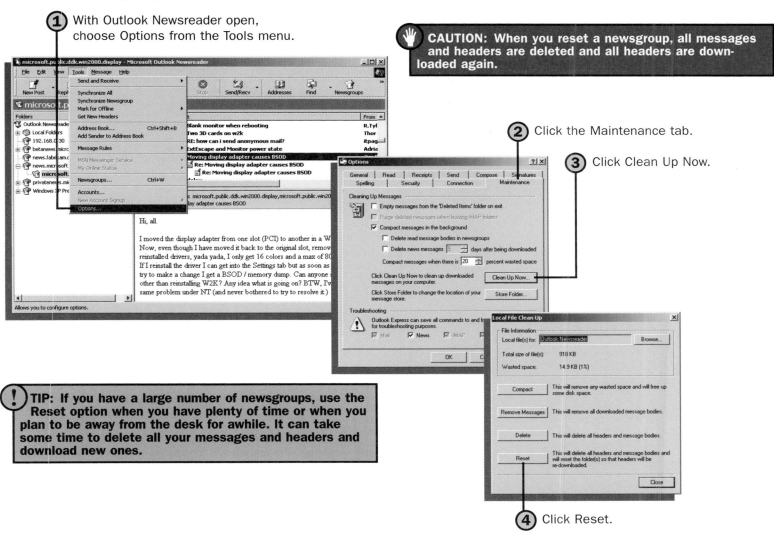

TIP: If you have a large number of newsgroups, use the Reset option when you have plenty of time or when you plan to be away from the desk for awhile. It can take some time to delete all your messages and headers and download new ones.

(4) Click Reset.

Synchronize a Newsgroup

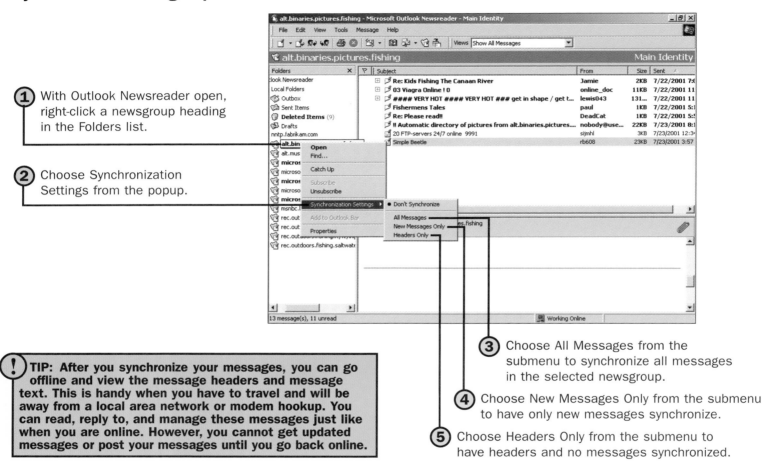

1. With Outlook Newsreader open, right-click a newsgroup heading in the Folders list.

2. Choose Synchronization Settings from the popup.

3. Choose All Messages from the submenu to synchronize all messages in the selected newsgroup.

4. Choose New Messages Only from the submenu to have only new messages synchronize.

5. Choose Headers Only from the submenu to have headers and no messages synchronized.

!️ **TIP: After you synchronize your messages, you can go offline and view the message headers and message text. This is handy when you have to travel and will be away from a local area network or modem hookup. You can read, reply to, and manage these messages just like when you are online. However, you cannot get updated messages or post your messages until you go back online.**

!️ **TIP: For a quick way to synchronize your newsgroups, choose Synchronize Newsgroups from the Tools menu.**

Working with Contacts

Staying in contact with others is part of life and an important task in business. You should always try to stay in touch with those closest to you and those you rely on as clients and customers. Whether it's your best friend from high school, a client you've worked with for years, or a new customer, you need a way to store all the information about each one of them.

Outlook's Contact feature enables you to save personal and business contact information, including phone numbers, addresses, e-mail addresses, Web site information, and personal data. Instead of being a glorified card file to store your information in, Contacts is a full-featured database that lets you use automatic dialing to call a contact, import data from other contact managers or databases (such as Microsoft Access), create new messages to a contact, set up distribution lists for contacts, and more. Outlook gives you several ways to view your contacts as well. For example, you can view contacts using address cards, group contacts by category, or list them by their phone numbers. As with other folders, Outlook also lets you create custom views.

This section explores the Contacts folder. In it you learn how to create and sort contacts and use them for a variety of tasks. You will learn how to send e-mail messages to contacts, work with contacts in your address book, add files to a contact, and much more.

Adding a New Contact

You can add contacts in Outlook's Contacts folder in three ways: by typing in new information about someone, by using information you've entered for another contact, or by using information from an e-mail message. In the latter case, for example, you can quickly create a new contact by using the information from a message that you've received.

Use E-Mail Message Information

(1) With the Inbox showing, select the message that has the contact information you want to save. If you don't have the preview pane displayed, open the message to access the From field.

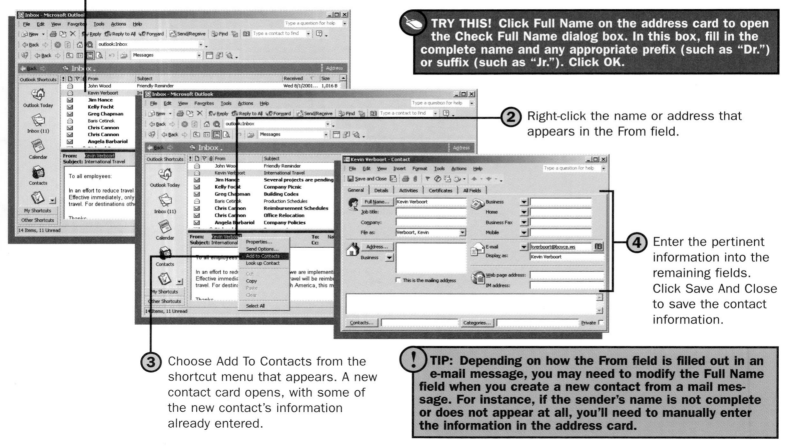

TRY THIS! Click Full Name on the address card to open the Check Full Name dialog box. In this box, fill in the complete name and any appropriate prefix (such as "Dr.") or suffix (such as "Jr."). Click OK.

(2) Right-click the name or address that appears in the From field.

(4) Enter the pertinent information into the remaining fields. Click Save And Close to save the contact information.

(3) Choose Add To Contacts from the shortcut menu that appears. A new contact card opens, with some of the new contact's information already entered.

TIP: Depending on how the From field is filled out in an e-mail message, you may need to modify the Full Name field when you create a new contact from a mail message. For instance, if the sender's name is not complete or does not appear at all, you'll need to manually enter the information in the address card.

Use the Contact Window

(1) Click the Contacts icon on the Outlook Bar to display the Contacts folder.

(2) Double-click the contact you want to open.

CAUTION: When entering a contact's e-mail address, be sure you type it in correctly. An incorrect address will prevent your messages from being sent successfully. Take the time when entering a contact's e-mail address to double-check it for accuracy. You can, of course, change it later but it's best to make sure it's correct now.

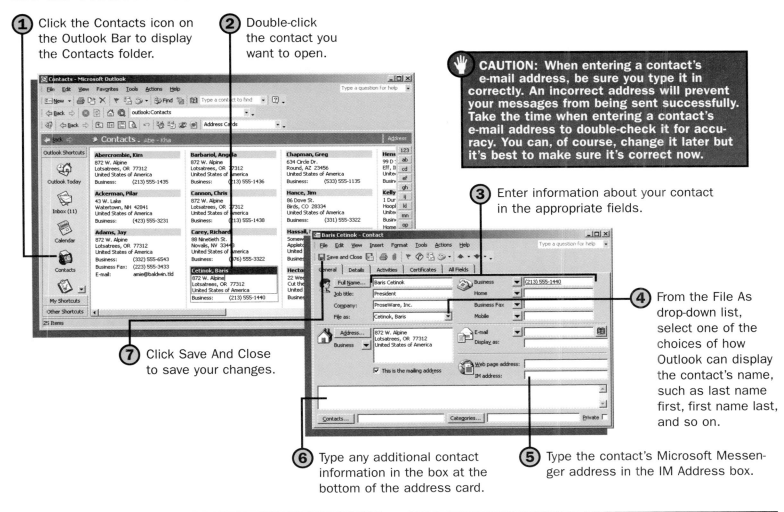

(3) Enter information about your contact in the appropriate fields.

(4) From the File As drop-down list, select one of the choices of how Outlook can display the contact's name, such as last name first, first name last, and so on.

(7) Click Save And Close to save your changes.

(6) Type any additional contact information in the box at the bottom of the address card.

(5) Type the contact's Microsoft Messenger address in the IM Address box.

TIP: The Contacts icon appears in the Outlook Shortcuts section of the Outlook Bar. If it is not displaying, click Outlook Shortcuts in the Outlook Bar.

TIP: To ensure the AutoDialer feature works correctly, enter phone numbers as numbers instead of using letters.

Inserting Items into a Contact Record

You can add items, objects, and files to a contact by using the Item command on the Insert menu. For example, you can add an e-mail message to a contact for future reference, insert an attachment, or insert a Microsoft Excel worksheet. This enables you to access these items from the contact card. You can add a new, empty item and then modify it right in the Outlook item. Or you can insert an existing document.

Add an Outlook Item

① Open a contact, and choose Item from the Insert menu.

② Click the Outlook folder in which the item you want to insert is located.

⑤ Click OK to insert the item into the contact address card.

④ Select the format of the item: text only, attachment, or shortcut.

③ Select an item in the Items list.

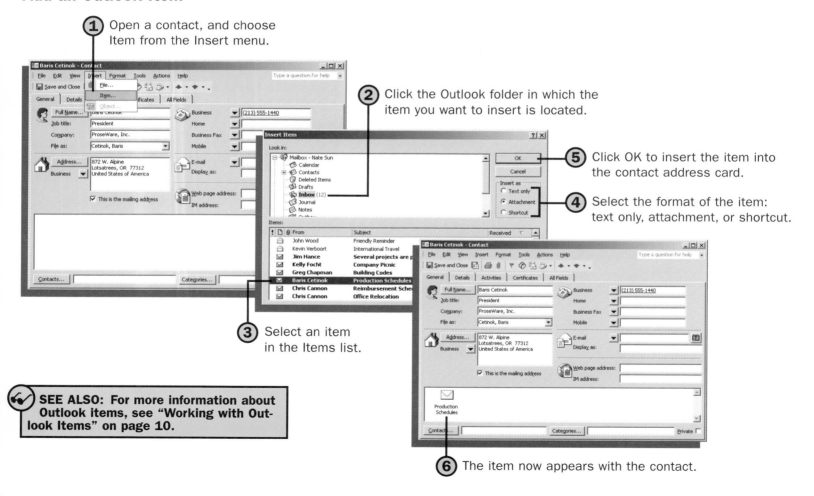

⑥ The item now appears with the contact.

SEE ALSO: For more information about Outlook items, see "Working with Outlook Items" on page 10.

Add a File

(1) Open a contact, and choose File from the Insert menu.

TIP: After you insert a file into a contact's card, you can open it to view, edit, or print it. To do this, double-click the file's icon in the address card to launch the file within its associated application.

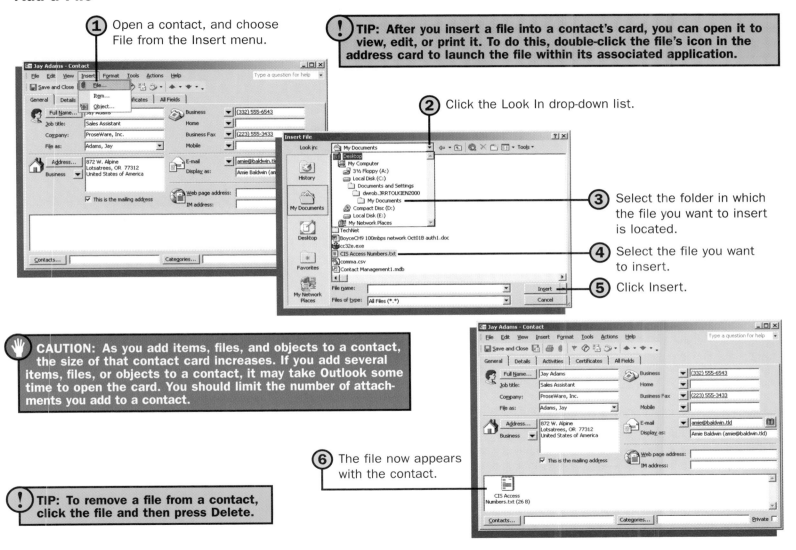

(2) Click the Look In drop-down list.

(3) Select the folder in which the file you want to insert is located.

(4) Select the file you want to insert.

(5) Click Insert.

CAUTION: As you add items, files, and objects to a contact, the size of that contact card increases. If you add several items, files, or objects to a contact, it may take Outlook some time to open the card. You should limit the number of attachments you add to a contact.

(6) The file now appears with the contact.

TIP: To remove a file from a contact, click the file and then press Delete.

Viewing Your Contacts Folder

Outlook lets you view your contacts as a single address card or all at once, moving through your Contacts folder as if it were an electronic phone book or address book. Another way to look at your contact information is through the Outlook Address Book, which lists contacts alphabetically.

Use the Contacts Folder

SEE ALSO: One task that no one wants to face is typing in all their contacts a second time. This is why it's a good idea to set up a backup schedule to make sure your contacts are backed up at least once a week. For information on backing up and restoring Outlook Contacts, see "Backing Up and Restoring a Data File" on page 212.

1 Click the Contacts icon on the Outlook Bar.

2 Click the Current View drop-down list on the Advanced toolbar. (If the Advanced toolbar is not showing, select Toolbars from the View menu and then click Advanced.)

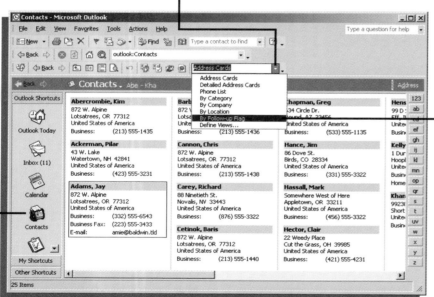

3 Select the view type you want to use to view the contact information in the Contacts folder. You can choose from the following list:

- Address Cards
- Detailed Address Cards
- Phone List
- By Category
- By Company
- By Location
- By Follow-Up Flag

TRY THIS! To see how Outlook displays your contact information in different formats, select each of the views in the Current View drop-down list. When you see one that you like, such as the Detailed Address Cards, keep it so that the next time you open the Contacts folder that view is showing.

Use the Address Book

(1) Choose Address Book from the Tools menu.

(2) Choose New Entry from the File menu.

(3) Click New Contact in the Select The Entry Type dialog box.

(4) Click OK.

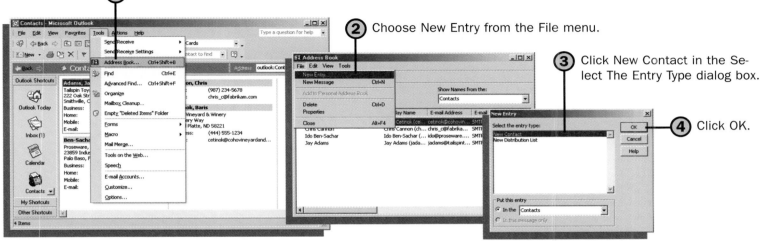

(5) Add the new contact information to the appropriate fields.

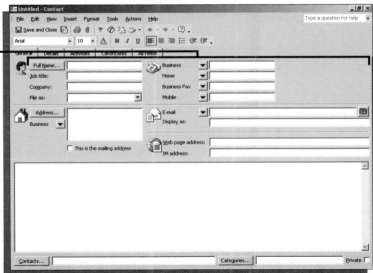

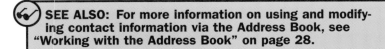

(!) **TIP:** You can add distribution lists to the Contacts folder using the Address Book. Rather than clicking New Contact in the Select The Entry Type dialog box, click New Distribution List. The new distribution list appears in the Contacts folder alongside individual entries.

SEE ALSO: For more information on using and modifying contact information via the Address Book, see "Working with the Address Book" on page 28.

Viewing Contact Information

After you create a contact, you can view it in the Contacts folder or open it in its own address card. In the Contacts folder you can see the contact's name, some phone information, and the first fifteen or sixteen characters of the e-mail address. To see a contact's full set of information, you must display the address card. When you view contact information in an address card, you can print the information, view activities associated with a contact, and display a map to his or her address.

Print Contact Information

① Click the Contacts folder in the Outlook Bar.

② Double-click the contact name you want to print.

SEE ALSO: For more information on printing your contacts, see "Viewing Your Contacts Folder" on page 110.

③ Click Print from the File menu.

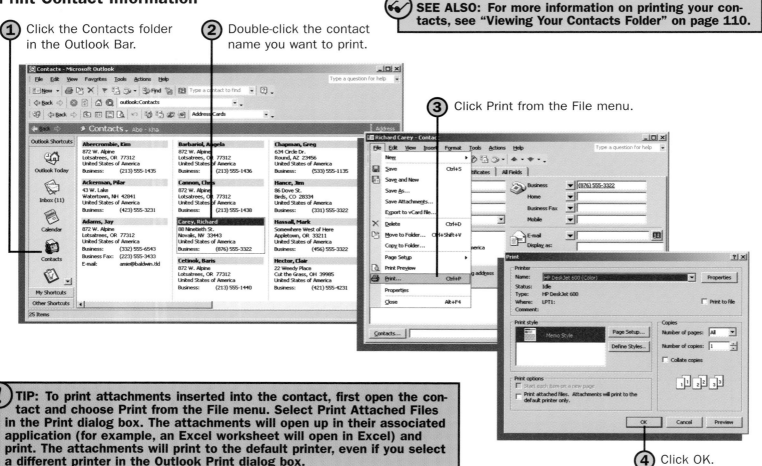

④ Click OK.

TIP: To print attachments inserted into the contact, first open the contact and choose Print from the File menu. Select Print Attached Files in the Print dialog box. The attachments will open up in their associated application (for example, an Excel worksheet will open in Excel) and print. The attachments will print to the default printer, even if you select a different printer in the Outlook Print dialog box.

Use the Activities Tab

1 Click the Contacts icon on the Outlook Bar.

2 Double-click the contact name you want to view.

3 Click the Activities Tab.

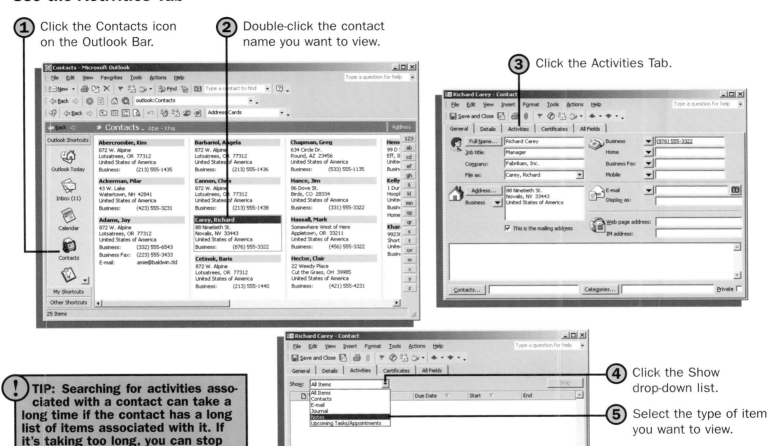

4 Click the Show drop-down list.

5 Select the type of item you want to view.

TIP: Searching for activities associated with a contact can take a long time if the contact has a long list of items associated with it. If it's taking too long, you can stop the search at any time by clicking the Stop button on the right-hand side of the Activities tab.

Display a Map

1 Click the Contacts icon on the Outlook Bar.

2 Double-click the contact for which you want to display a map.

3 Click the down-arrow under the Address button, and select the contact address (home address, business address, or other) for which you want a map.

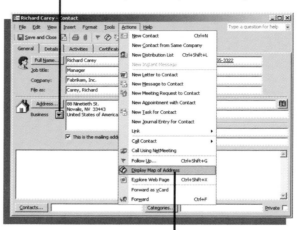

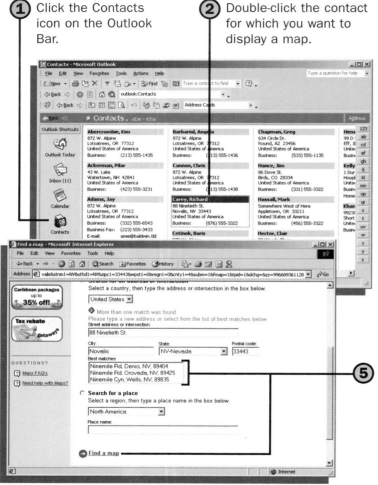

4 Click Display Map Of Address from the Actions menu. Outlook will connect to the Expedia.com Web site to search for a map of the address.

5 Select an address in the Best Matches list, or click the Find A Map hyperlink to search for a map of another address.

> **! TIP:** To see a map for an address, you must have Internet access and the address must be located in the United States.

> **✋ CAUTION:** Not all addresses are available from the Expedia.com Web site. If the address you are looking for is not found, modify the information you entered on the Find A Map Web page. Click the Find A Map hyperlink to begin the search again.

Updating an Existing Contact

You can store a great deal of information about a person or company in a single address card. For many contacts, however, you probably will start by entering only the most critical information. Later you'll need to update the information. Outlook makes it easy to do so. Simply open the Contacts folder, locate the contact you wish to update, open the contact card for that person, and make your changes.

> **TIP:** When viewing contacts using the Address Cards and Detailed Address Cards views, you can click the letter buttons on the right side of the window to jump to contacts whose names start with that letter. For example, click the letter "m" to jump to contacts named "Mitchell," "Mosley," and so on.

Use the Contacts Folder

(1) Click the Contacts folder icon on the Outlook Bar.

(2) Select Current View on the View menu, and then select a view type.

> **SEE ALSO:** For information on using contacts in e-mail messages, see "Writing and Sending E-Mail" on page 25.

> **SEE ALSO:** For information on customizing Outlook's appearance, see "Setting Contact and Journal Options" on page 228.

(3) Click in the scroll bar to navigate through the list of contacts.

(4) Double-click a contact to open its form for updating.

Finding a Contact

Outlook makes it easy to find contacts. You can search for them using the Find tool, you can use the Find A Contact box, or simply scroll through the list of your contacts. With Outlook you don't even have to know the complete name of the person you are looking up, since searching for part of a name will bring up any name that matches that string.

Scroll Through the Contacts Folder

1 Click the Contacts folder icon on the Outlook Bar.

2 Select Current View from the View menu, and then select Address Cards from the submenu.

> **! TIP:** If your Contacts folder is really large, scrolling through the list of contacts is not the most efficient way to locate a contact. Instead use the Find A Contact box or the Find tool to locate the contact.

> **✋ CAUTION:** Be careful when viewing contacts in the Contacts folder. If you press Delete after clicking on a contact, you'll delete the contact. If this happens, select Undo Delete from the Edit menu.

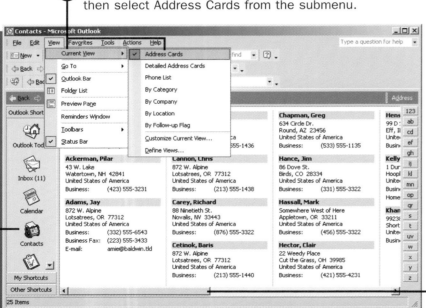

3 Move the scroll bar at the bottom of the Contacts folder to scroll through your contacts.

Use the Find A Contact Box

① Click the Contacts folder icon on the Outlook Bar.

② Click Find on the Standard toolbar.

! TIP: To show your entire list of contacts again, click Clear.

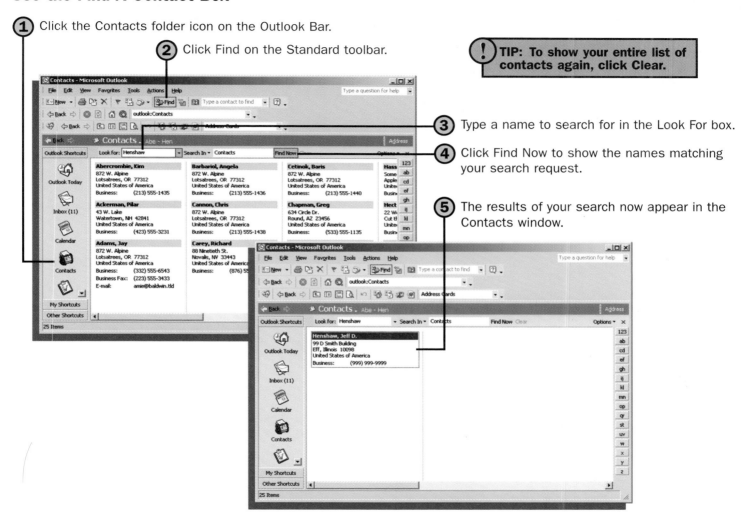

③ Type a name to search for in the Look For box.

④ Click Find Now to show the names matching your search request.

⑤ The results of your search now appear in the Contacts window.

 SEE ALSO: For information on finding names in the Address Book, see "Find a Name In the Address Book" on page 29.

Use the Find Tool

(1) Click the Contacts folder icon on the Outlook Bar.

! TIP: Another way to display the Advanced Find dialog box is to click the Find button on the Standard toolbar, click the Options drop-down list, and then click Advanced Find.

(2) Choose Advanced Find from the Tools menu.

(3) Enter a word or phrase in the Search For The Word(s) field.

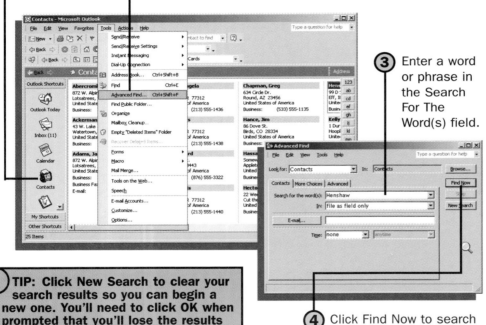

! TIP: Click New Search to clear your search results so you can begin a new one. You'll need to click OK when prompted that you'll lose the results of the previous search.

(4) Click Find Now to search for contacts matching the search criteria.

! TIP: You can use the Advanced Find dialog box to find contacts using a number of search criteria. For example, you can search for contacts who have a specific e-mail address or domain name in the e-mail address. This is handy if you know that a contact has a domain name of @business.com but are not sure of her name or e-mail address. Simply enter "@business.com" in the E-Mail field, and press Enter.

Organizing Your Contacts

When you have only a dozen or so contacts, finding and managing them is fairly easy. You can simply open the Contacts folder, scroll through the list and find what you're looking for. However, once the Contacts folder grows, you need to organize your contacts to make them easier to find and update. Outlook provides three ways to organize your contacts. You can use folders to store related contacts, use categories to set up relationships between contacts, or use views to sort contacts in ways that make sense to you.

TRY THIS! Once you create a folder for contacts, you can drag existing contacts to your new folder to organize them as necessary. For example, create a folder named "Project Team" in the Contacts folder. Open the Folder List so you can see the new folder, but keep the focus on the Contacts folder. Drag members from your project team into the Project Team folder. You now can quickly see who is on your team by clicking this folder.

Use Folders

(1) Click the Contacts icon on the Outlook Bar.

(2) Choose Folder from the File menu, and then select New Folder from the submenu.

CAUTION: When you create a new folder for contacts, make sure the Contact Items option is selected in the Folder Contains drop-down list. If it is not, Outlook will not store contacts in the correct format and you may lose information.

(3) Type a name for the folder in the Name field.

(4) Click the Folder Contains drop-down list, and select Contact Items.

(5) Click OK.

(6) Click Yes if you want the new folder to appear in your Outlook Bar, or No if you don't.

(7) Click on the Personal Folders menu to see your new folder.

(8) Click on the new folder to select it.

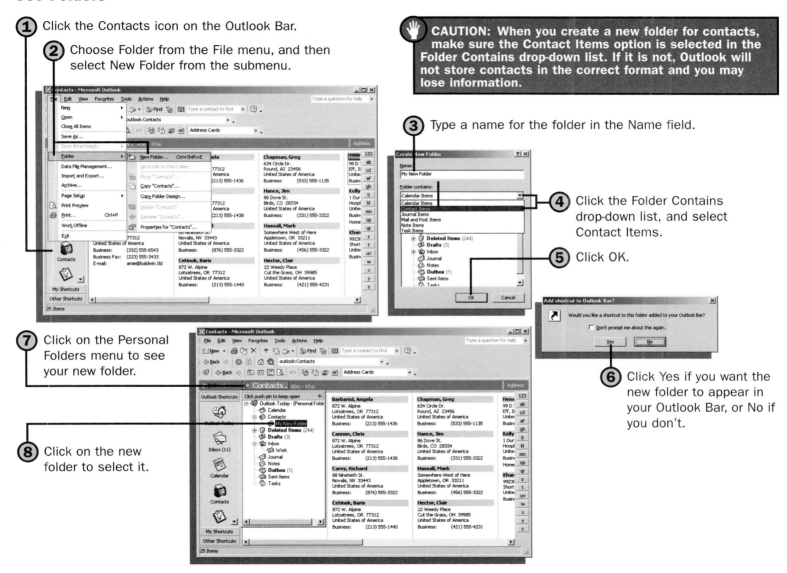

Use Categories

(1) Click the Contacts icon on the Outlook Bar.

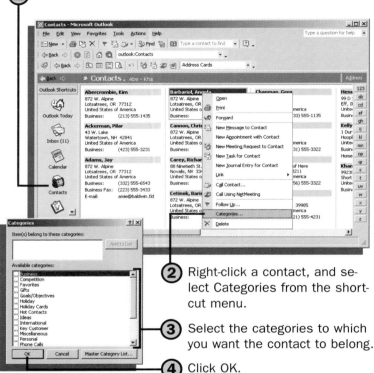

(2) Right-click a contact, and select Categories from the short-cut menu.

(3) Select the categories to which you want the contact to belong.

(4) Click OK.

! TIP: You can create your own categories by clicking Master Category List on the Categories dialog box. Enter a name for the category in the New Category box, and click Add. Click OK to display the category in the Categories dialog box.

SEE ALSO: For more information on Outlook Categories, see "Using Categories" on page 188.

Use Views

(1) Click the Contacts icon on the Outlook Bar.

(2) Choose Current View from the View menu.

(3) Click a view type.

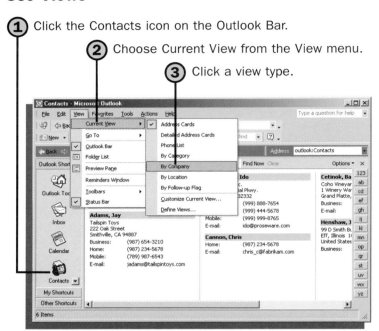

TRY THIS! Create a customized view by selecting Customize Current View from the Current View submenu. Click Filter, and specify the filtering criteria for your custom view. For example, if you want Outlook to show only those contacts that have a specific e-mail domain name, enter that domain name in the Email field.

SEE ALSO: For more information on sorting contacts, see "Setting Contact and Journal Options" on page 228.

Communicating with Contacts

Microsoft Outlook makes it easy to communicate with your contacts. You can open the Contacts folder and create a new e-mail message while viewing a contact's address card, or you can use Outlook's AutoDialer feature to call a contact. Finally, Outlook can address a letter or envelope to your contact using the name, address, and other information that you've entered.

> **TRY THIS!** You can add your own information to the letter. Click on the Sender Info tab, and type your name in the Sender's Name box. Also fill out your return address in the Return Address area and click Finish.

Write a Letter to a Contact

> **!** **TIP:** To write a letter to a contact, you must have Microsoft Word 2002 installed on your system.

① Click the Contacts icon on the Outlook Bar.

③ Choose New Letter To Contact from the Actions menu to start Microsoft Word's Letter Wizard.

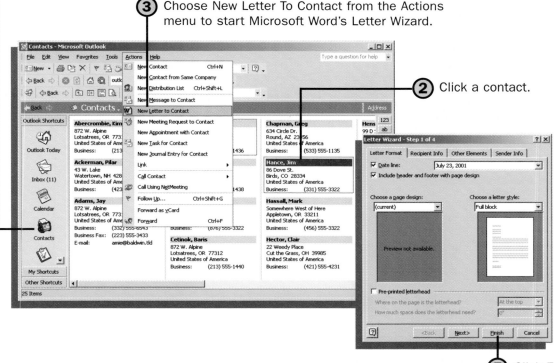

② Click a contact.

④ Work through the four steps of the Letter Wizard to create a new letter.

⑤ Click Finish when you're ready for Word to create the letter.

E-Mail a Contact

① Click the Contacts icon on the Outlook Bar.

③ Choose New Message To Contact from the Actions menu.

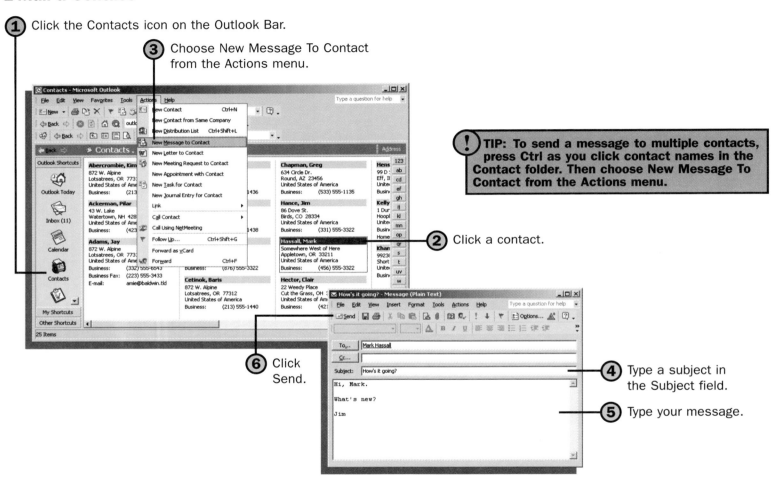

TIP: To send a message to multiple contacts, press Ctrl as you click contact names in the Contact folder. Then choose New Message To Contact from the Actions menu.

② Click a contact.

⑥ Click Send.

④ Type a subject in the Subject field.

⑤ Type your message.

CAUTION: If you select a contact that does not have an e-mail address, you will receive an error message that the selected contact does not have an e-mail address or that another problem exists. You can click OK to continue, but you will not be able to send the message to that contact until you provide a valid e-mail address.

Telephone a Contact

① Click the Contacts icon on the Outlook Bar.

② Click the Dial button on the Standard toolbar.

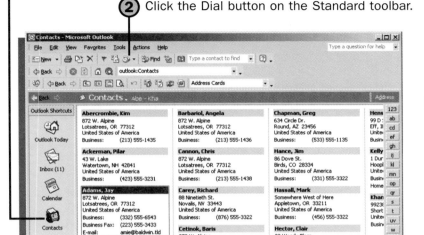

③ Click Start Call in the New Call dialog box. Pick up your telephone handset when the other phone begins to ring.

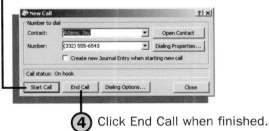

④ Click End Call when finished.

⚠ TIP: You can have Outlook keep a Journal entry for the phone call by selecting Create New Journal Entry When Starting New Call. This is handy if you need to track call information, including who you call, when you call them, and the length of time the call takes.

🖱 TRY THIS! You can modify a contact from the New Call dialog box. Click Open Contact to display the contact's address card. Edit the card as necessary, then click Save And Close.

⚠ TIP: You must have a telephone or headset connected to your modem for the AutoDialer option to work.

Scheduling Meetings and Tasks for a Contact

The Contacts folder provides tools to let you schedule meetings and assign tasks to contacts. Meetings are appointments you invite others to and schedule resources for, like meeting rooms and overhead projectors. With Outlook, you can select the contacts that you want to invite to a meeting and then let Outlook send messages to them inviting them to the meeting. You also can set up appointments with a contact in the same way, including recurring appointments that occur at the same time every day, week, month, or quarter.

Request a Meeting with a Contact

(1) Click the Contacts icon on the Outlook Bar.

(3) Choose New Meeting Request To Contact from the Actions menu.

TRY THIS! You can set meeting reminders using the Meeting window. Select Reminder and choose a time you want the reminder to display. Click the sound icon to pick a sound file that plays when the reminder is activated.

TIP: Setting up meetings and appointments for contacts works best on networks on which Microsoft Exchange Server is installed.

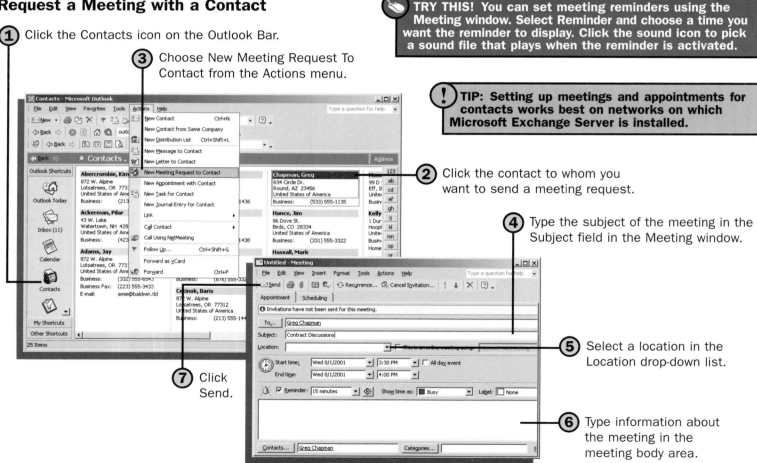

(2) Click the contact to whom you want to send a meeting request.

(4) Type the subject of the meeting in the Subject field in the Meeting window.

(7) Click Send.

(5) Select a location in the Location drop-down list.

(6) Type information about the meeting in the meeting body area.

Set up an Appointment with a Contact

(1) Click the Contacts icon on the Outlook Bar.

(3) Choose New Appointment With Contact from the Actions menu.

(!) TIP: To set up a schedule for a recurring appointment, click the Recurrence button on the Standard toolbar of the Appointment window. Select the appointment time, how often the appointment should recur, and the recurrence pattern (such as "every Friday at 8 AM").

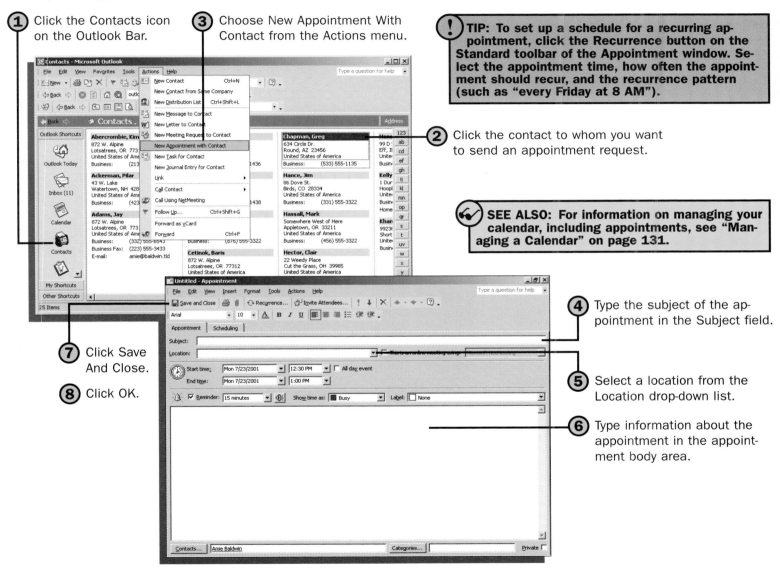

(2) Click the contact to whom you want to send an appointment request.

SEE ALSO: For information on managing your calendar, including appointments, see "Managing a Calendar" on page 131.

(7) Click Save And Close.

(8) Click OK.

(4) Type the subject of the appointment in the Subject field.

(5) Select a location from the Location drop-down list.

(6) Type information about the appointment in the appointment body area.

Assigning Tasks to a Contact

You can set up a task to be completed by a contact. This can be handy for managers who need to allocate tasks to coworkers. When you assign a task, Outlook can send a message or task request to that contact and inform him or her of the newly assigned task. The recipient will then have the option of accepting or rejecting the task.

> **! TIP: Tasks appear on the TaskPad. You can access this by clicking the Calendar icon on the Outlook Bar.**

Record a Task for the Contact

1 Click the Contacts icon on the Outlook Bar.

2 Click a contact.

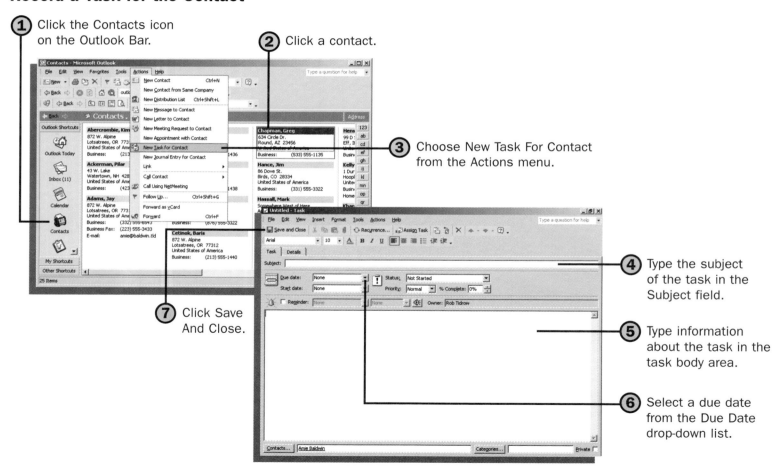

3 Choose New Task For Contact from the Actions menu.

4 Type the subject of the task in the Subject field.

5 Type information about the task in the task body area.

6 Select a due date from the Due Date drop-down list.

7 Click Save And Close.

Associating Items with Contacts

Items can be associated ("linked") with contacts so that any modifications to the original item will be reflected in the item when you open it from the contact card. This is different from inserting an item because, when you insert an item into contact, the item will not reflect any changes made to the original item.

SEE ALSO: For information on inserting items in your calendar, see "Inserting Items, Objects, and Files in a Calendar Item" on page 144.

Connect an Item to a Contact

(1) Click the Contacts icon in the Outlook Bar.   **(2)** Click a contact.

TIP: To connect multiple items to a contact, click Apply and then click the next item you want to connect. Click Apply to continue adding items, or OK when you're done.

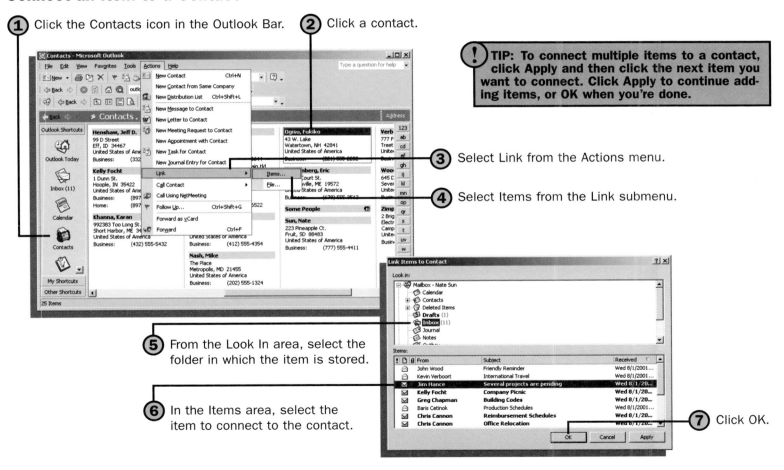

(3) Select Link from the Actions menu.

(4) Select Items from the Link submenu.

(5) From the Look In area, select the folder in which the item is stored.

(6) In the Items area, select the item to connect to the contact.

(7) Click OK.

Sharing Contact Information

As you build your contact list, you may want to share it with others in your company or among your circle of friends. Outlook enables you to share contact information by forwarding it as a Contact item or as a *vCard*. A vCard is a virtual business card that you can share with other Outlook users.

SEE ALSO: For information on importing items into Outlook, see "Importing and Exporting Items" on page 208.

Forward a Contact Item

(1) Click the Contacts icon on the Outlook Bar.

(2) Click the contact you want to share.

TIP: When the recipient receives the message with the forwarded contact item, he can import the information into Outlook.

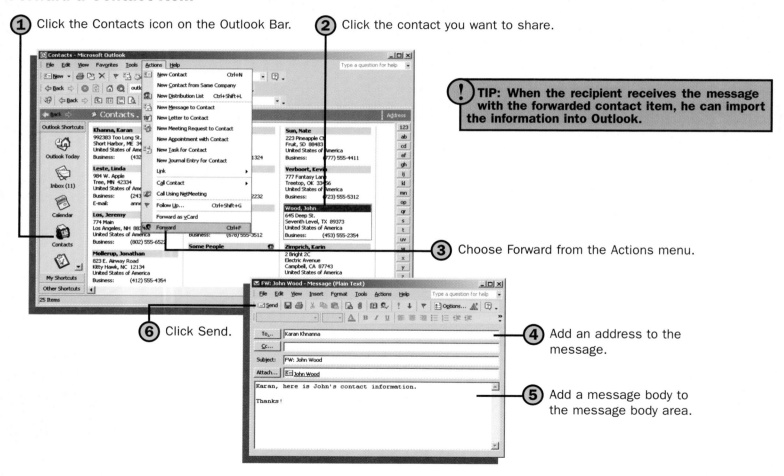

(3) Choose Forward from the Actions menu.

(6) Click Send.

(4) Add an address to the message.

(5) Add a message body to the message body area.

Forward a vCard

(1) Click the Contacts icon in the Outlook Bar.

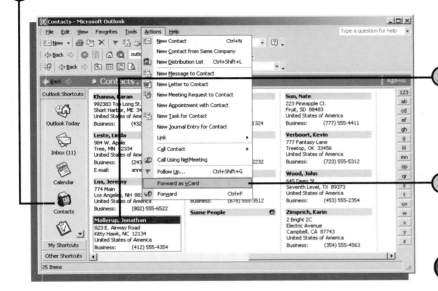

(2) Click the contact you want to share.

(3) Choose Forward As vCard from the Actions menu.

> **✋ CAUTION:** If the Forward As vCard command is not available on the Actions menu, your system doesn't support this feature. Use the Forward command from the Actions menu to send the contact information as a Contact item.

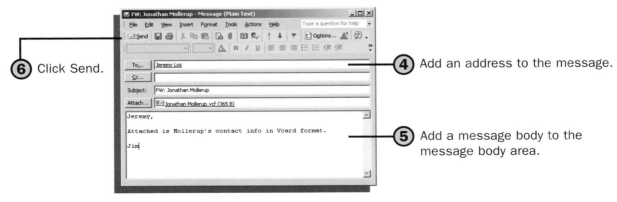

(6) Click Send.

(4) Add an address to the message.

(5) Add a message body to the message body area.

Recording Journal Entries

Outlook allows you to record Journal entries for contacts from within the Contacts folder. For example, you can create a Journal entry about a telephone conversation you had with a customer. The entry can include the name of the person you spoke with, the time it took place, the length of the call, the topic of conversation, and other information.

Log a Telephone Call

① Click the Contacts icon on the Outlook Bar.

② Click a contact.

! TIP: Click the Start Timer button to have Outlook keep track of when you start recording information about a person. Then click Pause Timer when you quit working with the person. Outlook keeps a running tab of the length of time you work on this contact. This is handy for anyone who must keep close track of time they spend with each client or customer.

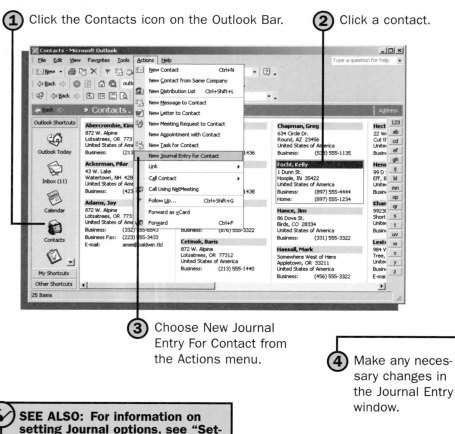

③ Choose New Journal Entry For Contact from the Actions menu.

④ Make any necessary changes in the Journal Entry window.

⑤ Click Save And Close.

⊘ SEE ALSO: For information on setting Journal options, see "Setting Contact and Journal Options" on page 228.

8) Managing a Calendar

Microsoft Outlook's calendar simplifies the burden of keeping and maintaining a schedule of meetings, appointments, events, and tasks. At a glance, you can quickly see your agenda in daily, monthly, or yearly views. With Outlook, you won't have any excuses for missing a lunch date or forgetting a meeting.

Outlook enables you to keep track of recurring meetings or events so that you don't have to manually enter these items each time they take place. For example, you might have a weekly staff meeting that takes place every Friday morning from 9:00–10:00 AM. Make it a recurring meeting, and Outlook blocks out that day and time. Similarly, if your PTA meets every third Wednesday of the month at 7:00 PM, you can set Outlook to schedule that meeting as well.

Outlook includes a reminder alarm that will display a message prior to your Calendar items so you won't forget a meeting, appointment, or To Do task. For example, you can set up Outlook to display a reminder of an upcoming meeting two or three days before the meeting. This way if you need to prepare a presentation, document, or other item for the meeting you give yourself ample time to do so. You then can "snooze" the reminder so it goes off again but perhaps only three hours prior to the meeting.

Viewing Your Calendar

With Outlook's calendar you're not stuck with one view—you can view your calendar in several different formats. Day View shows you an hour-by-hour view of your daily schedule, while Month View shows you what the entire month looks like. The Date Navigator is a small calendar with which you can navigate quickly to a specific day, week, or month, while the TaskPad is an electronic to-do list that keeps track of items you want to get done during the course of a day or week.

Use the Date Navigator

TRY THIS! To see today's date, click the Today button on the Standard toolbar. If the current month is showing in the Date Navigator, click the boxed date to display today's date.

① Click the Calendar icon on the Outlook Bar.

② Click the Day button on the Standard toolbar.

③ Click a day on the Date Navigator to display it in the Calendar view.

④ Click to the left of a week on the Date Navigator to display that week in the Calendar view.

⑤ Click the right arrow on the Date Navigator to move to the next month.

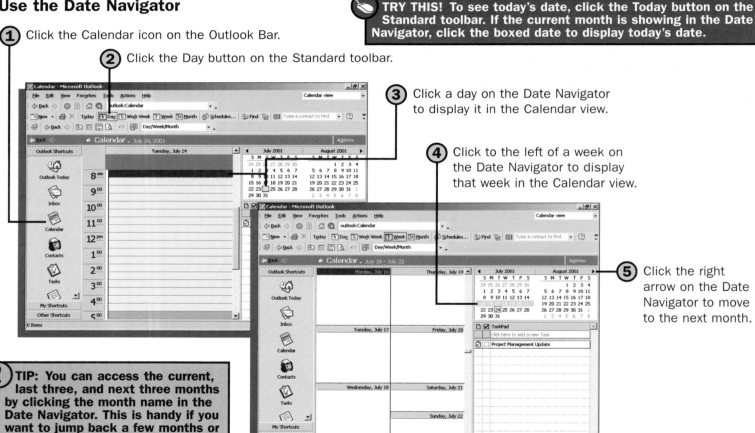

TIP: You can access the current, last three, and next three months by clicking the month name in the Date Navigator. This is handy if you want to jump back a few months or jump forward a month or two.

Use the Calendar View

1 Click the Calendar icon on the Outlook Bar.

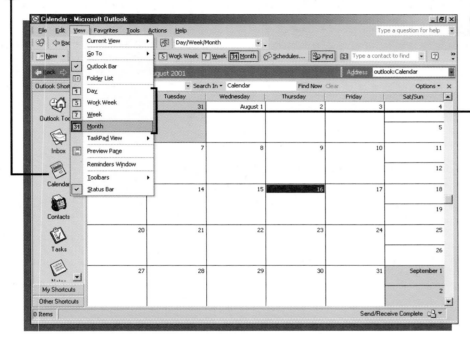

! TIP: To return to today's date, right-click inside a view and choose Today from the shortcut menu that appears.

2 Choose a type of view from the View menu.

- Click Day to see an hourly breakdown of your day.

- Click Work Week to see a work week's schedule by hour.

- Click Week to see a week's schedule.

- Click Month to see a month's schedule.

! TIP: If viewing Day, Work Week, or Week, you can make more room on the screen by dragging to the left of the TaskPad and Date Navigator.

Use the TaskPad View

(1) Click the Calendar icon on the Outlook Bar.

(2) Choose TaskPad View from the View menu.

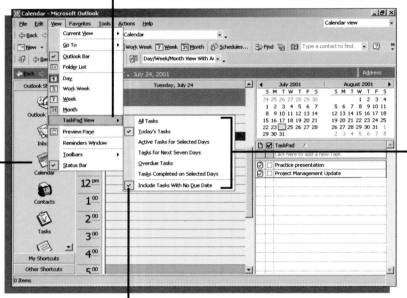

(3) Choose a view from the TaskPad View submenu:

- Choose All Tasks to display all your tasks.

- Choose Today's Tasks to display tasks you want to complete today.

- Choose Active Tasks for Selected Days to display tasks assigned for the days displaying in the Calendar View.

- Choose Tasks For Next Seven Days to display tasks assigned for the next seven days.

- Choose Overdue Tasks to display tasks that are overdue.

- Choose Tasks Completed On Selected Days to display tasks you've completed on the days showing in the Calendar View.

(4) Choose Include Tasks With No Due Dates if you would like tasks that do not have a due date to display.

SEE ALSO: For information on setting task schedules, see "Using the TaskPad" on page 154.

TIP: Depending on the options and schedules you've set for your tasks, some TaskPad views may be blank.

Recording an Appointment

An appointment in Outlook is an activity you enter for a specific time that, unlike a meeting, does not involve other people or resources. When you schedule an appointment, you block out a day, a time, and a location for that appointment to occur. Outlook also makes it easy to set a reminder that flashes on your screen and plays a sound file to alert you to the appointment.

Describe the Appointment

① Click the Calendar icon on the Outlook Bar.

② Choose New from the File menu.

③ Choose Appointment from the New submenu.

TRY THIS! If you'd like to add extended information about an appointment, click in the text area at the bottom of the Appointment window. Type a longer description here, such as directions to the appointment location, important information about the appointment, and so on.

TIP: You can print your appointments to the default printer by clicking the Print button on the Standard toolbar.

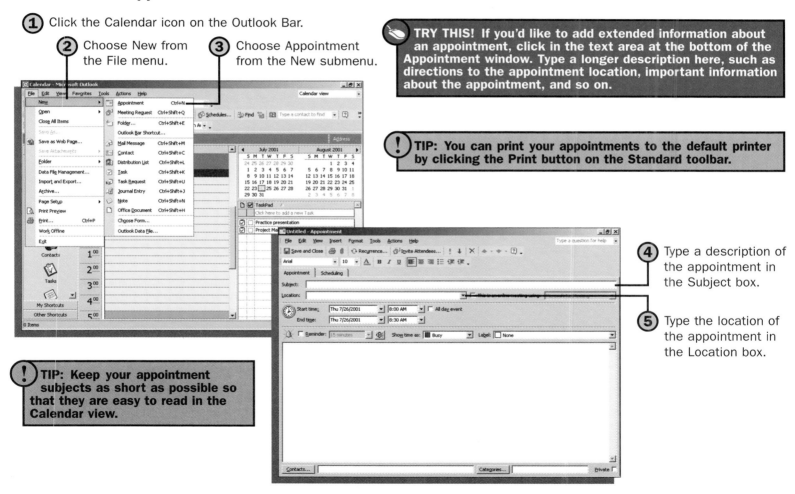

④ Type a description of the appointment in the Subject box.

⑤ Type the location of the appointment in the Location box.

TIP: Keep your appointment subjects as short as possible so that they are easy to read in the Calendar view.

Schedule the Appointment

1 Create a new appointment.

2 Add a subject for the appointment.

3 Click the down arrow to the right of the Start Time date, and select the day of the appointment.

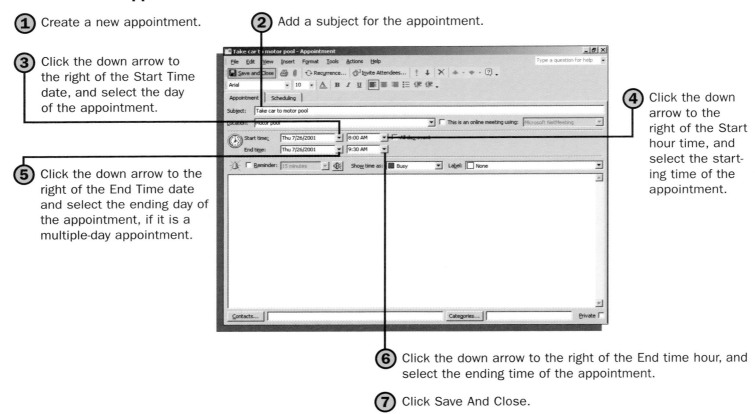

4 Click the down arrow to the right of the Start hour time, and select the starting time of the appointment.

5 Click the down arrow to the right of the End Time date and select the ending day of the appointment, if it is a multiple-day appointment.

6 Click the down arrow to the right of the End time hour, and select the ending time of the appointment.

7 Click Save And Close.

! TIP: If you use Outlook on a network running Microsoft Exchange Server, you can share your appointment information with other users. This way they know when you're busy and can schedule meetings with you based on this information.

! TIP: To categorize the appointment, click the Categories button. Select the categor(ies) you want to assign to this appointment, and then click OK.

Recognizing an Event

An event is an activity that runs for 24 hours or longer. An example of an event is a week-long conference or seminar you attend. Events display as banners at the top of the day and run from midnight to midnight, so they do not take up blocks of time. This allows you to schedule appointments or meetings during the day.

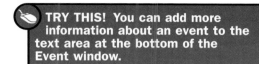
TRY THIS! You can add more information about an event to the text area at the bottom of the Event window.

Describe the Event

(1) Click the Calendar icon on the Outlook Bar.

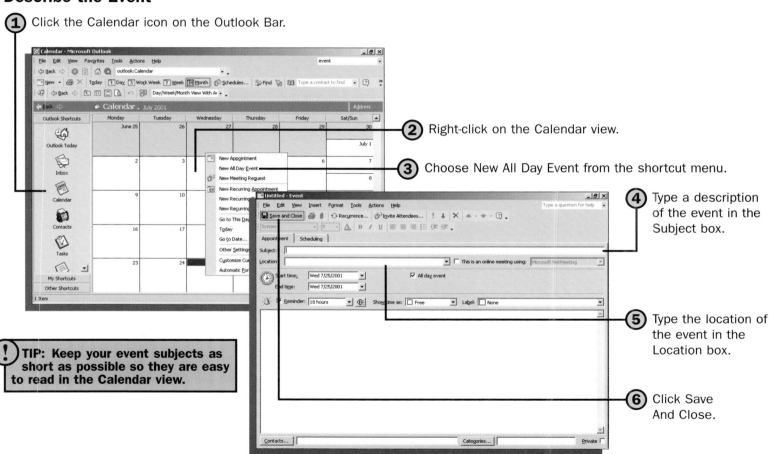

(2) Right-click on the Calendar view.

(3) Choose New All Day Event from the shortcut menu.

(4) Type a description of the event in the Subject box.

(5) Type the location of the event in the Location box.

(6) Click Save And Close.

TIP: Keep your event subjects as short as possible so they are easy to read in the Calendar view.

Schedule the Event

① Create a new event.

② Add a subject for the event.

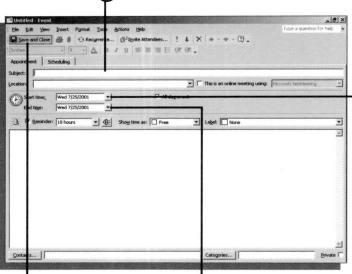

③ Click the Start Time down arrow and select the starting day of the event.

⑤ Click Save And Close.

④ Click the End Time down arrow and select the ending day of the event, if it is a multiple-day event.

 SEE ALSO: For information on setting up contacts, see "Working with Contacts" on page 105.

! **TIP:** You may already have events entered in your Calendar folder. When you create a new contact in the Contacts folder and include a birthday or anniversary for the contact, Outlook schedules that date as an event in the calendar.

Setting Up a Meeting

A meeting is an activity that involves other people and resources. A resource can be a conference room, VCR, slide projector, conference call equipment, laptop computer, or other equipment. Usually a meeting involves you and at least two other people. Outlook sends a meeting invitation to every person you designate, and they have the option of accepting or rejecting the request.

! **TIP:** If you're on a network and want to use the Meeting Planner to set up a meeting and its resources, choose Plan A Meeting from the Actions menu. Add attendees to the All Attendees list by typing them in or clicking the Add Others button and selecting names from your Address Book.

TRY THIS! When you type your meeting subject, keep it short but descriptive. "Team Meeting" may not be enough if people are members of multiple teams. Use something specific, like "Development Team Meeting," for your description.

Describe the Meeting

1 Click the Calendar icon on the Outlook Bar.

2 Right-click on the Calendar view.

3 Choose New Meeting Request from the shortcut menu.

6 Type a description of the meeting in the Subject box.

7 Type the location of the meeting in the Location box.

8 Click Send.

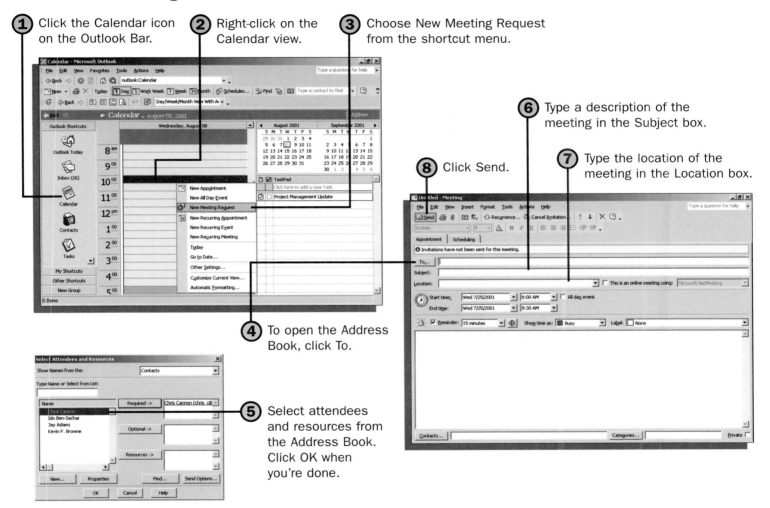

4 To open the Address Book, click To.

5 Select attendees and resources from the Address Book. Click OK when you're done.

Schedule the Meeting

(1) Create a new meeting.

(2) Add a subject for the meeting.

(7) Click Save And Close.

(3) Click the down arrow closest to Start Time, and select the starting date.

(4) Click the down arrow to the right of the time, and select the starting time of the meeting.

(5) Click the down arrow closest to End Time, and select the ending day of the meeting, if it is a multiple-day meeting.

(6) Click the down arrow to the right of the time, and select the ending time of the meeting.

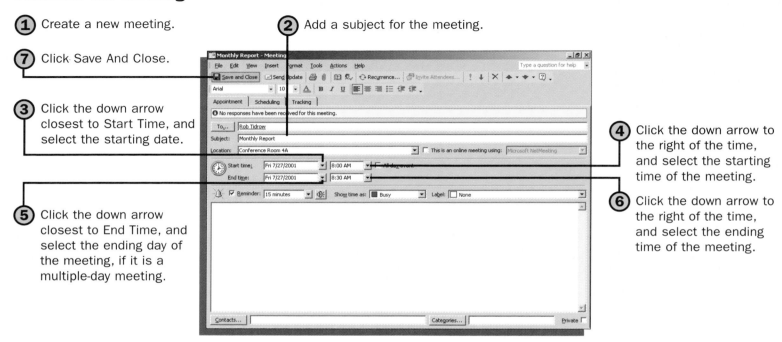

CAUTION: Make sure that your attendee list has correct e-mail addresses. If you attempt to send the meeting request to someone not in one of your address books, Outlook prompts you that the person cannot be validated.

SEE ALSO: For information on the Address Book and adding new contacts, see "Working with Contacts" on page 105.

TIP: Outlook provides the Meeting Planner to help you set up meetings with other people in your organization. Meeting Planner is designed so that you can see other people's schedules if they are connected to the same local area network.

Updating Calendar Information

Outlook makes it easy to edit a meeting, appointment, or event information saved in the Calendar folder. You might, for instance, need to modify the time an appointment starts or ends, change where a meeting is held, or adjust the date of an event. When you change a meeting you can send new meeting messages to attendees to announce the change.

Change an Appointment

> **TRY THIS!** Make an appointment recurring by clicking the Recurrence button and filling out the Appointment Recurrence information. For instance, set the time for the appointment to occur from 8:00 AM to 10:00 AM for every Thursday.

> **TIP:** Any date that has a meeting, appointment, or event shows up as bold on the Date Navigator. Click that date to switch to the day, week, or month in which that activity occurs.

① Click the Calendar icon on the Outlook Bar.

② Double-click the appointment you want to change.

④ Click Save And Close.

③ Make changes to the appointment.

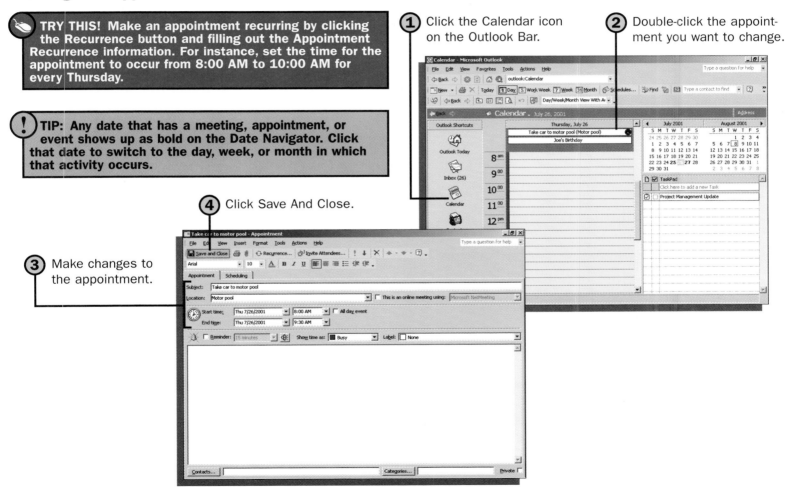

Update Event Information

1 Click the Calendar icon on the Outlook Bar.

2 Double-click the event you want to change.

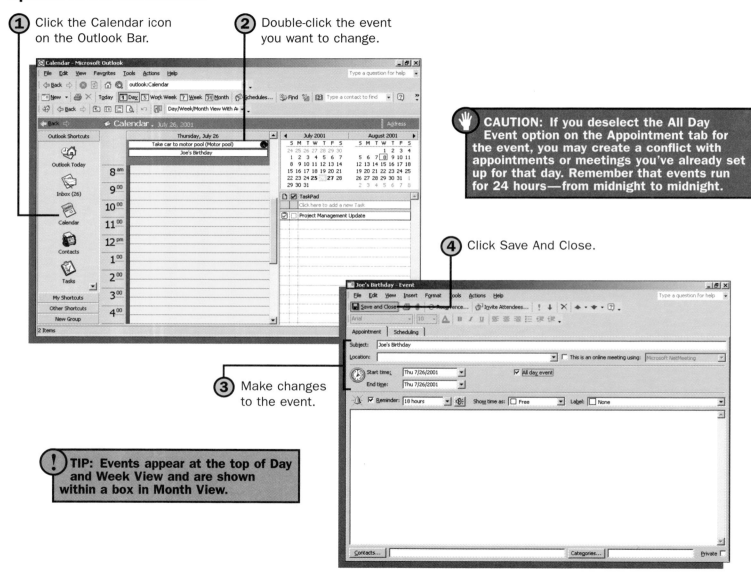

CAUTION: If you deselect the All Day Event option on the Appointment tab for the event, you may create a conflict with appointments or meetings you've already set up for that day. Remember that events run for 24 hours—from midnight to midnight.

4 Click Save And Close.

3 Make changes to the event.

TIP: Events appear at the top of Day and Week View and are shown within a box in Month View.

Reschedule a Meeting

(1) Open the meeting you want to change.

(4) Click Save and Close.

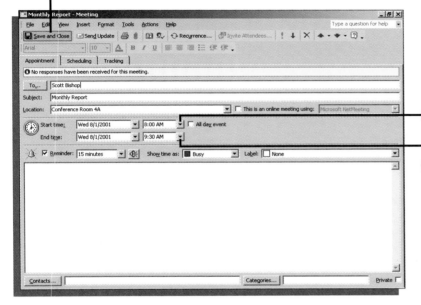

(2) Click the Start Time drop-down list, and select the new start time.

(3) Click the End Time drop-down list, and select the new end time.

> **! TIP: Use the Tracking tab to see which attendees have responded to your meeting request.**

> **✋ CAUTION: When you change the time for a meeting, a warning appears at the top of the Appointment tab saying that no responses have been received for the meeting. Click the Send Update button and Outlook sends an update message to the recipients, who need to reply to the revised meeting invitation.**

Inserting Items, Objects, and Files in a Calendar Item

Outlook enables you to insert items, objects, and files into your Calendar items. For example, you may have a meeting to which you want to take an important document. You can insert the document into the meeting item so that you don't forget to take it with you. Similarly, you can add Outlook items like contacts to a calendar item.

Add an Outlook item

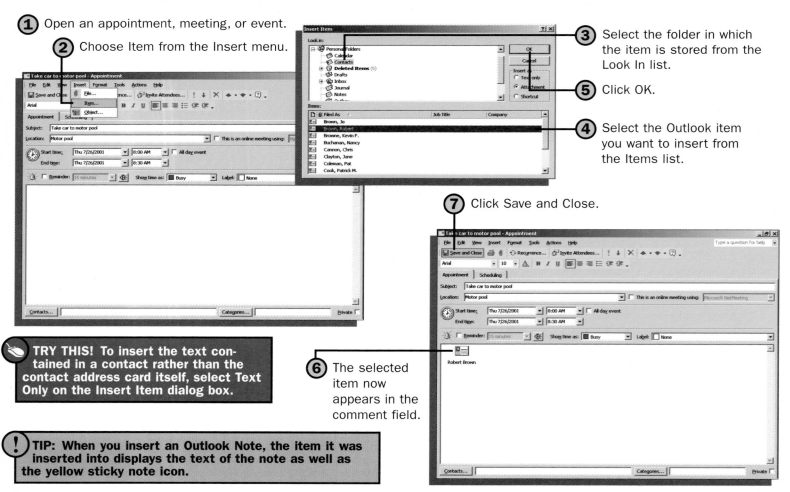

(1) Open an appointment, meeting, or event.

(2) Choose Item from the Insert menu.

(3) Select the folder in which the item is stored from the Look In list.

(5) Click OK.

(4) Select the Outlook item you want to insert from the Items list.

(7) Click Save and Close.

(6) The selected item now appears in the comment field.

TRY THIS! To insert the text contained in a contact rather than the contact address card itself, select Text Only on the Insert Item dialog box.

TIP: When you insert an Outlook Note, the item it was inserted into displays the text of the note as well as the yellow sticky note icon.

Add a File

(1) Double-click an appointment, meeting, or event.

(2) Choose File from the Insert menu.

(3) Select the file you want to insert.

(4) Click Insert.

(6) Click Save And Close.

(5) The added file appears in the comment field.

> **! TIP:** To delete a file, item, or object from a Calendar item, select the item and press Delete.

Add an Object

1 Click the Calendar icon on the Outlook Bar.

2 Double-click an appointment, meeting, or event.

3 Choose Object from the Insert menu.

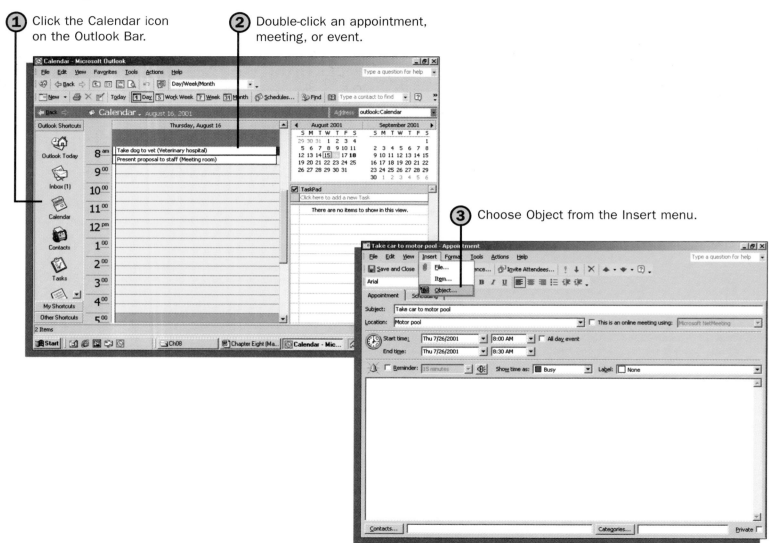

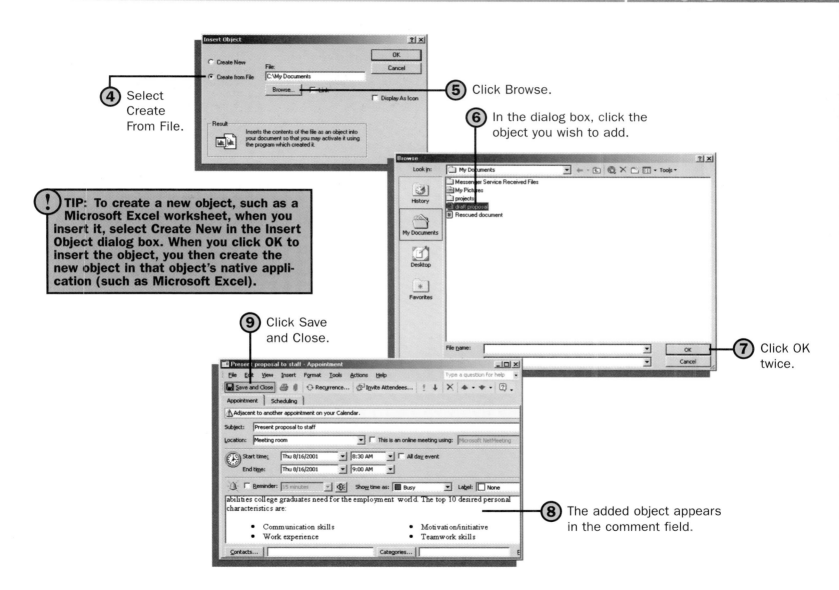

4 Select Create From File.

5 Click Browse.

6 In the dialog box, click the object you wish to add.

! TIP: To create a new object, such as a Microsoft Excel worksheet, when you insert it, select Create New in the Insert Object dialog box. When you click OK to insert the object, you then create the new object in that object's native application (such as Microsoft Excel).

9 Click Save and Close.

7 Click OK twice.

8 The added object appears in the comment field.

Working with Reminders

You can have Outlook display a reminder of upcoming appointments, events, or meetings. The reminder displays in a message box and can sound an alarm to alert you. You can use any sound included with Windows, or use a sound that you've downloaded from the Internet and saved to your hard disk.

> **!** TIP: You can set up reminders for meetings and events by following the same sequence of steps shown here for appointments.

Set Up a Reminder

1 Open the appointment, meeting, or event for which you want to set a reminder.

3 Click Save And Close. You will be reminded of the appointment at the scheduled time.

2 Select Reminder.

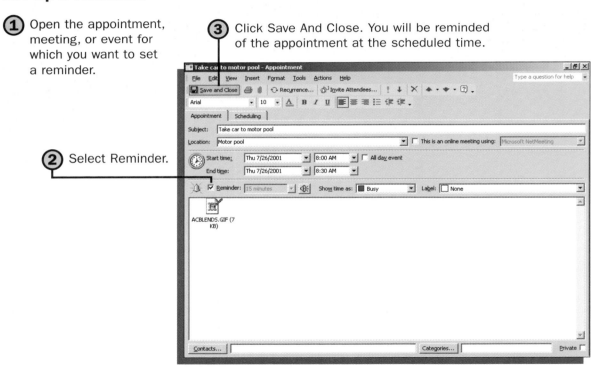

> **!** TIP: Reminders display even if the Calendar item is overdue. For example, if an event was set for Saturday and you didn't turn on your computer that day, the next time you start Windows the reminder for that event will display. You can disable the reminder at that point.

Specify How Reminders Work

(1) Open the appointment for which you want to set a reminder.

(7) Click Save and Close.

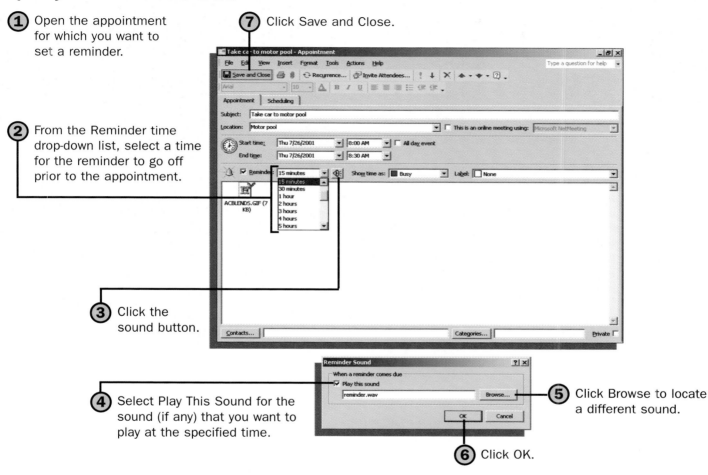

(2) From the Reminder time drop-down list, select a time for the reminder to go off prior to the appointment.

(3) Click the sound button.

(4) Select Play This Sound for the sound (if any) that you want to play at the specified time.

(5) Click Browse to locate a different sound.

(6) Click OK.

> **TRY THIS!** When the Reminder box displays for a Calendar item, you click the Snooze button to delay the reminder for a time. You also can cancel the reminder by clicking the Dismiss button on the Reminder box.

Sharing Calendar Information

Outlook enables you to share Calendar information with others. You can forward a Calendar item by e-mail to users on an Exchange server, or you can forward an iCalendar to any user over the Internet. You should use iCalendar when you're scheduling meetings with people who are not signed on to an Exchange server.

Forward a Calendar Item

1 Open a meeting item by double-clicking it in the Calendar.

2 Choose Forward from the Actions menu.

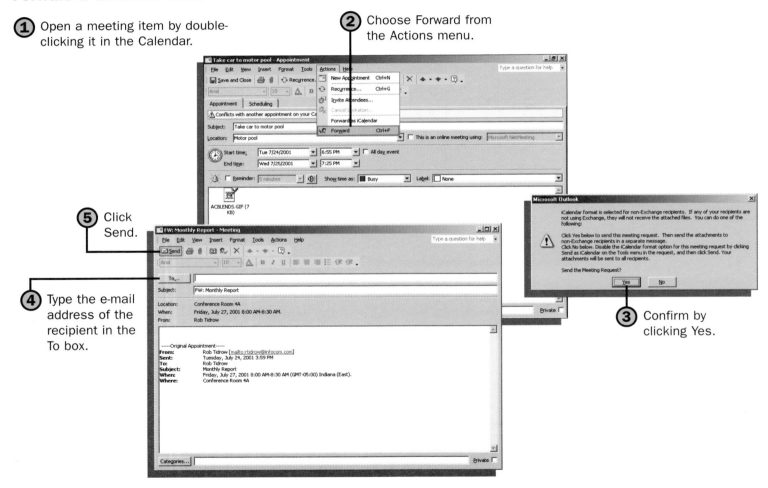

5 Click Send.

4 Type the e-mail address of the recipient in the To box.

3 Confirm by clicking Yes.

Forward an iCalendar

1 Open a meeting item by double-clicking it in the Calendar.

2 Choose Forward As iCalendar from the Actions menu.

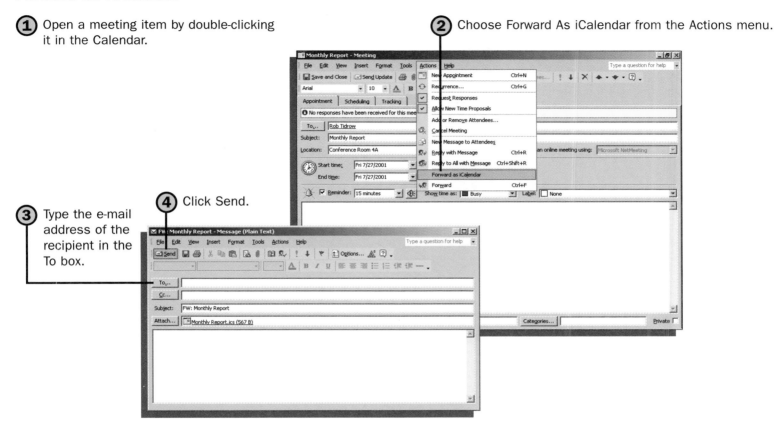

4 Click Send.

3 Type the e-mail address of the recipient in the To box.

> **! TIP:** iCalendar is for people who do not use Microsoft Exchange Server. If you want to forward a Calendar item to someone on an Exchange Server network, use the Forward command on the Actions menu.

> **! TIP:** If you forward a calendar item that has an attachment, that attachment is forwarded along with the Calendar item.

Printing Calendars

Outlook makes it easy to print your calendars. You can print your appointment calendar, such as your daily or weekly appointments, meetings, and events. Or you can print an individual calendar item, such as a meeting item.

Print your Appointment Calendar

1 Click the Calendar icon on the Outlook Bar.

2 Choose Print from the File menu.

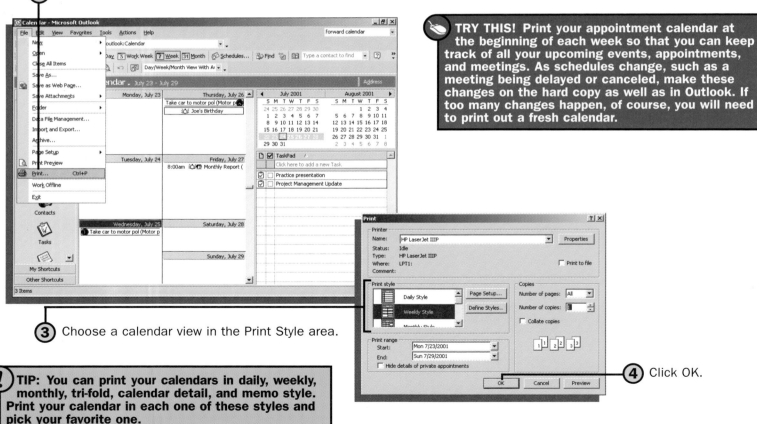

> TRY THIS! Print your appointment calendar at the beginning of each week so that you can keep track of all your upcoming events, appointments, and meetings. As schedules change, such as a meeting being delayed or canceled, make these changes on the hard copy as well as in Outlook. If too many changes happen, of course, you will need to print out a fresh calendar.

3 Choose a calendar view in the Print Style area.

4 Click OK.

> TIP: You can print your calendars in daily, weekly, monthly, tri-fold, calendar detail, and memo style. Print your calendar in each one of these styles and pick your favorite one.

Print a Calendar Item

(1) Click the Calendar icon on the Outlook Bar.

(2) Double-click the Calendar item you want to print.

(3) Choose Print from the File menu.

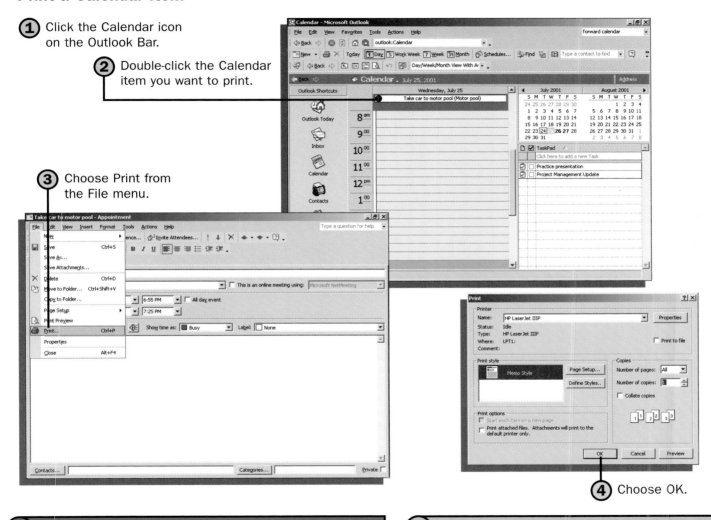

(4) Choose OK.

Using the TaskPad

The Outlook TaskPad is just like a little notebook that sits on your desk, where you can write your to-do list. The nice thing about the one in Outlook, however, is that it stays in one spot—you don't have to look for it under a ton of papers or industry magazines. In the TaskPad you can add a task, mark a task completed when you finish it, and delete a task.

Add a Task

1 Click the Calendar icon on the Outlook Bar.

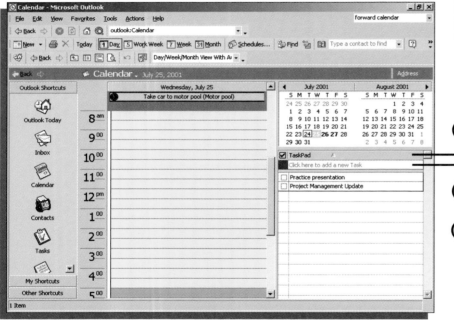

TRY THIS! Double-click a task and set the Priority setting to High. Click Save and Close. By right-clicking on the TaskPad bar, choosing Customize Current View, and editing the Fields and Sort options, you can sort tasks by priority level: High, Normal, and Low.

4 If you have multiple tasks, click the TaskPad bar to sort your tasks.

2 Click in the Click Here To Add New Task area in the TaskPad, and type a new task.

3 Press Enter.

Mark a Task as Complete

1 Click the Calendar icon on the Outlook Bar.

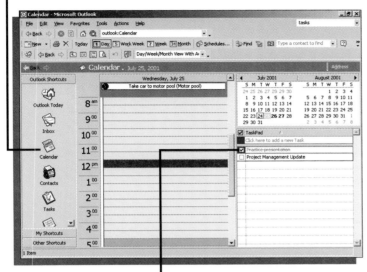

2 Select the checkbox to the left of the completed task to mark the task as complete (it shows up with strikethrough formatting through the task name).

> **TRY THIS!** Open a task, and set a reminder for it. When the reminder is activated, Outlook prompts you that you must complete the task by a specified date and time.

> **TIP:** If you mark a task as complete and later decide that it is incomplete, click the checkbox to the left of the task to clear it.

Delete a Completed Task

1 Click the Calendar icon on the Outlook Bar.

3 Click Delete.

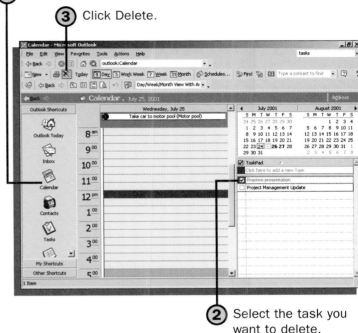

2 Select the task you want to delete.

> **CAUTION:** You are not given a warning that the task is deleted before it's gone. When you press Delete, it's removed from the TaskPad. Choose Undo Delete from the Edit menu if you want to restore the deleted task.

Working with Tasks

Most of us at some time or another have written a to-do list—a list of tasks we needed to perform. Maybe you put together a list of the improvements or repairs you wanted to make to your house. Maybe it was something simpler like a list of errands to run. Whatever the case, having a list of the tasks you need to complete can be valuable for keeping you on track.

Microsoft Outlook includes a feature to help you stay on track. The Tasks folder stores your to-do list. You can create tasks for yourself, assign them a due date, and easily mark them as completed. You can create one-time tasks or recurring tasks. Outlook also lets you assign tasks to others and receive status updates on the tasks from the people to whom you've assigned them. This section explains how to use the Tasks folder to create and manage one-time and recurring tasks, as well as assign tasks to others.

Viewing Your Tasks

Outlook includes a Tasks folder that you can use to store your tasks and tasks that you assign to others. The Tasks folder offers a handful of ways to view and work with your tasks, including the Task List and the TaskPad. The default view for the Tasks folder is the Simple List view, which shows whether the task is complete, the name (subject) of the task, and the due date.

Open the Task Item Window

(1) Click the Tasks icon on the Outlook Bar to open the Tasks folder.

> **TIP:** When you create a task, Outlook doesn't set up a reminder for the task, but you can add one later. Open the task, click the Task tab, select the Reminder checkbox, and then select the date and time for the reminder from the two drop-down lists beside the Reminder checkbox.

(2) Double-click a task to open the task's form.

(3) Click the Details tab to display additional task information.

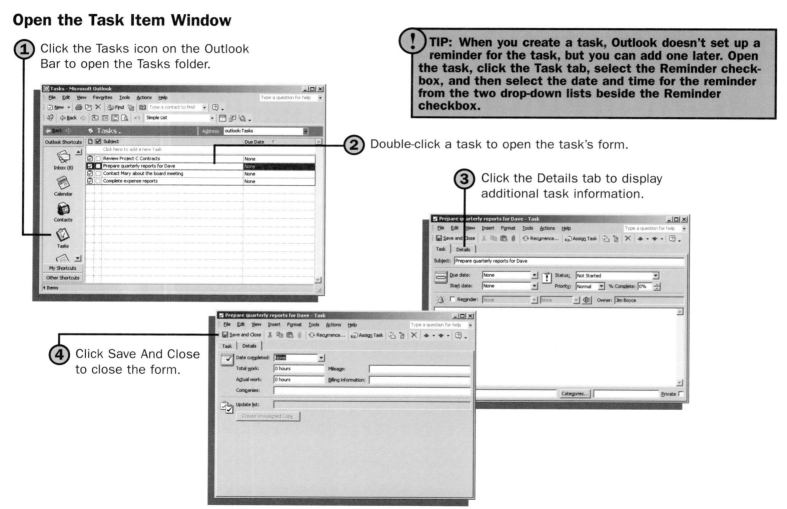

(4) Click Save And Close to close the form.

Use the Task List

(1) In Outlook, click the Tasks icon on the Outlook Bar to open the Tasks folder.

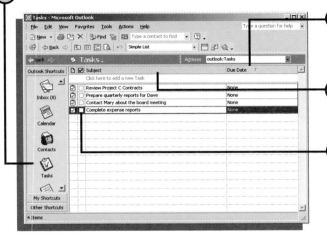

(2) When the Tasks folder opens, click the Due Date column to sort the list by due date.

(3) Click the Subject column to restore the default sort method.

(4) Select the checkbox beside the task's subject to mark the task as complete. Select it again to remove the check and mark the task as incomplete.

> **(!) TIP:** You can add and remove columns from the Task List to show the task data most important to you. Right-click the column header and select Field Chooser. In the Field Chooser dialog box, click a column and drag it to the column header. To remove a column, drag it from the column header to the Field Chooser dialog box.

Use the TaskPad

(1) Click the Calendar icon on the Outlook Bar to open the Calendar folder.

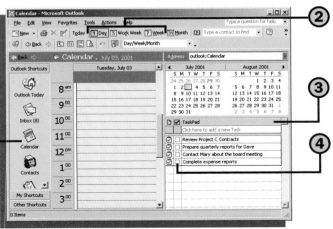

(2) Click Day, Work Week, or Week on the Standard toolbar.

(3) View the tasks in the TaskPad.

(4) Click the checkbox beside a task to mark it as complete. Click the checkbox again to clear the check and mark the task as incomplete.

> **(!) TIP:** The Outlook Today view includes a simplified task list that shows the subject and completion status. You can click on a task's subject to open the task to view its details or modify it. Click the checkbox beside a task to mark it as complete.

> **(✓) SEE ALSO:** The Outlook Today view is built using HTML, the same language used to design Web pages. If you have some knowledge of HTML, you can create a custom Outlook Today view. See *Microsoft Outlook 2002 Inside Out* (Redmond, WA: Microsoft Press, 2001).

Adding a Task

Tasks can be added to your Tasks folder in one of two ways: you can create the task yourself or accept a task that someone else has assigned to you. If you create the task yourself, you can create it by using the New menu, or you can create it through the Tasks folder.

Set the Task Name and Due Date

1 Click the Tasks icon on the Outlook Bar to open the Tasks folder.

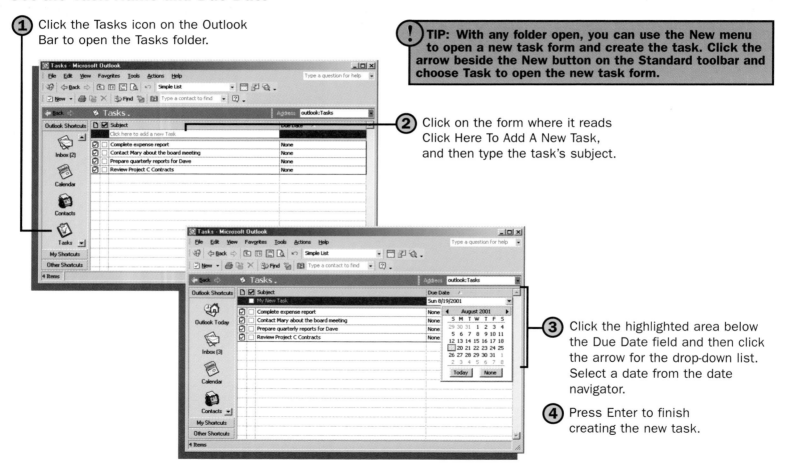

TIP: With any folder open, you can use the New menu to open a new task form and create the task. Click the arrow beside the New button on the Standard toolbar and choose Task to open the new task form.

2 Click on the form where it reads Click Here To Add A New Task, and then type the task's subject.

3 Click the highlighted area below the Due Date field and then click the arrow for the drop-down list. Select a date from the date navigator.

4 Press Enter to finish creating the new task.

Set Task Properties

(1) Click the Tasks icon on the Outlook Bar to open the Tasks folder.

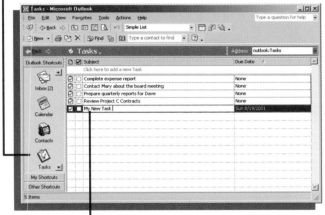

(2) Double-click the task whose properties you want to change to open the task form.

SEE ALSO: For more information on working with reminders, see "Working with Reminders" on page 148.

(3) Click the Task tab.

(4) Set properties for the task.

(5) Click the Details tab.

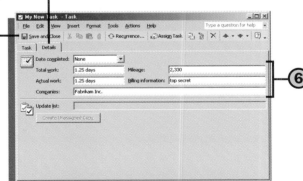

(7) Click Save And Close to close the form.

(6) Set additional properties for the task.

> **TRY THIS!** If you delegate an Outlook folder to other users, allowing them to open your folder and view the items in it, they can see all items not marked private. Use the Private checkbox on the Task tab to prevent your delegates from seeing the task in your task list.

> **TIP:** When you set a reminder for a task, Outlook doesn't assign a sound for the reminder—it only displays the reminder in the Reminders dialog box when the specified time arrives. You can click the speaker button on the Task tab of the program's properties to select a sound file for Outlook to play when it displays the reminder.

Working with Recurring Tasks

Some tasks are *recurring* tasks—they repeat on a regular basis. For example, maybe you have to prepare a set of reports every Friday that summarizes the week's sales or other information. Or perhaps you need to back up your files every week. Although a recurring task shows up only once in the task list, it appears in the TaskPad when the assigned due date falls in the TaskPad's range. If you set a reminder for the task, you'll receive the reminder for each recurrence of the task.

Create a Recurring Task

(1) Click the Tasks icon on the Outlook Bar to open the Tasks folder.

(2) Click New on the Standard toolbar to open a form for the new task.

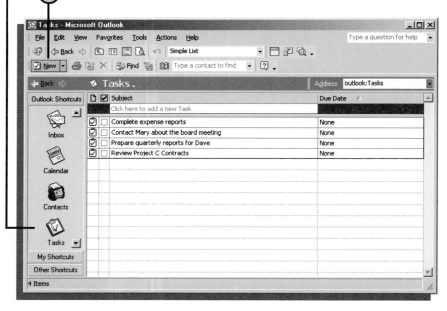

TRY THIS! You can make a recurring task nonrecurring by opening a task's form, clicking Recurrence on the toolbar to open the Task Recurrence dialog box, and then clicking Remove Recurrence.

TIP: If you set a recurring task with no end date, you'll still be able to revise the task's properties to make it end after a specified number of occurrences or specified date. Just open the task's properties, click Recurrence to open the Task Recurrence dialog box, choose the desired end option, and click OK. Then click Save And Close to save the changes.

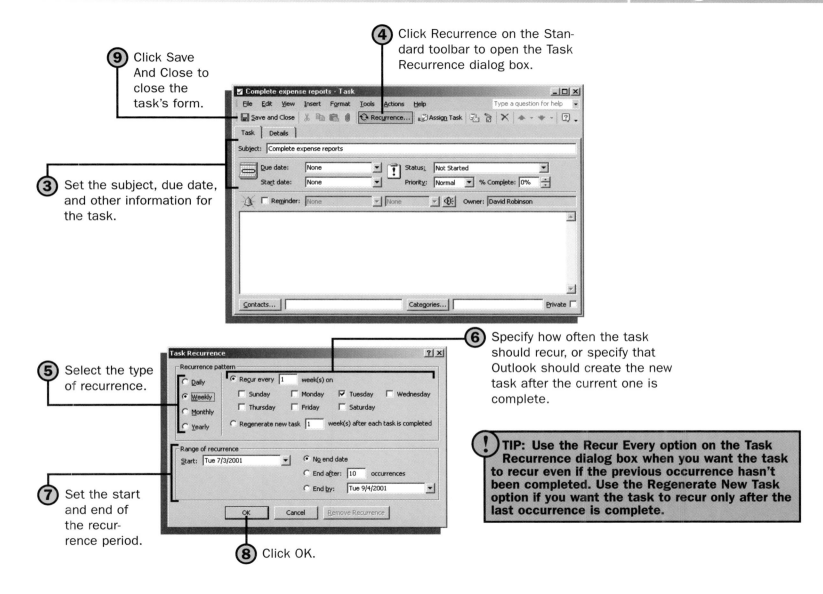

④ Click Recurrence on the Standard toolbar to open the Task Recurrence dialog box.

⑨ Click Save And Close to close the task's form.

③ Set the subject, due date, and other information for the task.

⑤ Select the type of recurrence.

⑦ Set the start and end of the recurrence period.

⑥ Specify how often the task should recur, or specify that Outlook should create the new task after the current one is complete.

! TIP: Use the Recur Every option on the Task Recurrence dialog box when you want the task to recur even if the previous occurrence hasn't been completed. Use the Regenerate New Task option if you want the task to recur only after the last occurrence is complete.

⑧ Click OK.

Modifying and Updating a Task

You can modify a task at any time to change any property, including subject, due date, recurrence, and so on. Another change you'll want to make to tasks is to mark them as complete. This allows you to see at a glance which of your tasks are complete and which are not. You can also change the view of the Tasks folder to show only tasks that are complete, only tasks that are overdue, only those that are incomplete, and so on. In addition to marking tasks as complete, you'll probably want to delete completed tasks and send status updates for tasks that are assigned to you.

Mark a Task as Complete

(1) Click the Tasks icon on the Outlook bar to open the Tasks folder.

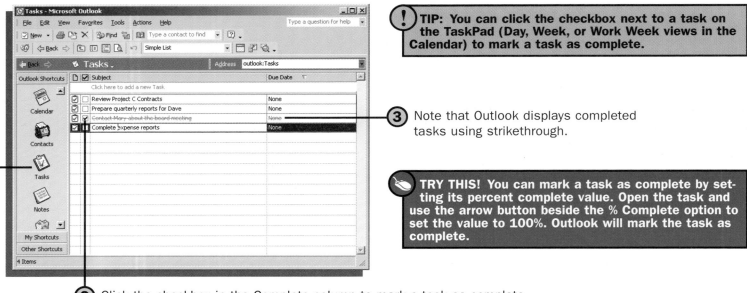

! **TIP:** You can click the checkbox next to a task on the TaskPad (Day, Week, or Work Week views in the Calendar) to mark a task as complete.

(3) Note that Outlook displays completed tasks using strikethrough.

TRY THIS! You can mark a task as complete by setting its percent complete value. Open the task and use the arrow button beside the % Complete option to set the value to 100%. Outlook will mark the task as complete.

(2) Click the checkbox in the Complete column to mark a task as complete.

Delete a Completed Task

(1) With the task list or the TaskPad displayed, select the task.

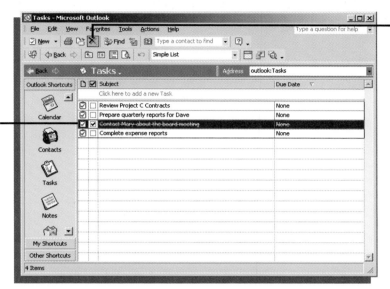

(2) Click the Delete button on the Standard toolbar to delete the task.

(!) TIP: You can delete any task, whether or not the task is marked as complete. Use the same method to delete an incomplete task that you use to delete a complete task.

(!) TIP: When you delete a task, Outlook places the task in the Deleted Items folder. If you deleted the wrong task or decided you didn't want to delete it after all, you can restore it to the Tasks folder. Open the Deleted Items folder and drag the task to the Tasks icon on the Outlook Bar. You can also right-click a task in the Deleted Items folder, choose Move To Folder, select the Tasks folder, and click OK to move it back.

Send a Status Report for an Assigned Task

① Click the Tasks icon on the Outlook Bar to open the Tasks folder.

② Double-click the task to open its form.

③ Make changes to the task's properties as needed and click Save on the File menu to save the changes.

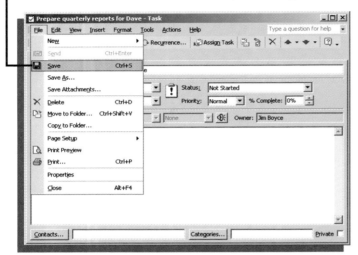

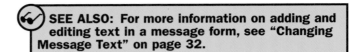 **SEE ALSO:** For more information on adding and editing text in a message form, see "Changing Message Text" on page 32.

SEE ALSO: For more information on assigning tasks to others, see "Assigning a Task to Someone Else" on page 168.

SEE ALSO: For more information on addressing e-mail messages and working with the address book, see "Writing an E-Mail Message" on page 26.

TIP: Outlook fills in the status information in the body of the update message for you. You can edit this text if needed. Just highlight the text you want to change and type the replacement text.

4 Choose Send Status Report on the Actions menu to open the Task Status Report message form.

5 Outlook adds the update address list; click To or Cc to add addresses for people not included in the update list.

7 Click Send to send the message.

6 Click in the body of the message and add notes or comments as desired.

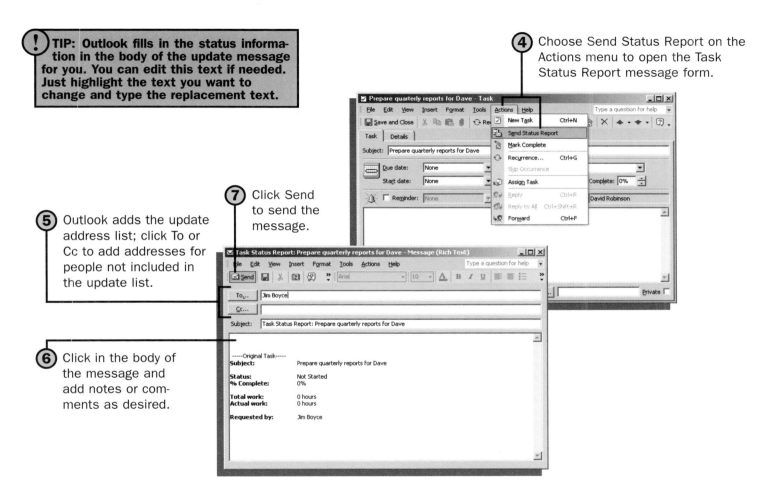

TRY THIS! You can send a copy of a status report to a person not on the update list without letting the people on the list know that you've copied that person. Just use the Bcc field to address the message to the other person. If Outlook isn't currently showing the Bcc field, open a message form and choose Bcc Field from the View menu to display it. The Bcc Field command is available on the View menu only if you are using Outlook as your e-mail editor, rather than Microsoft Word.

Assigning a Task to Someone Else

If you manage others and use Outlook in your organization for e-mail and collaboration, you'll probably want to assign tasks to others. Outlook sends the task assignment as an e-mail message and the assignee has the option of accepting or rejecting the task. When you assign a task you define a status update distribution list. The people on that list receive status reports when the assignee makes changes to the task.

Assign a Task

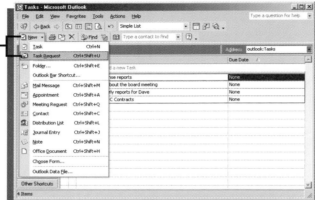

(1) Click the arrow beside New on the Standard toolbar and choose Task Request to open a new task form that includes message address fields.

> **!** **TIP: When you assign a task to another person, a copy of the task request message goes into your Sent Items folder. If you open the message, its form shows a status message indicating that Outlook is waiting for a response from the assignee. This message changes after the assignee either accepts or rejects the task.**

(2) Use the properties on the Task tab to define the task.

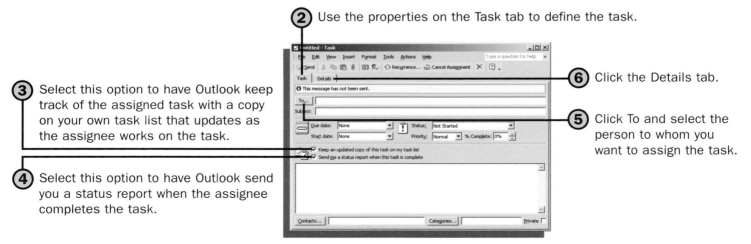

(3) Select this option to have Outlook keep track of the assigned task with a copy on your own task list that updates as the assignee works on the task.

(4) Select this option to have Outlook send you a status report when the assignee completes the task.

(6) Click the Details tab.

(5) Click To and select the person to whom you want to assign the task.

(8) Click Send.

(7) Add other information for the task.

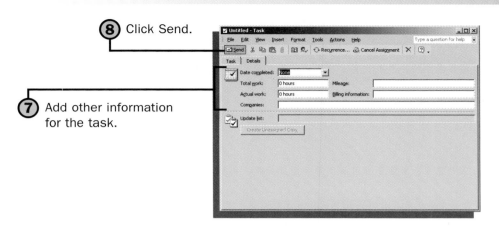

SEE ALSO: For information on how to include a document with a task you assign to someone else, see "Inserting Items into a Task" on page 170.

Accept or Reject an Assigned Task

(1) Click the Inbox icon on the Outlook Bar to open the Inbox.

(2) Click a message to select it. If the preview pane is not open, double-click the message to open it.

TRY THIS! If you want to "pass the buck" and assign the task to someone else, open the task, click Assign Task on the standard toolbar, and assign the task by typing in someone's name or selecting a name from your address list.

TIP: When you reassign a task that someone has assigned to you and that third person accepts the task, Outlook sends an acceptance notice to you and to the task's originator. The status update list then includes the originator's address and yours, so you receive status updates along with the originator.

TIP: When you accept or reject a task, Outlook deletes the task request message from your Inbox. You can't control this behavior to prevent Outlook from deleting the message. However, Outlook does keep copies in your Sent Items folder of task requests that you create.

(3) Click Accept to accept the task, or Decline to decline the task.

Inserting Items into a Task

When you create a task—whether you create the task for yourself or assign it to someone else—you might want to add items to the task. For example, assume you're going to assign a task to someone else, and that person needs a copy of a Word document to perform the task. You can attach the document to the task. Or perhaps you need to include some contacts with a task. Whatever the case, it's easy to insert Outlook items, objects, and files in a task.

Add an Outlook item

① Click the Tasks icon on the Outlook Bar to open the Tasks folder.

② Double-click a task to open its form.

③ Choose Item from the Insert menu to open the Insert Item dialog box.

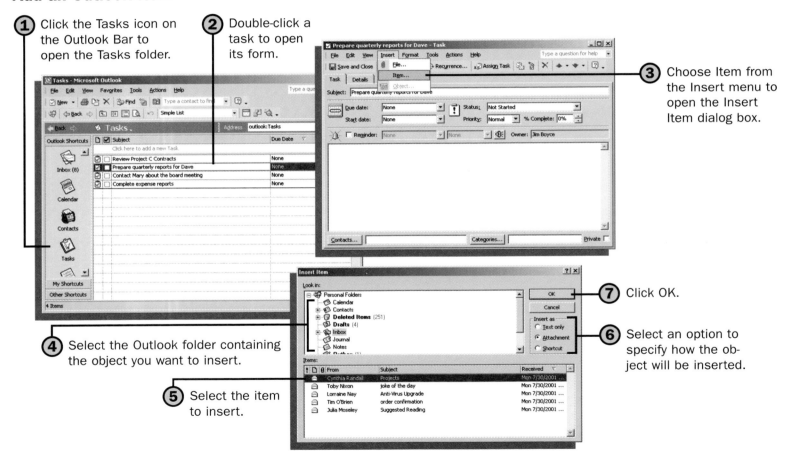

④ Select the Outlook folder containing the object you want to insert.

⑤ Select the item to insert.

⑥ Select an option to specify how the object will be inserted.

⑦ Click OK.

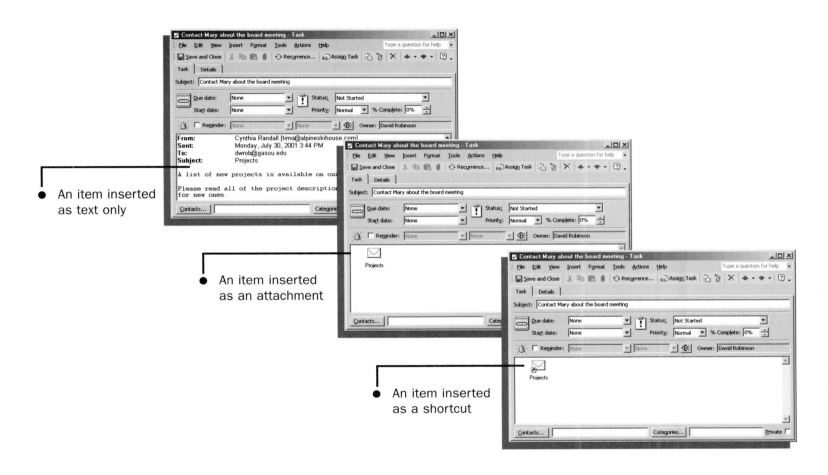

- An item inserted as text only
- An item inserted as an attachment
- An item inserted as a shortcut

⚠ **TIP:** If you insert the item as text only or as an attachment, the item data itself is attached to the task. You can save storage space by inserting a shortcut to the item. Double-clicking the shortcut then opens the item from its original location. In most cases, though, you can't insert a shortcut to an item in a task that you are assigning to someone else and still have that person be able to open the item, because they typically won't have access to the Outlook folder where it's located.

Add a File

① Click the Tasks icon to open the Tasks folder.

② Double-click a task to open its form.

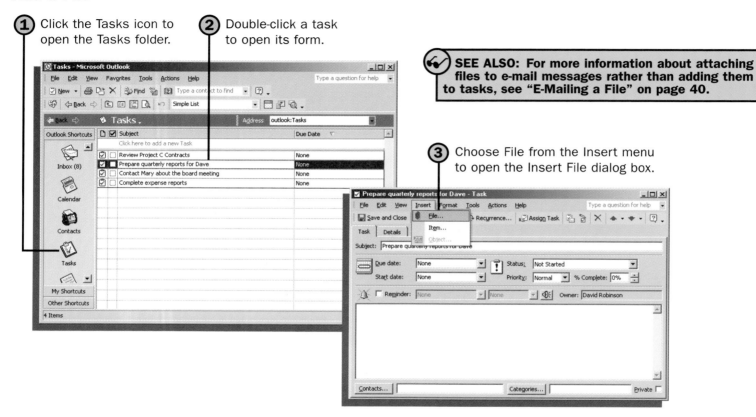

SEE ALSO: For more information about attaching files to e-mail messages rather than adding them to tasks, see "E-Mailing a File" on page 40.

③ Choose File from the Insert menu to open the Insert File dialog box.

TRY THIS! You can insert a file as a hyperlink rather than as an attachment, which allows the task to be opened from its source rather than included in the task. The main benefit to this is you don't duplicate the document but instead create a shortcut to it. To insert a hyperlink in a task, open the task and choose File from the Insert menu. Select the file, click the arrow beside the Insert button, and then choose Insert As Hyperlink.

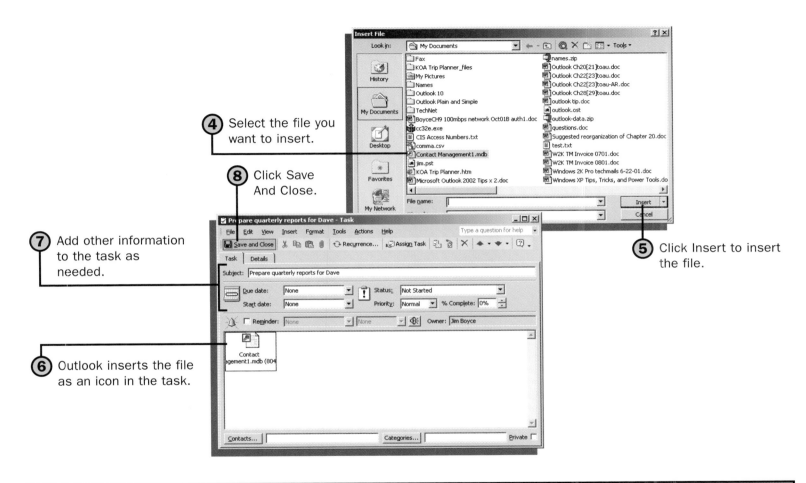

④ Select the file you want to insert.

⑧ Click Save And Close.

⑦ Add other information to the task as needed.

⑤ Click Insert to insert the file.

⑥ Outlook inserts the file as an icon in the task.

TIP: When you insert a file as a hyperlink, Outlook inserts the path to the document. If you insert a file from your local computer, the path uses the local drive letter. This works fine for creating hyperlinks to documents you use, but doesn't work when assigning a task to someone else, because clicking the link on their end will cause Outlook to try to open the file from their computer. However you can link files on network servers in tasks that you assign, as long as you're viewing the server through a UNC path rather than a mapped drive. A UNC path has the form \\server\folder, where *server* is the name of the server and *folder* the name of the shared folder on the server where the document is located.

Sharing Task Information

Sometimes you might need to share a task with someone else. For example, you might need to include information about a task in a written report. Or perhaps you need to print a list of tasks to include in an information packet for a staff meeting. Outlook gives you several ways to share tasks, including printing them and sending them through e-mail messages.

Print a Task List

(1) Open the Tasks folder and choose Print from the File menu.

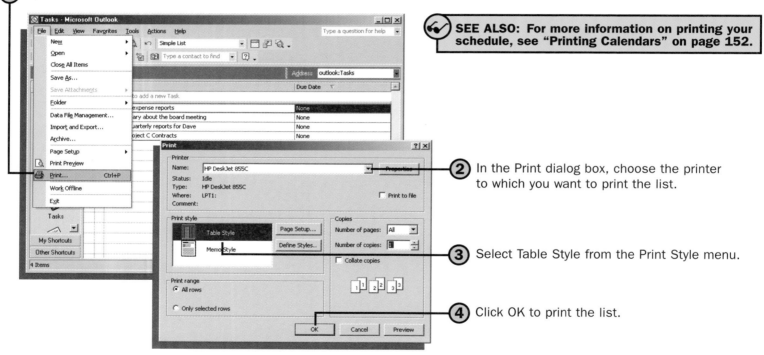

 SEE ALSO: For more information on printing your schedule, see "Printing Calendars" on page 152.

(2) In the Print dialog box, choose the printer to which you want to print the list.

(3) Select Table Style from the Print Style menu.

(4) Click OK to print the list.

TRY THIS! Sometimes you might not want to include all of your tasks in the printed list. Open the Tasks folder, hold down the Ctrl key, and click on the tasks you want included in the list. Choose Print from the File menu, select the printer, and then select Only Selected Rows. Click OK to print the selected tasks.

Print a Task Item

(1) Open the Tasks folder and open the task you want to print.

(2) Choose Print from the File menu.

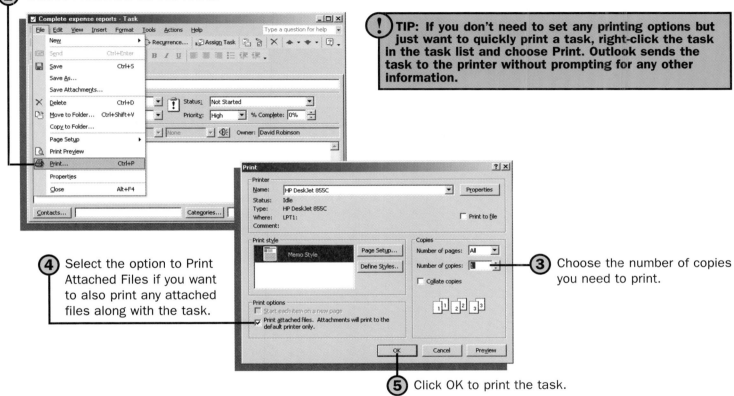

TIP: If you don't need to set any printing options but just want to quickly print a task, right-click the task in the task list and choose Print. Outlook sends the task to the printer without prompting for any other information.

(4) Select the option to Print Attached Files if you want to also print any attached files along with the task.

(3) Choose the number of copies you need to print.

(5) Click OK to print the task.

SEE ALSO: For more information about attaching files to a task, see "Add a File" on page 172.

Forward a Task

1 Open the Tasks folder, right-click a task, and choose Forward to open a message with the task as an attachment.

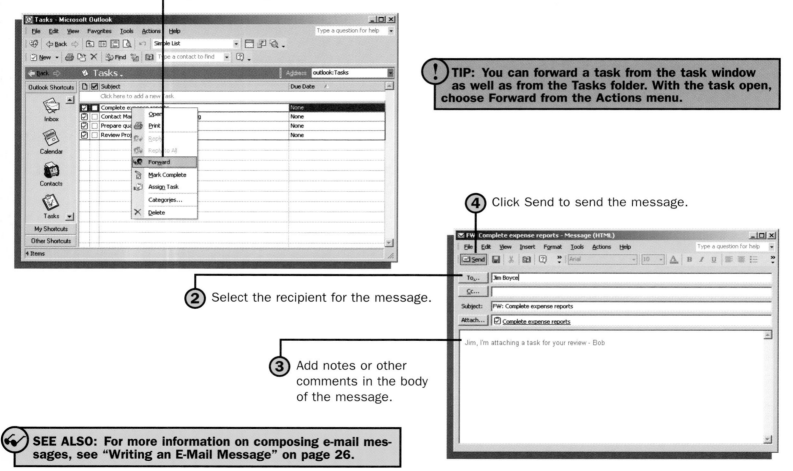

TIP: You can forward a task from the task window as well as from the Tasks folder. With the task open, choose Forward from the Actions menu.

4 Click Send to send the message.

2 Select the recipient for the message.

3 Add notes or other comments in the body of the message.

SEE ALSO: For more information on composing e-mail messages, see "Writing an E-Mail Message" on page 26.

Working with Notes

If you're like most people, you probably have lots of notes littering your desk or stuck to your monitor, and they help you organize your day (or they would, if the notes themselves weren't so disorganized). Some of those notes are probably important enough that you'd have a hard time getting by without them.

You can get organized and clean up your desk at the same time by switching to using Outlook to keep track of all your notes. Outlook provides a Notes folder you can use to create and view electronic notes. As with other Outlook items, you can print these notes, save them on your computer, and even stick them right on your Windows desktop.

This section explains how to work with the Notes folder in Outlook. You will learn how to create and view notes, edit and delete them, and use different colors for your notes. You'll also learn how to cut and copy notes, print them out (when you simply must have a hard copy), and attach them to e-mail messages.

Viewing Notes

As with other types of items, Outlook provides a folder specifically for working with notes. You can create additional notes folders if you like, or just work with the main Notes folder. The initial view for the Notes folder shows the notes as icons with the first few lines of the note text underneath the icon. When you click on a note to select it, Outlook shows more of the text.

> **SEE ALSO:** For more information on creating other folders in Outlook for storing notes, see "Organizing with Folders" on page 190.

Open the Notes Folder

1 Click the Notes icon on the Outlook Bar to open the Notes folder.

3 Choose Current View from the View menu, then choose Notes List. This will cause the first three lines of each note to be displayed.

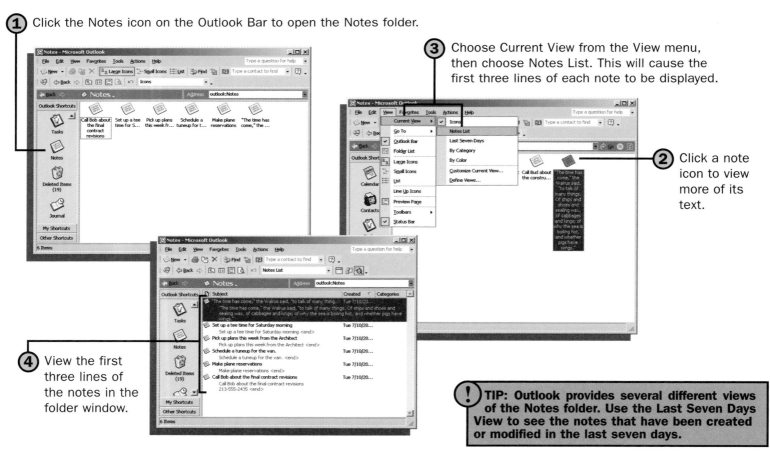

2 Click a note icon to view more of its text.

4 View the first three lines of the notes in the folder window.

> **TIP:** Outlook provides several different views of the Notes folder. Use the Last Seven Days View to see the notes that have been created or modified in the last seven days.

Read a Note

(1) Click the Notes icon on the Outlook Bar to open the Notes folder.

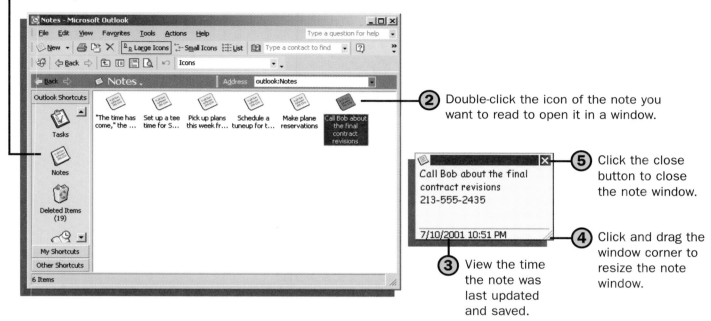

(2) Double-click the icon of the note you want to read to open it in a window.

(5) Click the close button to close the note window.

(4) Click and drag the window corner to resize the note window.

(3) View the time the note was last updated and saved.

⚠ TIP: You can click on the small note icon in the upper left corner of the note's window to perform any of several commands on the note, such as saving it, changing its color, and more.

🔍 SEE ALSO: For information on how to change the color of a note, see "Customizing the Notes Folder" on page 182.

Creating a Note

Working with notes is one of the easiest tasks in Outlook. Notes are little more than text files, and creating a new note is as easy as creating a file with NotePad or WordPad. Outlook opens an empty window when you start a new note, ready for your text. You can easily edit a note to change its contents or add more text. Finally, when you don't need the note anymore you can easily delete it.

> **! TIP:** You can insert blank lines in a note simply by pressing Enter.

Add a Note

(1) Click the Notes icon on the Outlook Bar to open the Notes folder.

(2) Click New on the Standard toolbar to open a new note window.

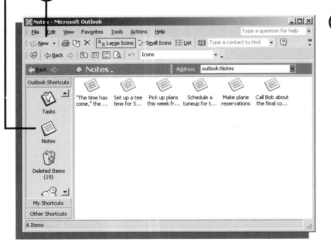

(3) Start typing the note text in the note window. You can insert blank lines by pressing Enter.

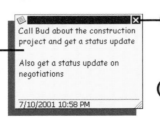

(4) Click the close button to save the changes and close the note window.

(5) Outlook adds an icon to the Notes window for the new note.

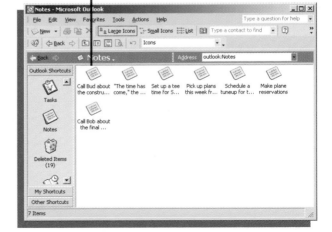

> **TRY THIS!** To see how the note date and time feature works, start by creating a new note. Type some text and notice the date and time at the bottom of the window. Close the note and wait a few minutes. When you reopen the note you will see that the time has not changed.

Delete a Note

(1) Click the Notes icon on the Outlook Bar to open the Notes folder.

(3) Click the Delete button on the Standard toolbar.

[Screenshot of Notes - Microsoft Outlook window]

File   Edit   View   Favorites   Tools   Actions   Help   Type a question for help

New ▾ | 🖨 | ✂ | ✖ | Large Icons   Small Icons   List | Type a contact to find ▾ | ❓ »

⊕ ⇐ Back ⇒ | ⬆ | 📄 📑 📰 📇 | ↶ Icons ▾

← Back ⇒   📝 Notes .   Address   outlook:Notes

Outlook Shortcuts

📝 Tasks

📝 Notes

🗑 Deleted Items (19)

My Shortcuts

Other Shortcuts

7 Items

Call Bud about the constru...   "The time has come," the ...   Set up a tee time for S...   Pick up plans this week fr...   Schedule a tuneup for the van.   Make plane reservations

Call Bob about the final co...

(2) Click to select the note you want to delete.

> ⚠ **TIP:** You can select a note and then press Delete on the keyboard to delete it. You can also select more than one note and delete them at the same time.

> 🖱 **TRY THIS!** As with other Outlook items, notes you delete are placed in the Deleted Items folder. You can recover the notes if needed by opening the Deleted Items folder and dragging the notes back to the Notes folder.

> ⚠ **TIP:** Hold down the Ctrl key while clicking notes to select multiple notes for deletion.

Customizing the Notes Folder

Unlike most other Outlook folders, the Notes folder offers only a few settings. You can change the color Outlook uses for new notes, the note font, and the initial window size for new notes. You can change the font used by all notes but not the font used by individual notes. In other words, all notes have the same font and font size. However, you can set note color individually.

Change Note Color

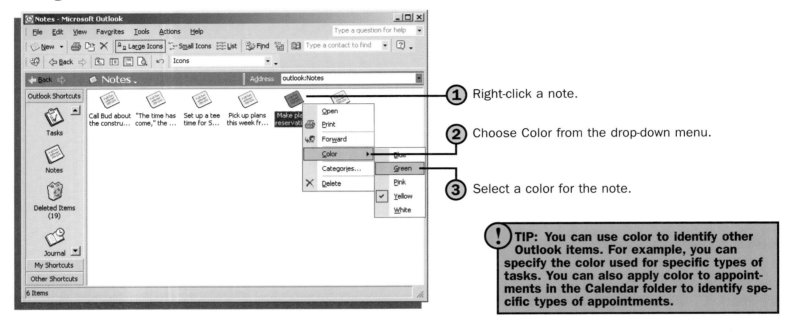

1. Right-click a note.

2. Choose Color from the drop-down menu.

3. Select a color for the note.

> **TIP:** You can use color to identify other Outlook items. For example, you can specify the color used for specific types of tasks. You can also apply color to appointments in the Calendar folder to identify specific types of appointments.

Change the Notes Folder View

(1) Click Small Icons on the Standard toolbar.

SEE ALSO: For more information on working with different views, see "Viewing Items and Folders" on page 18.

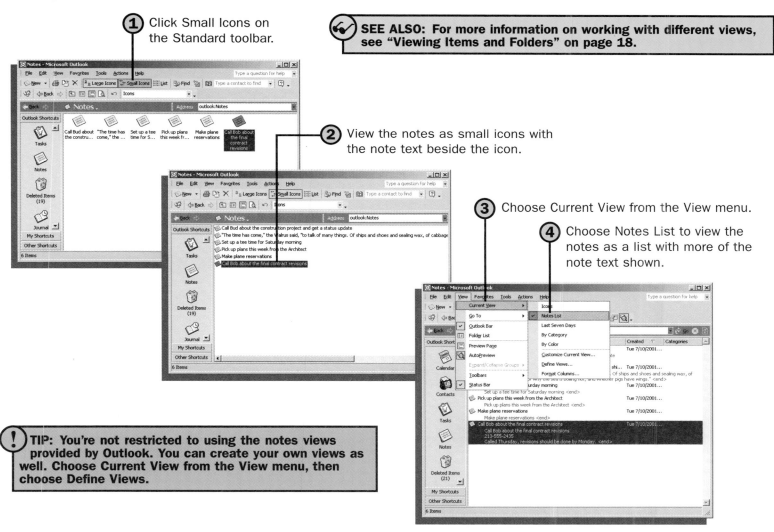

(2) View the notes as small icons with the note text beside the icon.

(3) Choose Current View from the View menu.

(4) Choose Notes List to view the notes as a list with more of the note text shown.

TIP: You're not restricted to using the notes views provided by Outlook. You can create your own views as well. Choose Current View from the View menu, then choose Define Views.

Sharing Notes

You can share notes with others in a handful of different ways, just as you can share other Outlook items. For example, you can e-mail a note to someone or print it to save a hard copy or send with a report. You can also use the Clipboard to copy notes to other Outlook items or other programs.

E-Mail a Note

1 Open the Notes folder and select the note you want to send as e-mail.

2 Choose Forward from the Actions menu to open a message window with the note attached to the message.

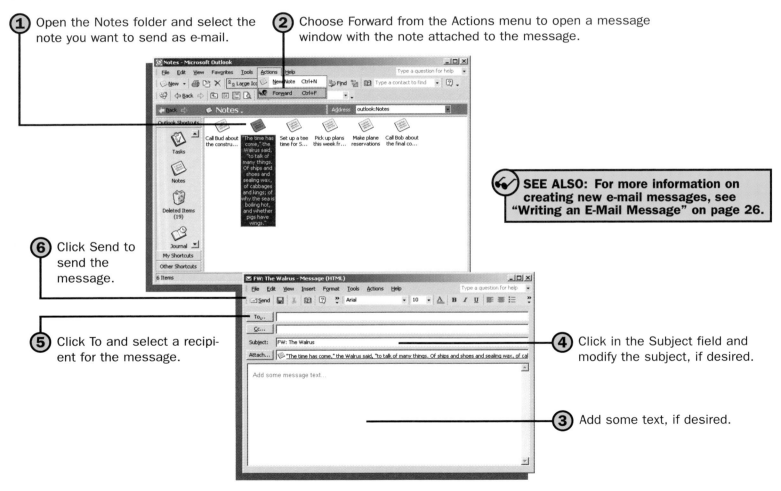

> **SEE ALSO:** For more information on creating new e-mail messages, see "Writing an E-Mail Message" on page 26.

6 Click Send to send the message.

5 Click To and select a recipient for the message.

4 Click in the Subject field and modify the subject, if desired.

3 Add some text, if desired.

Print a Note

(1) Open the Notes folder and select the note you want to print.

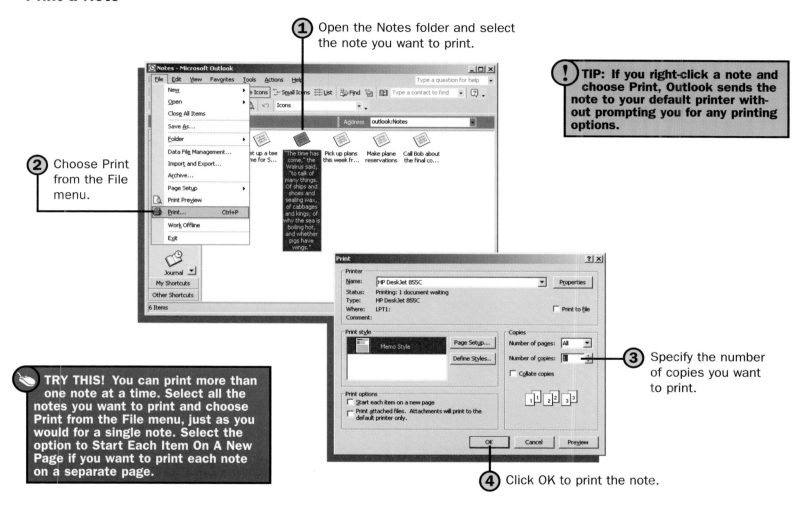

(!) TIP: If you right-click a note and choose Print, Outlook sends the note to your default printer without prompting you for any printing options.

(2) Choose Print from the File menu.

(3) Specify the number of copies you want to print.

(✎) TRY THIS! You can print more than one note at a time. Select all the notes you want to print and choose Print from the File menu, just as you would for a single note. Select the option to Start Each Item On A New Page if you want to print each note on a separate page.

(4) Click OK to print the note.

Copy or Cut a Note

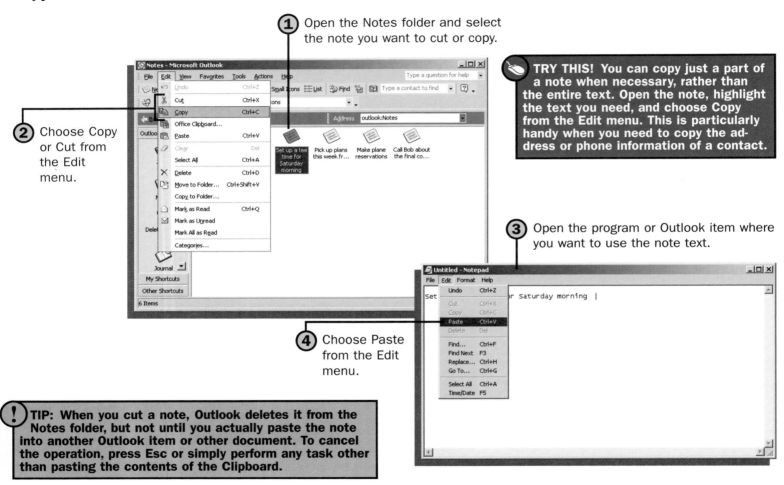

① Open the Notes folder and select the note you want to cut or copy.

② Choose Copy or Cut from the Edit menu.

TRY THIS! You can copy just a part of a note when necessary, rather than the entire text. Open the note, highlight the text you need, and choose Copy from the Edit menu. This is particularly handy when you need to copy the address or phone information of a contact.

③ Open the program or Outlook item where you want to use the note text.

④ Choose Paste from the Edit menu.

TIP: When you cut a note, Outlook deletes it from the Notes folder, but not until you actually paste the note into another Outlook item or other document. To cancel the operation, press Esc or simply perform any task other than pasting the contents of the Clipboard.

Managing Items and Folders

Microsoft Outlook 2002 provides several ways you can manage your Outlook items and folders, including organizing items in categories, creating and using folders to store items, using the Mailbox Cleanup Tool, and using the Journal to organize your work. For example, you can create folders to store e-mail messages relating to projects on which you work, making it easier to locate those messages when you need them.

Categories let you organize and sort your data in Outlook. You might assign a project category to all items for a specific project, then set up a view in each Outlook folder that displays the items grouped by category. This helps you quickly locate items associated with a specific project.

The Journal is another important feature in Outlook. You can use the Journal folder to keep track of documents, phone calls, meetings, and other items and events that occur during the day. Outlook can even record many items in the Journal.

This section covers how to manage your items and folders in Outlook 2002. It covers how to categorize items, organize folders, delete items, clean up folders, and create a Journal.

Using Categories

Categories are keywords or phrases that help you manage Outlook items, such as contacts, e-mail messages, journal entries, and meetings. With categories, you can set up relationships between items stored in different places in Outlook. For instance, you can categorize a piece of e-mail and a meeting reminder as business items. Then when you sort, filter, or search for all your business-related items, that e-mail message and meeting reminder will appear.

Categorize an Item

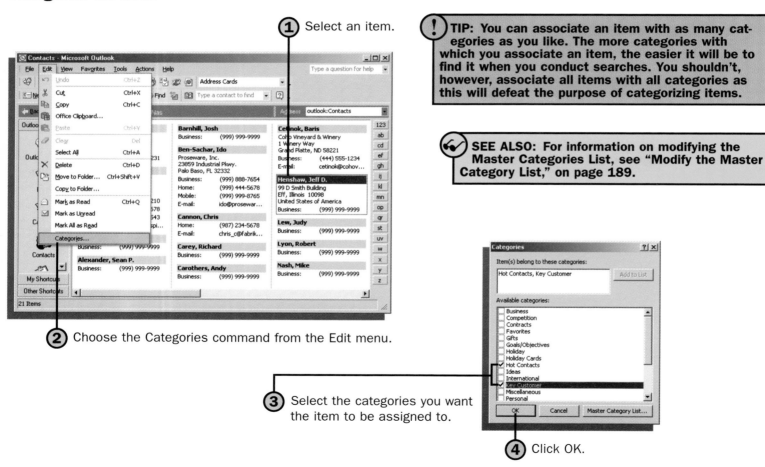

① Select an item.

TIP: You can associate an item with as many categories as you like. The more categories with which you associate an item, the easier it will be to find it when you conduct searches. You shouldn't, however, associate all items with all categories as this will defeat the purpose of categorizing items.

SEE ALSO: For information on modifying the Master Categories List, see "Modify the Master Category List," on page 189.

② Choose the Categories command from the Edit menu.

③ Select the categories you want the item to be assigned to.

④ Click OK.

Modify the Master Category List

① Select an item.

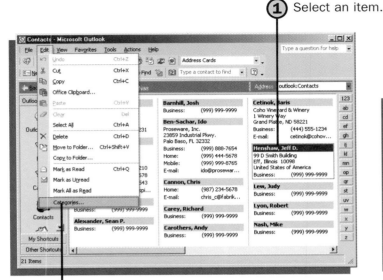

② Choose the Categories command from the Edit menu.

③ Click Master Category List.

④ Type a new category name in the New Category box, and click Add.

⚠ **CAUTION:** If you assign a category to an item and then remove it from the Master Category list, the category is not deleted from that item. You can still sort, view, or filter items based on deleted categories.

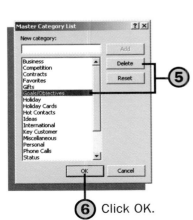

⑤ Select a category, and click Delete to remove it from the Master Category List.

⑥ Click OK.

Organizing with Folders

Outlook 2002 uses folders to let you store items, such as e-mail messages and notes. Outlook folders are similar to the folders you can create and modify in Windows Explorer. The Inbox folder, for example, is the default location for your incoming e-mail messages. The Outbox folder, on the other hand, stores your outgoing e-mail messages until you send them.

Create a New Folder

① In Outlook, choose New from the File menu and then Folder from the submenu.

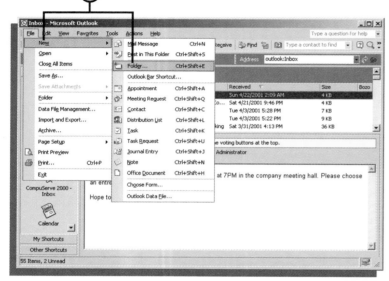

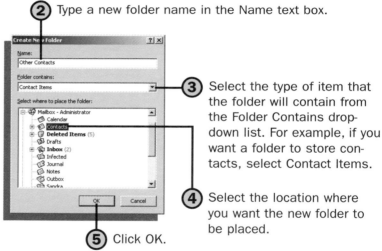

② Type a new folder name in the Name text box.

③ Select the type of item that the folder will contain from the Folder Contains drop-down list. For example, if you want a folder to store contacts, select Contact Items.

④ Select the location where you want the new folder to be placed.

⑤ Click OK.

> **TIP:** You can create *subfolders*, which are folders within folders. Subfolders can help you manage your items in Outlook by letting you organize items in ways that help you do your work. For example, you can set up subfolders under the Inbox folder relating to the projects on which you currently are working. As you receive e-mail relating to those projects, you can move the item from the Inbox to the appropriate subfolder.

SEE ALSO: For information on Outlook folders, see "Exploring Outlook Folders" on page 9.

Move Items to a Folder

(1) In the Outlook main window, choose the item you want to move.

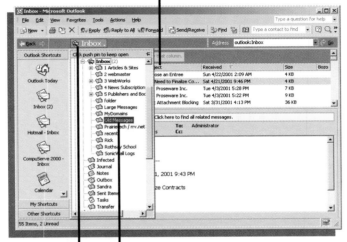

(3) Continue holding down the mouse button, and drop the item on the folder where you want the item moved.

(2) Click and drag the item from the Outlook main window to the Folder List button to open the folder list.

TRY THIS! When you're moving or copying an item, drag it with the right mouse button pressed instead of the left. When you drop the item on a new folder, a shortcut menu appears. Choose Move, Copy, or Cancel to complete the operation.

Copy Items to a Folder

(1) In the Outlook main window, choose the item you want to copy.

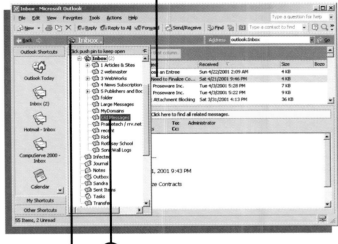

(3) Drop the item on the folder where you want the item copied.

(2) Press and hold down the Ctrl key, then click and drag the item from the Outlook main window to the Folder List button to open the folder list.

CAUTION: Sometimes when you move an item you may drop it into the wrong folder. If you do this, don't panic. Choose Undo Move from the Edit menu immediately after you move the item. Outlook will return the item to its location prior to the move.

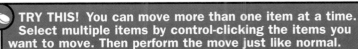
TRY THIS! You can move more than one item at a time. Select multiple items by control-clicking the items you want to move. Then perform the move just like normal.

Cleaning Up Folders

You should get in the habit of cleaning out unwanted e-mail messages, old contacts, and other items by deleting them or moving them to other folders. Outlook 2002 provides the Mailbox Cleanup tool to help you manage your mailbox. This tool lets you set the size of your mailbox to increase Outlook's performance and to make managing mailbox items easier.

Use the Mailbox Cleanup Tool

1 In Outlook, choose Mailbox Cleanup from the Tools menu.

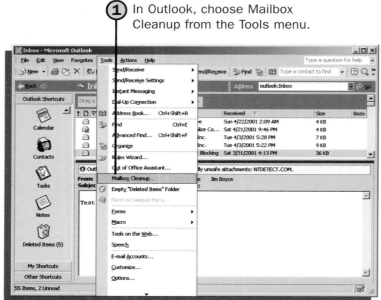

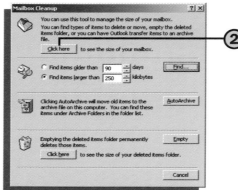

2 Click the button labeled Click Here to display the Folder Size dialog box.

3 View the size of your mailbox and other Outlook folders.

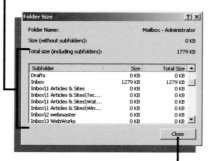

SEE ALSO: For information on setting AutoArchive options, see "Set the AutoArchive Options" on page 214.

4 Click Close to close the Folder Size dialog box and return to the Mailbox Cleanup dialog box.

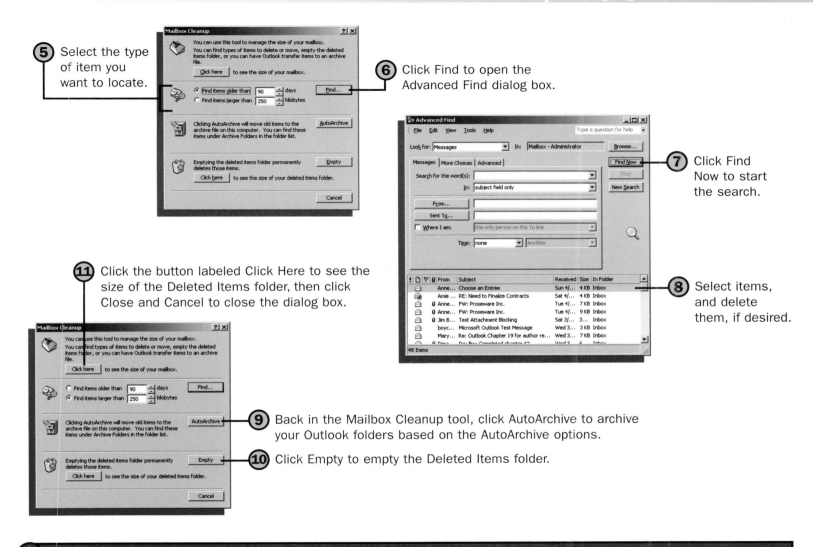

5 Select the type of item you want to locate.

6 Click Find to open the Advanced Find dialog box.

7 Click Find Now to start the search.

8 Select items, and delete them, if desired.

11 Click the button labeled Click Here to see the size of the Deleted Items folder, then click Close and Cancel to close the dialog box.

9 Back in the Mailbox Cleanup tool, click AutoArchive to archive your Outlook folders based on the AutoArchive options.

10 Click Empty to empty the Deleted Items folder.

CAUTION: Depending on the AutoArchive options set for a folder, messages older than a specific date may be removed from your current folders and placed in the Archive Folders. If you want to access a message that has been moved to these folders, open the folders from the Folder List pane and view the message in the main Outlook window.

Deleting Items

Over time your Outlook folders may become cluttered with too many items and become unmanageable. Outlook allows you to delete items from their current folder when you no longer need them. When you delete an item, it is removed from its current folder and placed in the Deleted Items folder.

Deleting an Item

(1) In an Outlook folder, choose the item you want to delete.

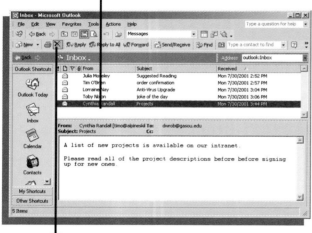

(2) Click Delete on the toolbar.

> ✋ **CAUTION:** When you delete an item from within Outlook, you are not given a prompt asking if you are sure you want to delete the item. Outlook just goes ahead and deletes it. Before deleting an item, open it to make sure it is the one you actually want to delete. If you delete an item by mistake, choose Undo from the Edit menu before continuing with any other tasks.

> 🧭 **SEE ALSO:** For information on managing the Inbox Folder, such as deleting unneeded messages, see "Managing the Inbox Folder" on page 51.

Emptying the Deleted Items Folder

(1) In the Outlook Bar, right-click the Deleted Items folder.

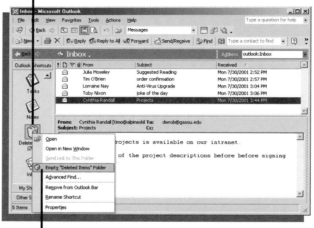

(2) Choose Empty "Deleted Items" Folder.

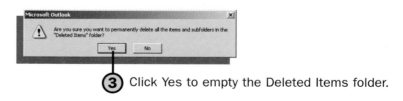

(3) Click Yes to empty the Deleted Items folder.

> 👆 **TRY THIS!** To set up Outlook to empty the Deleted Items folder when you exit Outlook, choose Options from the Tools menu. Click the Other tab, then select Empty The Deleted Items Folder Upon Exiting. Click OK.

Creating a Journal

Outlook Journal keeps track of when you worked on something in Outlook or in a supported application, such as Microsoft Word or Microsoft Access. The Journal keeps a timeline view of these actions and keeps track of conversations or other events you perform. You can configure the Journal to record activities you perform on an item, such as creating an e-mail message or updating a specific contact.

Keep a Journal

(1) In Outlook choose Options from the Tools menu.

> **SEE ALSO:** For information on setting which items and files get recorded in the Journal, see "Setting Contact and Journal Options" on page 228.

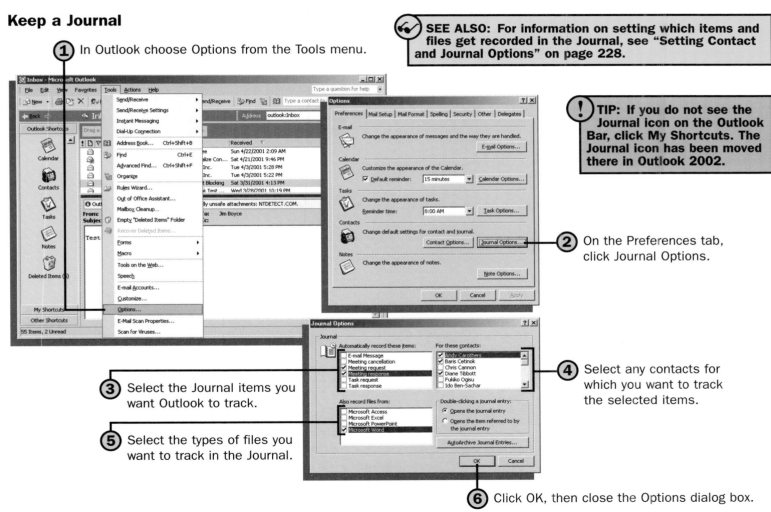

> **TIP:** If you do not see the Journal icon on the Outlook Bar, click My Shortcuts. The Journal icon has been moved there in Outlook 2002.

(2) On the Preferences tab, click Journal Options.

(3) Select the Journal items you want Outlook to track.

(4) Select any contacts for which you want to track the selected items.

(5) Select the types of files you want to track in the Journal.

(6) Click OK, then close the Options dialog box.

View the Journal

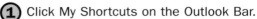

① Click My Shortcuts on the Outlook Bar.

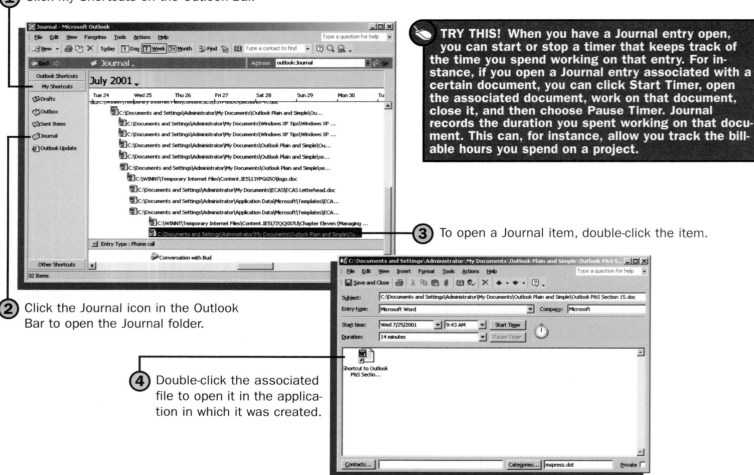

TRY THIS! When you have a Journal entry open, you can start or stop a timer that keeps track of the time you spend working on that entry. For instance, if you open a Journal entry associated with a certain document, you can click Start Timer, open the associated document, work on that document, close it, and then choose Pause Timer. Journal records the duration you spent working on that document. This can, for instance, allow you track the billable hours you spend on a project.

③ To open a Journal item, double-click the item.

② Click the Journal icon in the Outlook Bar to open the Journal folder.

④ Double-click the associated file to open it in the application in which it was created.

SEE ALSO: For information on using Journal entries to describe a telephone call, see "Recording Journal Entries" on page 130.

Using Outlook as a Desktop Manager

Much of the work you do with Outlook will be with Outlook items such as e-mail messages, appointments, tasks, and so on. In the average day, however, you probably work with folders and files outside of Outlook. For example, perhaps you need to create a new folder under My Documents to store documents for a particular project.

You can open drives, folders, and files from My Computer. You can also create new folders and files, move and copy files, delete files and remove folders, and perform other file and folder management tasks. If you're like most Microsoft Office users, however, you spend over 50% of your time in Outlook, so you might not want to exit Outlook to perform these tasks.

You can perform most folder and file management tasks right in Outlook. This saves you the trouble of minimizing or closing Outlook to open My Computer. While this might not seem like a major timesaver, the advantages extend beyond not having to open My Computer. For example, assume you have a large number of vCard files in a folder under My Documents and you want to add those contacts to your Contacts folder. You can open the folder right in Outlook and then simply drag the files to the Contacts icon on the Outlook Bar. You can perform similar tasks with other Outlook items. This section explains how to perform common folder and file tasks in Outlook, such as opening folders and files, copying files, and moving files.

Working with Drives and Folders

You can easily open your computer's drives—as well as folders stored on those drives—within Outlook. You can even open My Computer because it functions just like any other folder. You can open a folder to access a document stored there. Outlook doesn't show drives and file system folders by default, so to open them you need to use a different method than you would to open an Outlook folder.

Open a Drive

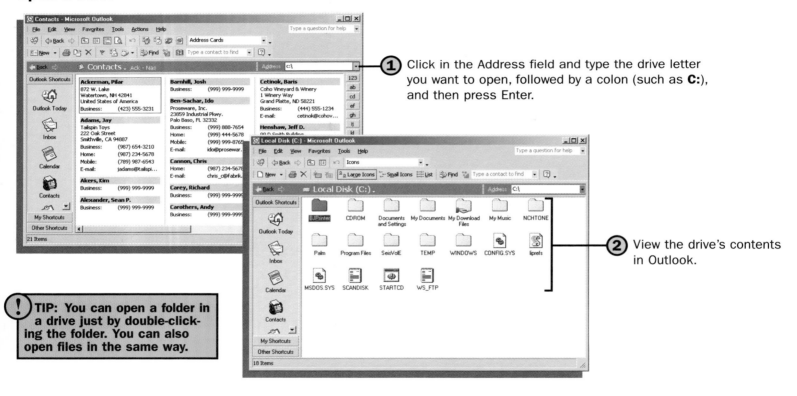

① Click in the Address field and type the drive letter you want to open, followed by a colon (such as **C:**), and then press Enter.

② View the drive's contents in Outlook.

> **! TIP:** You can open a folder in a drive just by double-clicking the folder. You can also open files in the same way.

> **TRY THIS!** You can open a shared network folder in the same way you open a local folder. Enter the path to the shared folder in the form *server**share*, where *server* is the name of the server sharing the folder and *share* is the name by which the folder is shared.

Open a Folder

SEE ALSO: For more information on Outlook's folders, see "Exploring Outlook's Folders" on page 9.

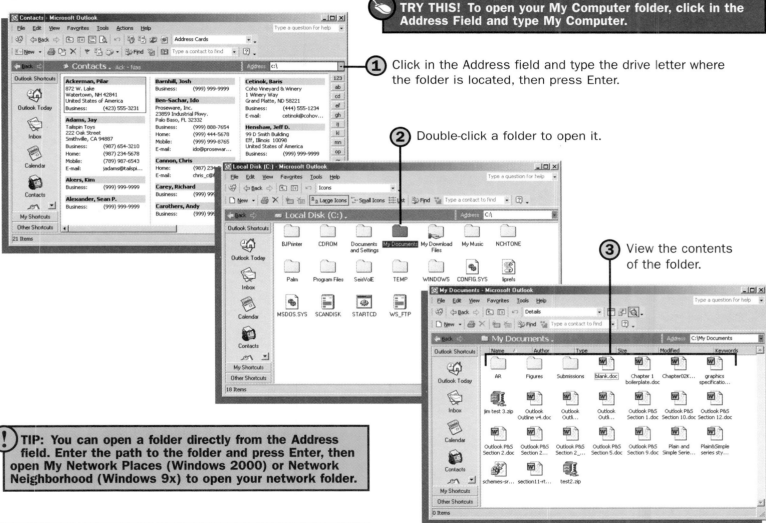

TRY THIS! To open your My Computer folder, click in the Address Field and type My Computer.

(1) Click in the Address field and type the drive letter where the folder is located, then press Enter.

(2) Double-click a folder to open it.

(3) View the contents of the folder.

TIP: You can open a folder directly from the Address field. Enter the path to the folder and press Enter, then open My Network Places (Windows 2000) or Network Neighborhood (Windows 9x) to open your network folder.

Working with Files

There are many file operations you can perform from within Outlook. For example, you can open document files created with other programs, including non-Office programs. You can also rename, copy, move, and delete files within Outlook. Performing these operations from Outlook saves you the trouble of exiting or minimizing Outlook to open My Computer and locate the file.

Open a File

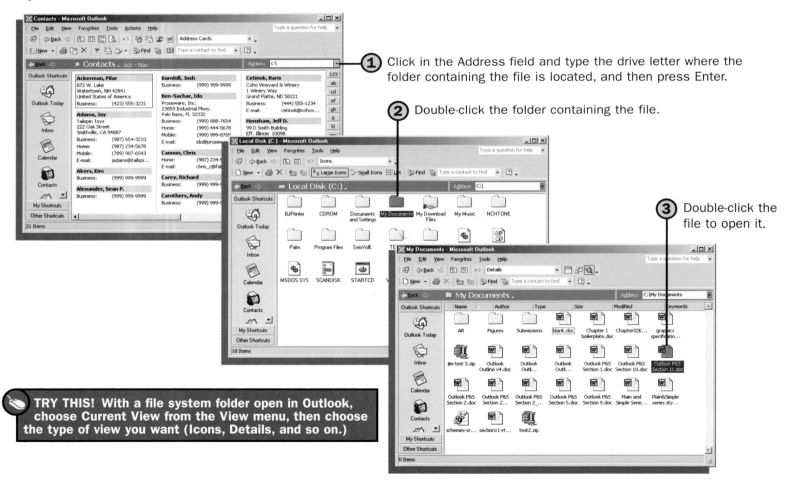

(1) Click in the Address field and type the drive letter where the folder containing the file is located, and then press Enter.

(2) Double-click the folder containing the file.

(3) Double-click the file to open it.

> **TRY THIS!** With a file system folder open in Outlook, choose Current View from the View menu, then choose the type of view you want (Icons, Details, and so on.)

Copy a File

① Use the Address field to open the folder where the file is located.

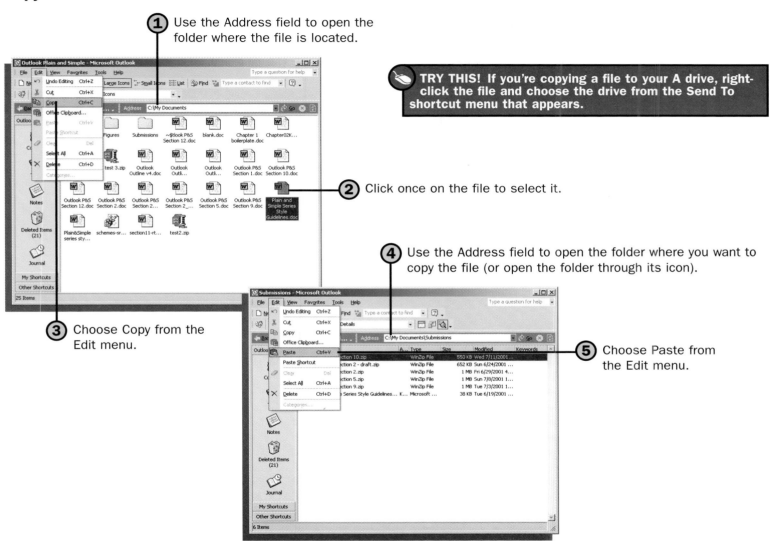

TRY THIS! If you're copying a file to your A drive, right-click the file and choose the drive from the Send To shortcut menu that appears.

② Click once on the file to select it.

③ Choose Copy from the Edit menu.

④ Use the Address field to open the folder where you want to copy the file (or open the folder through its icon).

⑤ Choose Paste from the Edit menu.

Delete a File

1 Use the Address field to open the folder where the file is located.

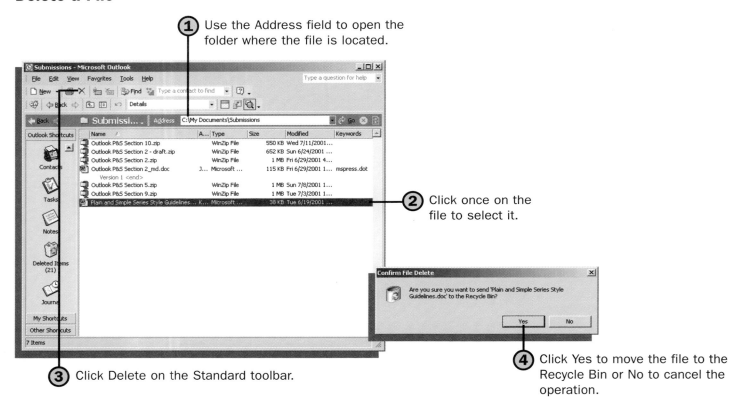

2 Click once on the file to select it.

4 Click Yes to move the file to the Recycle Bin or No to cancel the operation.

3 Click Delete on the Standard toolbar.

! TIP: If you prefer to bypass the Recycle Bin and delete the file immediately, hold down the Shift key when you click the Delete button on the toolbar.

Creating New Folders and Files

In addition to working with existing folders and files in Outlook, you can also create new folders and files. For example, you might want to create a new folder in My Documents to store the documents for a new project. Or maybe you want to create a new Word, Excel, or other Office document. You can perform these tasks from within Outlook.

Create a New Folder

① Use the Address field to open the folder where you would like to create the new folder.

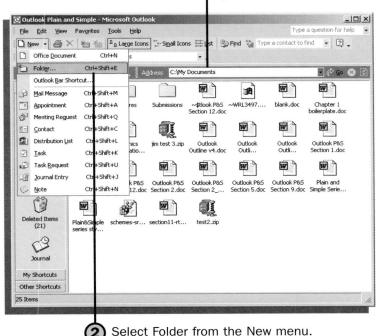

② Select Folder from the New menu.

TRY THIS! Right-click in a folder with Icon View selected and choose Other Settings to open the Format Icon View dialog box. Use this dialog box to select options that define the way icons are displayed, as well as other view options.

③ Type the name of the new folder.

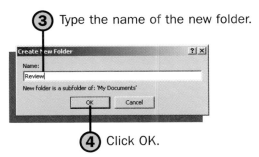

④ Click OK.

Create a New Office Document

① Use the Address field to open the folder where you want to create a new document.

② Click New on the Standard toolbar to open the New Office Document dialog box.

③ Click a tab to select the type of document you want to create.

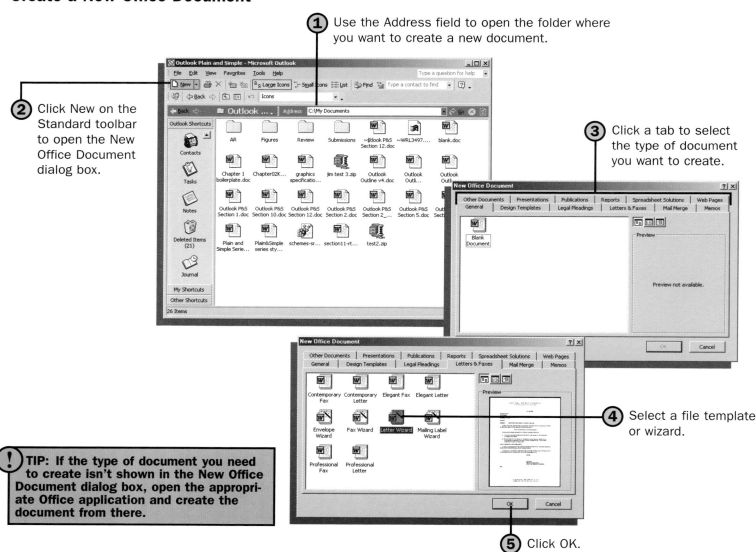

④ Select a file template or wizard.

⑤ Click OK.

> **TIP:** If the type of document you need to create isn't shown in the New Office Document dialog box, open the appropriate Office application and create the document from there.

Managing Your Outlook Files

Outlook stores your data in special types of files called *Outlook data files*. The main type of file is a personal folder file, or PST file. Outlook can store a complete set of Outlook folders—in addition to custom folders you add—in a PST file. For example, a particular PST might include Calendar, Inbox, and Tasks folders, along with custom folders.

In addition to storing data in PST files, Outlook can store data in an Exchange Server mailbox. The mailbox resides on the server rather than on your computer. When you open Outlook, the program contacts the server to display your data items. Open the Contacts folder, for example, and Outlook reads the data from the Contacts folder stored in your Exchange Server mailbox.

Sometimes your computer will not be able to communicate with the server because the server is off line or because you are working on a computer that isn't connected to the network. In these situations, Outlook can use a set of offline folders stored in an offline folder file, or OST file. Outlook stores data in the OST file and then synchronizes the changes with the mailbox the next time it is able to connect to the server.

This section explains how to perform several tasks with your Outlook data files, including adding new data files, using an existing file, and importing and exporting items. The section also explains how to back up and restore your Outlook data in a PST file and how to archive items.

Working with Outlook Data Files

Unless your only e-mail account is on an Exchange Server, Outlook creates a local data file for you when you set up your Outlook profile. When Exchange Server is the only account, Outlook stores all items in your Exchange Server mailbox. You can easily create a new PST file and then add or remove folders to it as needed.

Create a New Data File

1 In Outlook, choose Data File Management from the File menu to open the Outlook Data Files dialog box.

2 View the existing data files, if any, in the Data Files list.

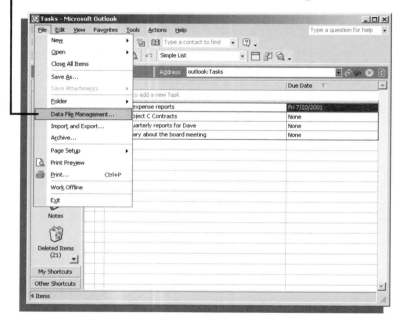

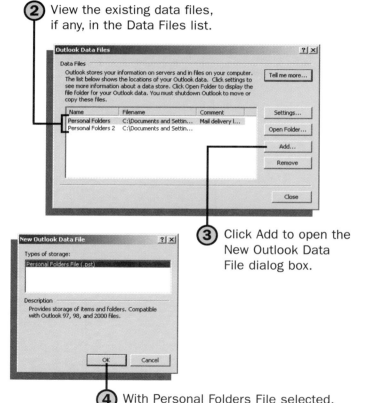

3 Click Add to open the New Outlook Data File dialog box.

4 With Personal Folders File selected, click OK to open the Create Or Open Outlook Data File dialog box.

> **SEE ALSO:** For more information on working with Outlook folders, see "Exploring Outlook's Folders" on page 9.

(5) Select a storage location for the file from the Save In drop-down list.

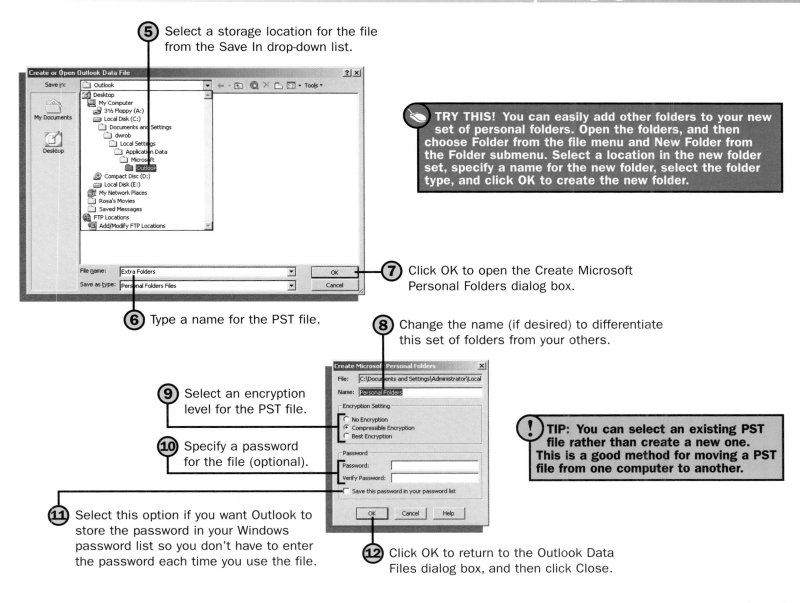

TRY THIS! You can easily add other folders to your new set of personal folders. Open the folders, and then choose Folder from the file menu and New Folder from the Folder submenu. Select a location in the new folder set, specify a name for the new folder, select the folder type, and click OK to create the new folder.

(7) Click OK to open the Create Microsoft Personal Folders dialog box.

(6) Type a name for the PST file.

(8) Change the name (if desired) to differentiate this set of folders from your others.

(9) Select an encryption level for the PST file.

(10) Specify a password for the file (optional).

TIP: You can select an existing PST file rather than create a new one. This is a good method for moving a PST file from one computer to another.

(11) Select this option if you want Outlook to store the password in your Windows password list so you don't have to enter the password each time you use the file.

(12) Click OK to return to the Outlook Data Files dialog box, and then click Close.

Importing and Exporting Items

Although you probably do much of your work in Outlook, occasionally you might want to move data into Outlook from other programs, or export data from Outlook to another program. Outlook makes it easy to import and export items. This section focuses on how to import and export items to and from PST files.

Import Items into Outlook

① Choose Import And Export from the File menu to open the Import And Export Wizard.

SEE ALSO: For more information on importing other types of data, see "Importing Data From Another Program" on page 15.

② Select Import From Another Program Or File, and click Next.

③ Select Personal Folder File, and click Next.

> **TIP:** Importing selected items from a PST file gives you an easy way to selectively copy Outlook items from one computer to another. Simply copy the PST file from the source computer to the destination computer, and then use the Import feature to import only those items you want on the other computer.

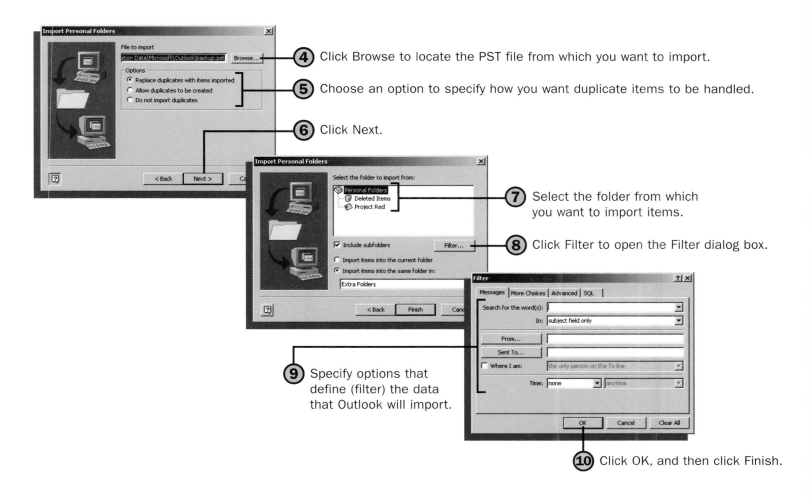

④ Click Browse to locate the PST file from which you want to import.

⑤ Choose an option to specify how you want duplicate items to be handled.

⑥ Click Next.

⑦ Select the folder from which you want to import items.

⑧ Click Filter to open the Filter dialog box.

⑨ Specify options that define (filter) the data that Outlook will import.

⑩ Click OK, and then click Finish.

Export Items from Outlook

(1) Choose Import And Export from the File menu to open the Import And Export wizard.

TIP: You don't have to export to a new PST file. You can export items to an existing PST file. This gives you a handy means of selectively backing up or archiving specific items. For example, you might back up selected items from your Exchange Server mailbox to a PST file on your local computer for safekeeping.

(2) Select Export To A File, and click Next.

(3) Select Personal Folder File, and click Next.

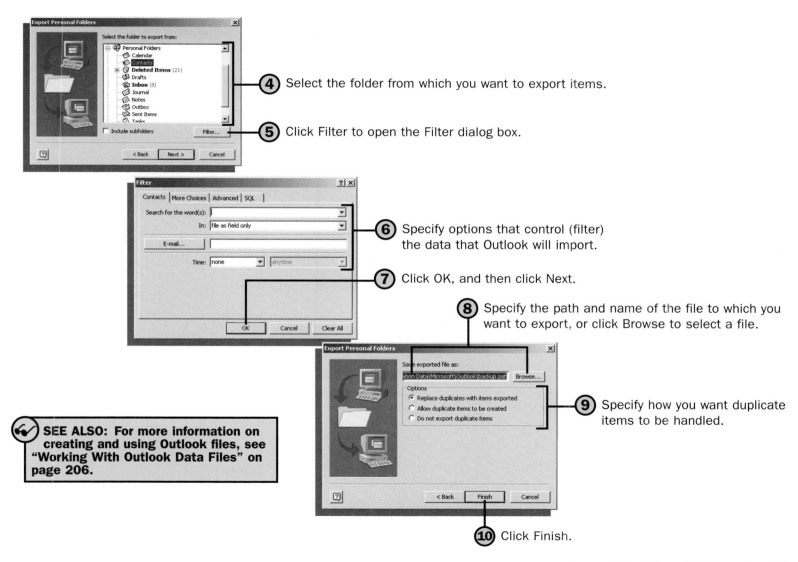

Select the folder from which you want to export items.

Click Filter to open the Filter dialog box.

Specify options that control (filter) the data that Outlook will import.

Click OK, and then click Next.

Specify the path and name of the file to which you want to export, or click Browse to select a file.

Specify how you want duplicate items to be handled.

SEE ALSO: For more information on creating and using Outlook files, see "Working With Outlook Data Files" on page 206.

Click Finish.

Backing Up and Restoring a Data File

If you use a set of personal folders in a PST file as your only data store or in addition to an Exchange Server mailbox, you should back up that PST file so your data will still be available if your computer experiences a problem such as a failed hard disk. Having the PST file backed up will allow you to restore the file and recover your data. You can back up smaller files to a floppy disk, but larger files must be backed up to your hard disk, a removable disk, or other media.

Back Up Outlook Data

1 Choose Data File Management from the File menu to open the Outlook Data Files dialog box.

> **! TIP:** You can use a backup program to back up the PST file if you don't want to copy it manually, or if you need to copy it to tape or CD-R/CD-RW. All versions of Windows include a Backup program in the Accessories menu that you can use to back up the file. CD-R and CD-RW drives usually include software you can use to copy files to a CD. The advantage to using a backup program to back up your PST file is that the backup program keeps track of the file's original location and will restore the file to that location by default. This saves you the trouble of trying to remember where the file was originally located.

2 Double-click the folder you want to back up to open the Personal Folders dialog box for the file.

3 Click in the Filename field, and use the arrow keys on the keyboard to view the whole path for the file. Make note of the file name and location.

4 Click OK and Close, and then close Outlook. You can now locate the file on your hard disk and manually create and store a backup copy in a safe location.

> **✋ CAUTION:** Don't back up your PST file to the same hard disk where it is currently located. If the disk fails, you will lose both copies of the file. Instead, back up the file to another hard disk if your computer has more than one or to another backup disk, CD, or tape.

> **! TIP:** Set up a regular backup schedule for your PST file, and make sure you back it up frequently to avoid losing any data.

Restore Outlook Data

1 Close Outlook, and then use My Computer to open the folder containing the backup file.

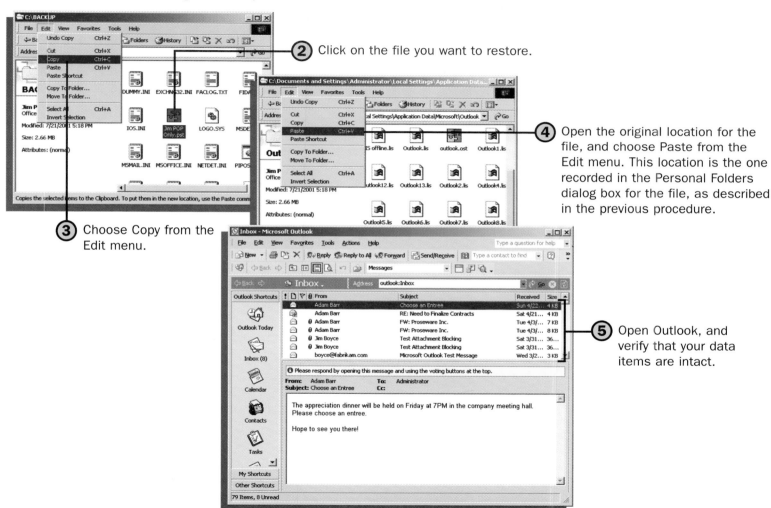

2 Click on the file you want to restore.

4 Open the original location for the file, and choose Paste from the Edit menu. This location is the one recorded in the Personal Folders dialog box for the file, as described in the previous procedure.

3 Choose Copy from the Edit menu.

5 Open Outlook, and verify that your data items are intact.

Archiving Outlook Data Files

Old messages, tasks, and other items have a tendency to pile up unless you clean them out. Outlook provides an AutoArchive feature that lets you specify how often Outlook should clean out old items, where it should place those items (or whether it should delete them), which items to move, and so on. If you choose to

archive items rather than delete them, Outlook places them in a PST file of your choosing. You can then recover them by opening that set of folders and copying the items back to your regular folders or by using the Import feature in Outlook to import from the archive file.

Set the AutoArchive Options

① Choose Options from the Tools menu to display the Options dialog box.

TIP: A network administrator can set retention policies that control your AutoArchive settings, preventing certain archive operations you might otherwise configure through your AutoArchive settings.

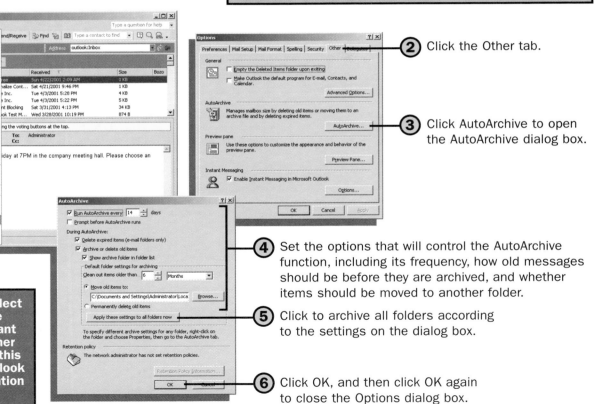

② Click the Other tab.

③ Click AutoArchive to open the AutoArchive dialog box.

④ Set the options that will control the AutoArchive function, including its frequency, how old messages should be before they are archived, and whether items should be moved to another folder.

⑤ Click to archive all folders according to the settings on the dialog box.

CAUTION: You should select the option Prompt Before AutoArchive Runs if you want to be able to control whether Outlook archives items. If this option is not selected, Outlook performs the archive operation without warning you.

⑥ Click OK, and then click OK again to close the Options dialog box.

Archive an Outlook Data File

1 Choose Archive from the File menu to open the Archive dialog box.

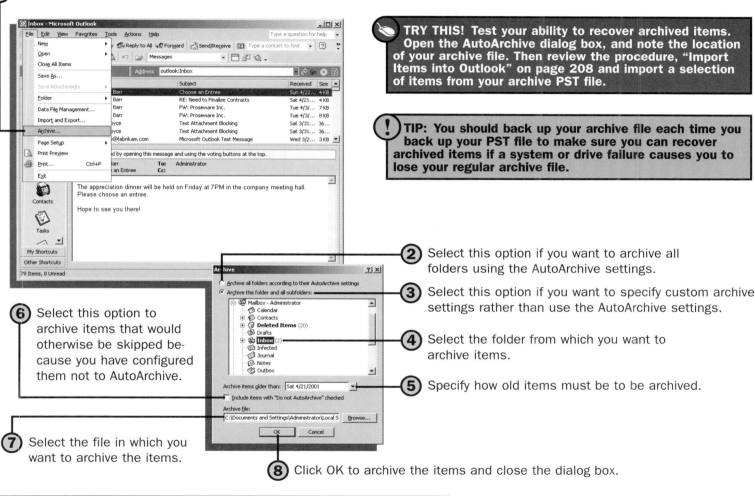

> **TRY THIS!** Test your ability to recover archived items. Open the AutoArchive dialog box, and note the location of your archive file. Then review the procedure, "Import Items into Outlook" on page 208 and import a selection of items from your archive PST file.

> **TIP:** You should back up your archive file each time you back up your PST file to make sure you can recover archived items if a system or drive failure causes you to lose your regular archive file.

2 Select this option if you want to archive all folders using the AutoArchive settings.

3 Select this option if you want to specify custom archive settings rather than use the AutoArchive settings.

4 Select the folder from which you want to archive items.

5 Specify how old items must be to be archived.

6 Select this option to archive items that would otherwise be skipped because you have configured them not to AutoArchive.

7 Select the file in which you want to archive the items.

8 Click OK to archive the items and close the dialog box.

> **SEE ALSO:** For more information on backing up PST files, see "Backing Up and Restoring a Data File" on page 212.

Working with Offline Folders

When you use an Exchange Server mailbox, Outlook stores your data in the mailbox. As long as the server is available, you can access your data. If the server is off line or you're not connected to the network, you can't continue working with your mailbox data unless you use a set of offline folders. Outlook uses the offline folders as a temporary storage location for your data until you can connect to the server once again. Then Outlook synchronizes any changes between the mailbox and the offline folders.

Enable Offline Folders

(1) Choose E-Mail Accounts from the Tools menu to open the E-Mail Accounts wizard.

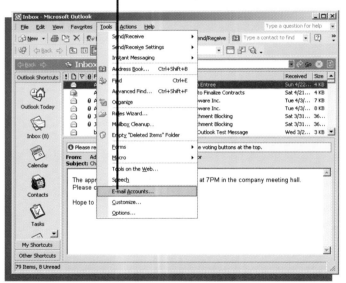

(!) TIP: You can either create a new OST file to store your offline folders or choose an existing OST file. If you choose an existing file, it must have been set up previously to work with your Exchange Server mailbox. You can't use an OST file that was set up for a different mailbox.

(2) Select View Or Change Existing E-Mail Accounts, and click Next.

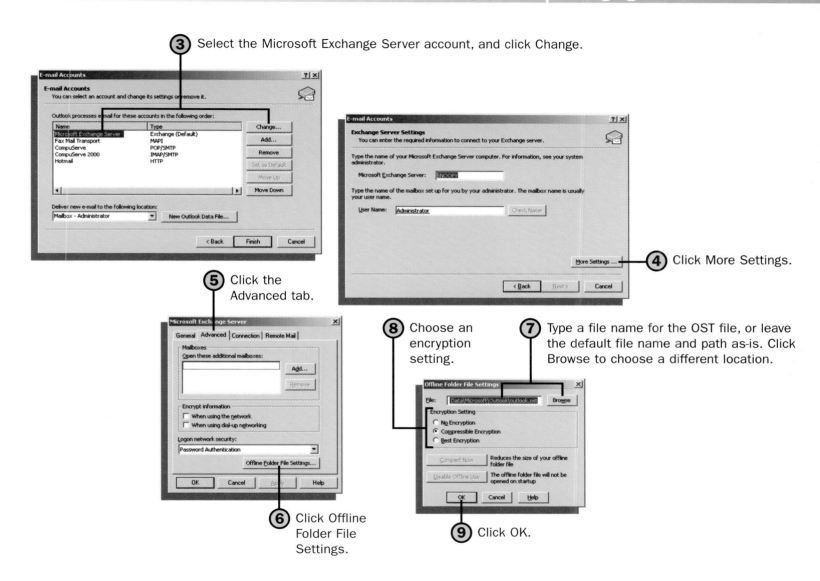

(3) Select the Microsoft Exchange Server account, and click Change.

(4) Click More Settings.

(5) Click the Advanced tab.

(8) Choose an encryption setting.

(7) Type a file name for the OST file, or leave the default file name and path as-is. Click Browse to choose a different location.

(6) Click Offline Folder File Settings.

(9) Click OK.

Synchronize Offline Folders

1 Choose Send/Receive from the Tools menu, and then choose Microsoft Exchange Server from the submenu.

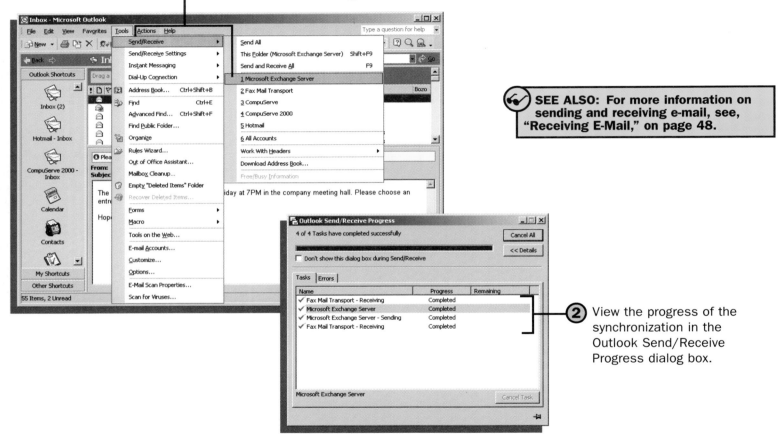

SEE ALSO: For more information on sending and receiving e-mail, see, "Receiving E-Mail," on page 48.

2 View the progress of the synchronization in the Outlook Send/Receive Progress dialog box.

Customizing Outlook

Although Microsoft Outlook can be used "out of the box," one of its finest features is its ability to be customized to look and work the way you work. For example, you can set up Outlook to sort incoming e-mail using rules. One rule, for instance, can store new messages from your team coordinator in a folder named "Team," while another rule can move junk mail to the Deleted Items folder when it arrives.

Microsoft Outlook can be customized a number of other ways. You can set up templates and choose formats for messages you create to customize outgoing mail messages. With Calendar, you can set up holiday schedules to match those recognized by your business or organization, set up your meeting schedule, and specify your work week. For example, if your work week differs from the traditional 8:00 to 5:00, Monday through Friday, you can change Outlook's Calendar views to match the days and hours you work.

You also can specify how Contact items are sorted and which items and files are recorded in the Journal. Finally, you can customize Outlook's toolbars, menus, and the Outlook Bar.

Customizing E-Mail Options

Outlook can help you manage your e-mail messages by applying rules to them. These rules tell Outlook where you want specific types of messages to be stored. For instance, if you want all messages from a specific user to be stored in a folder named "Project," you can set up a rule for that. You can also keep track of when messages that you send are delivered and read by their recipients. This is handy when you send a time-sensitive e-mail and you want to know when the recipients received and read the message.

Use Read and Delivery Receipts

1 Create a new e-mail message.

2 Click the Options button on the Standard toolbar.

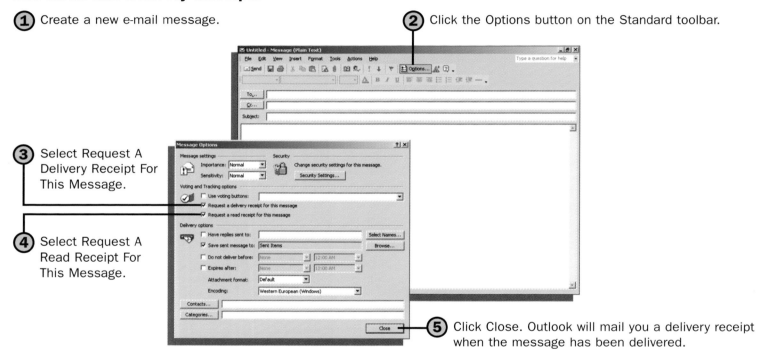

3 Select Request A Delivery Receipt For This Message.

4 Select Request A Read Receipt For This Message.

5 Click Close. Outlook will mail you a delivery receipt when the message has been delivered.

! **TIP: In the Message Options dialog box, you can set priority levels for an e-mail message. Click the Importance drop-down list, and select Low, Normal, or High. Low or High importance messages are sent at the same speed as Normal, but the recipient will see a symbol indicating the message's importance.**

TRY THIS! To set Outlook so all messages will have a delivery and read receipt, choose Options from the Tools menu and click E-Mail Options on the Preferences tab. Click Tracking Options, and select Read Receipt and Delivery Receipt.

Specify Rules for Handling Messages

(1) Click the Inbox icon on the Outlook Bar.

(2) Click the Organize button on the Standard toolbar.

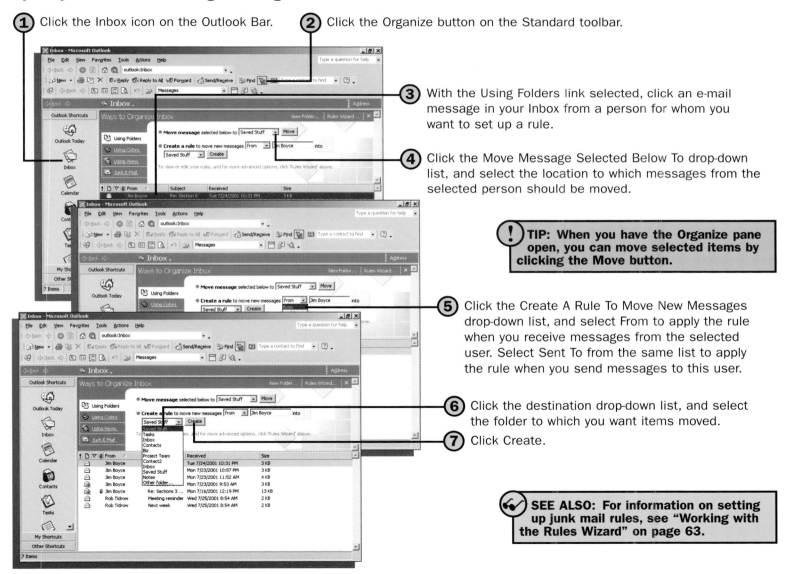

(3) With the Using Folders link selected, click an e-mail message in your Inbox from a person for whom you want to set up a rule.

(4) Click the Move Message Selected Below To drop-down list, and select the location to which messages from the selected person should be moved.

> **(!) TIP:** When you have the Organize pane open, you can move selected items by clicking the Move button.

(5) Click the Create A Rule To Move New Messages drop-down list, and select From to apply the rule when you receive messages from the selected user. Select Sent To from the same list to apply the rule when you send messages to this user.

(6) Click the destination drop-down list, and select the folder to which you want items moved.

(7) Click Create.

> **(✓) SEE ALSO:** For information on setting up junk mail rules, see "Working with the Rules Wizard" on page 63.

Choosing Message Formats

When you create new e-mail messages, you can specify the format in which the message should be created. The format you choose must be supported by the recipient of the message. Outlook also allows you to set up your environment so that all your messages use the same format. By default, the Plain Text format is used, but you can set Rich Text or HTML as the default.

Select a Format for the Open Message

SEE ALSO: For information on using Rich Text or HTML message formats, see "Formatting Message Text" on page 34.

1 Create a new message.

2 Choose a format from the Format menu:

- Choose Plain Text to create a message without formatting.

- Choose HTML to create a message with HTML support, such as embedded tables, inserted pictures, and live hyperlinks.

- Choose Rich Text to create a message with rich text formatting support, such as embedded objects, font specifications, and colored text.

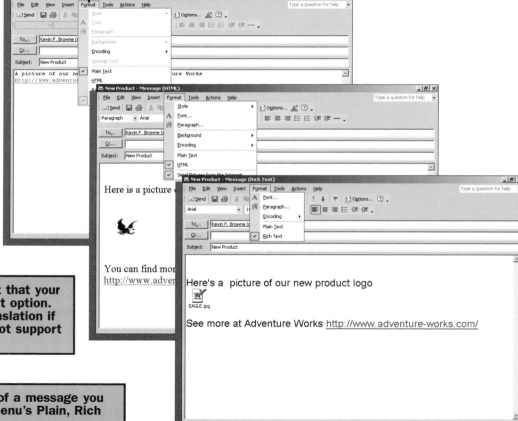

TIP: If you are not sure of the format that your recipient can read, use the Plain Text option. This ensures nothing is lost in the translation if your recipient's e-mail program does not support Rich Text or HTML messages.

TIP: You can change the formatting of a message you have received by using the Format menu's Plain, Rich Text, and HTML commands.

Select a Default Message Format

(1) With the Inbox icon selected on the Outlook Bar, choose Options from the Tools menu.

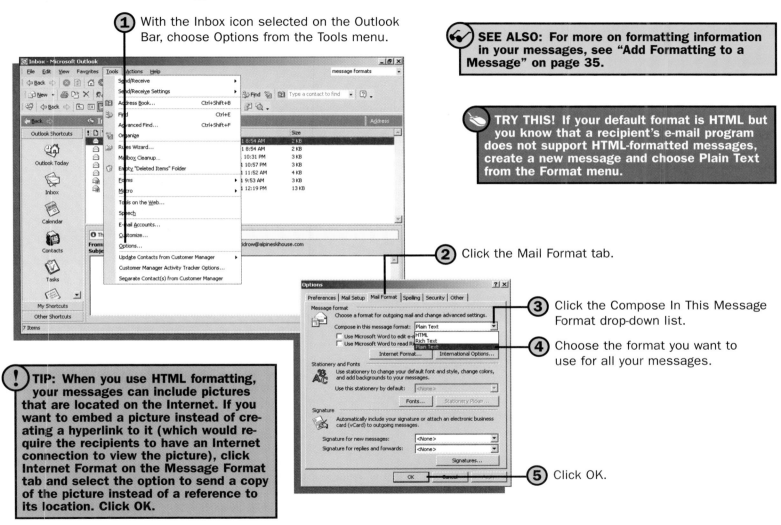

SEE ALSO: For more on formatting information in your messages, see "Add Formatting to a Message" on page 35.

TRY THIS! If your default format is HTML but you know that a recipient's e-mail program does not support HTML-formatted messages, create a new message and choose Plain Text from the Format menu.

(2) Click the Mail Format tab.

(3) Click the Compose In This Message Format drop-down list.

(4) Choose the format you want to use for all your messages.

(5) Click OK.

TIP: When you use HTML formatting, your messages can include pictures that are located on the Internet. If you want to embed a picture instead of creating a hyperlink to it (which would require the recipients to have an Internet connection to view the picture), click Internet Format on the Message Format tab and select the option to send a copy of the picture instead of a reference to its location. Click OK.

Using Message Templates

A message template (called stationery in Outlook 2002) is a predefined format you can use for your new messages. When you create a message, you can choose stationery that includes boilerplate text, formatting, and other features. For example, you can create stationery with your company's name and address appearing at the top of each message, and your company logo appearing at the bottom of each message.

Create a Message Template

(1) With the Inbox icon selected on the Outlook Bar, choose Options from the Tools menu.

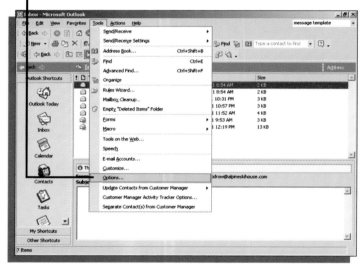

(2) Click the Mail Format tab.

(3) Click the Compose In This Message Format drop-down list, and select HTML.

(4) Click the Stationery Picker button.

(5) Click New.

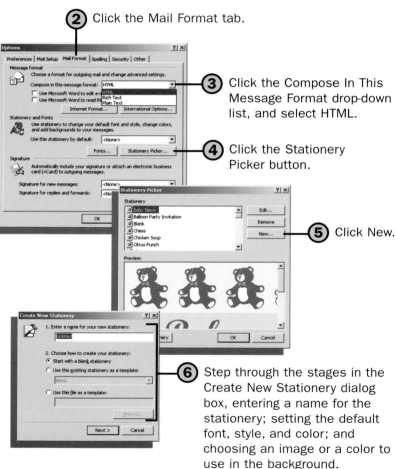

(6) Step through the stages in the Create New Stationery dialog box, entering a name for the stationery; setting the default font, style, and color; and choosing an image or a color to use in the background.

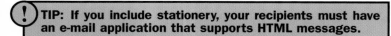

TRY THIS! In the Create New Stationery dialog box, select Use This Existing Stationery As A Template. Now you can simplify the creation process by basing your new stationery on an existing one.

TIP: If you include stationery, your recipients must have an e-mail application that supports HTML messages.

Use a Message Template

① With the Inbox icon selected on the Outlook Bar, choose New Mail Message Using from the Actions menu.

SEE ALSO: For more information on HTML stationery, see "Working with HTML Stationery" on page 37.

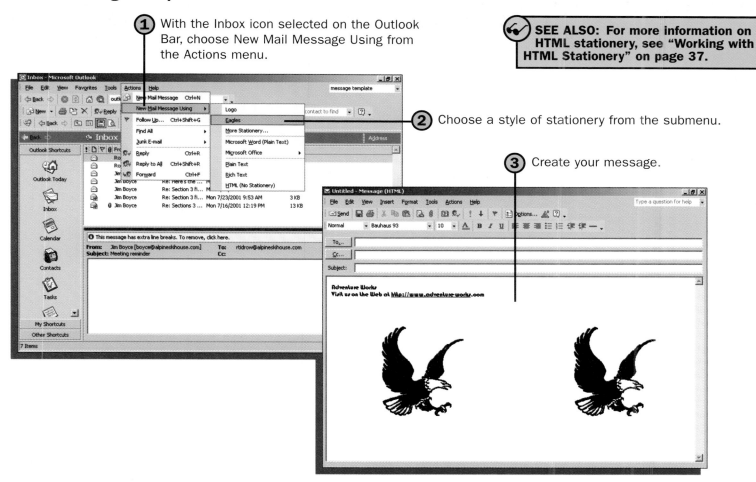

② Choose a style of stationery from the submenu.

③ Create your message.

TIP: If you want to pick different stationery from the New Mail Message Using submenu, choose More Stationery. In the Stationery Picker dialog box, choose the stationery you want and click OK.

Setting Calendar Options

Outlook enables you to change the way Calendar works. You can change the default Monday–Friday work week to one that is specific to your schedule (perhaps you work Wednesday–Saturday). You also can set up holidays that are not traditionally observed in the United States.

Describe the Work Week

1 With the Calendar icon selected on the Outlook Bar, choose Options from the Tools menu.

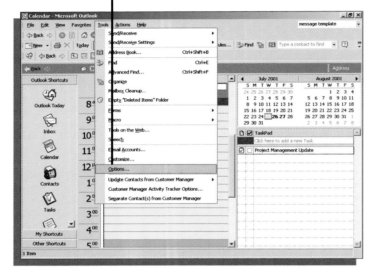

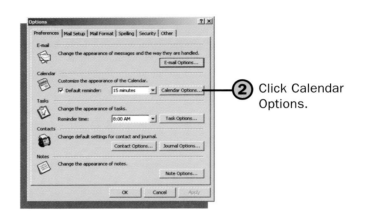

2 Click Calendar Options.

3 Select the days of the week that you work on.

4 Click the Start Time drop-down list, and select the time your work day begins. Do the same in the End Time list for the end of your work day.

5 Click OK.

TRY THIS! Change your work hours to begin at 10:00 P.M. and end at 7:00 A.M. Click the Calendar icon on the Outlook Bar and click the Day View button on the Standard toolbar. Notice how the 10–7 range is colored as your work day hours.

TIP: You can specify which day of the week is the first day for you. Click the First Day Of Week drop-down list, and click a day.

Add Holidays

(1) With the Calendar icon selected on the Outlook Bar, choose Options from the Tools menu.

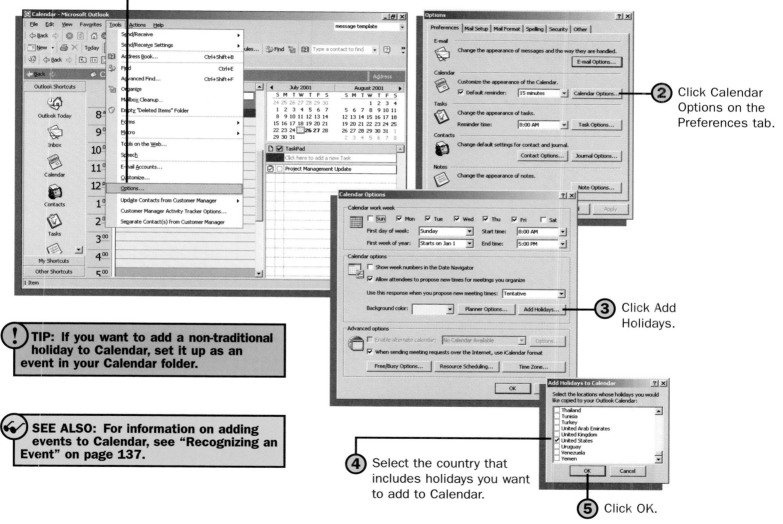

(2) Click Calendar Options on the Preferences tab.

(3) Click Add Holidays.

(4) Select the country that includes holidays you want to add to Calendar.

(5) Click OK.

TIP: If you want to add a non-traditional holiday to Calendar, set it up as an event in your Calendar folder.

SEE ALSO: For information on adding events to Calendar, see "Recognizing an Event" on page 137.

Setting Contact and Journal Options

You can set Outlook Contact options so that names in your Contacts folder are sorted in a way that suits your working style, such as by last name or by first name. You can also select which items get recorded in the Journal.

Describe How Contact Names Are Sorted

(1) With the Contacts icon selected on the Outlook Bar, choose Options from the Tools menu.

SEE ALSO: For information on using contacts, see "Working with Contacts" on page 105.

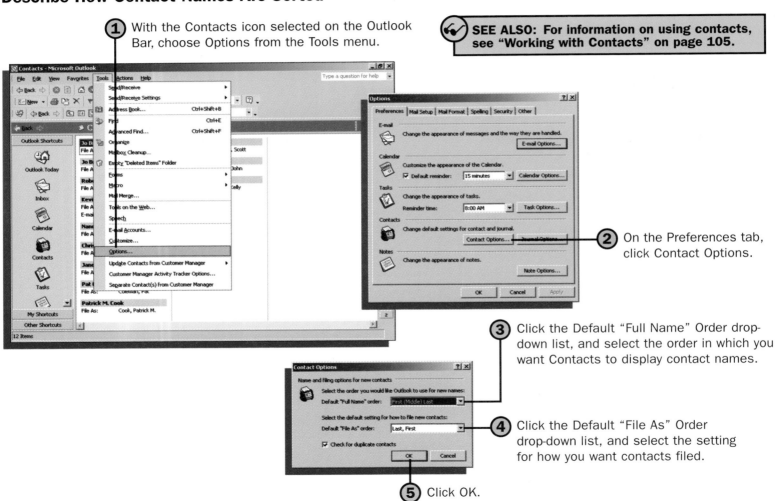

(2) On the Preferences tab, click Contact Options.

(3) Click the Default "Full Name" Order drop-down list, and select the order in which you want Contacts to display contact names.

(4) Click the Default "File As" Order drop-down list, and select the setting for how you want contacts filed.

(5) Click OK.

Select What Gets Recorded in the Journal

(1) With the Journal icon selected on the Outlook Bar, choose Options from the Tools menu.

SEE ALSO: For more information about Journal, see "Recording Journal Entries" on page 130.

TIP: To limit the amount of information Journal tracks, clear some of the settings in the Also Record Files From list. For instance, if you do not use Microsoft Access for critical data storage, clear the Microsoft Access option.

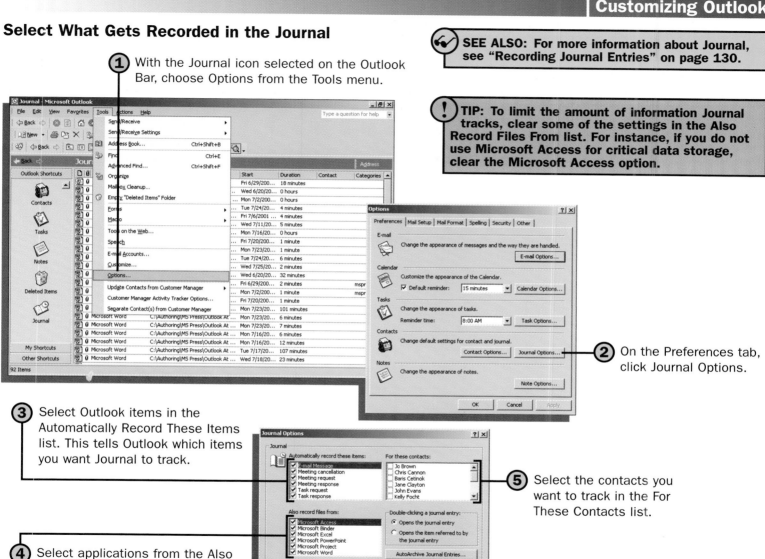

(2) On the Preferences tab, click Journal Options.

(3) Select Outlook items in the Automatically Record These Items list. This tells Outlook which items you want Journal to track.

(5) Select the contacts you want to track in the For These Contacts list.

(4) Select applications from the Also Record Files From list. This tells Outlook which program activity you want Journal to track.

(6) Click OK.

Customizing the Outlook Bar

The Outlook Bar includes icons you click to quickly open an Outlook folder. You can customize the Outlook Bar in several ways, by turning it off when you want more room to see items in Outlook, or by adding a shortcut group to the icons displayed in the bar.

Show or Hide the Outlook Bar

① Click on View on the menu bar to show the View menu.

② The Outlook Bar option displays with a check mark next to it if the Outlook Bar is currently displaying. The command works as a toggle: select Outlook Bar to hide it, and select it again to show it.

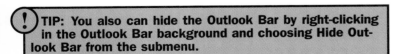

TIP: You also can hide the Outlook Bar by right-clicking in the Outlook Bar background and choosing Hide Outlook Bar from the submenu.

 SEE ALSO: To learn more about the Outlook Bar, see "Use the Outlook Bar" on page 9.

Add a Shortcut Group to the Outlook Bar

(1) Right-click the Outlook Bar background.

(2) Choose Add New Group from the submenu.

TRY THIS! Add several shortcut groups to help you access Outlook items you use often. For instance, first create a folder in which you store contacts that belong to a project team. Display the Folder List, and drag that folder to the shortcut group to create an icon there. When you want to open that folder, click its icon on the shortcut group.

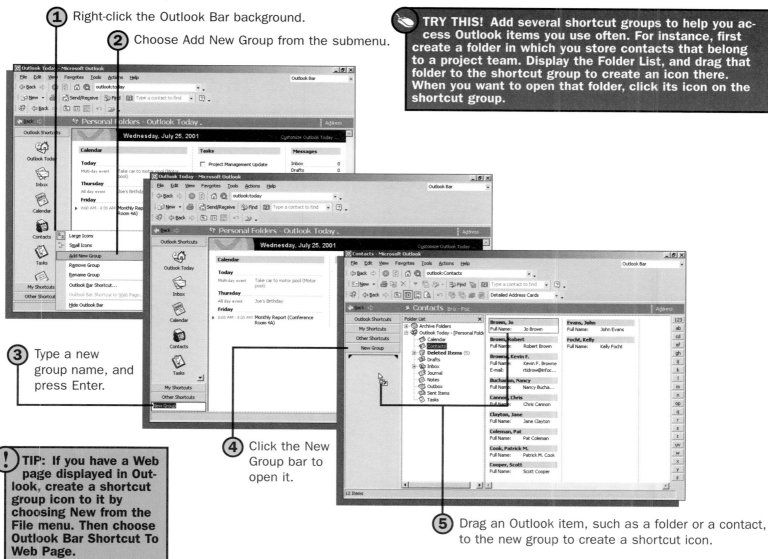

(3) Type a new group name, and press Enter.

TIP: If you have a Web page displayed in Outlook, create a shortcut group icon to it by choosing New from the File menu. Then choose Outlook Bar Shortcut To Web Page.

(4) Click the New Group bar to open it.

(5) Drag an Outlook item, such as a folder or a contact, to the new group to create a shortcut icon.

Customizing the Outlook Toolbars

Outlook includes several toolbars that contain dozens of toolbar buttons. Most users, however, use only a handful of toolbar buttons during any given Outlook session. Outlook enables you to remove or add toolbar buttons, and add or remove an entire toolbar.

Add or Remove a Toolbar

(1) Choose Toolbars from the View menu.

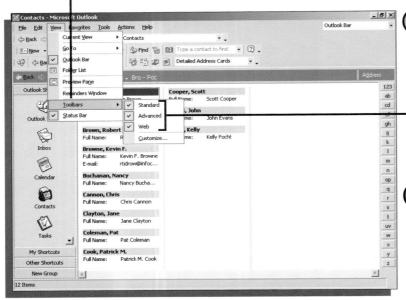

TIP: To quickly remove a toolbar, right-click a blank area on the toolbar and choose its name from the submenu.

(2) If a toolbar is displaying, it will have a check mark next to it. Select the toolbar to hide it. Select a non-checked toolbar to display it.

TRY THIS! To move a toolbar, click and hold the shaded bar at its left end and drag it to a different location.

CAUTION: Be selective when choosing the number of buttons you add to a toolbar. Unless you use a high screen resolution and have a large monitor, Outlook may not be able to display all the toolbar buttons at once.

TIP: To quickly add or remove a button to a toolbar, click the Toolbar Options arrow at the far right end of the toolbar. Select Add Or Remove Buttons, and then select the name of the toolbar (such as Standard) you would like to edit. You can then add or remove buttons from the list that appears.

Create a New Toolbar

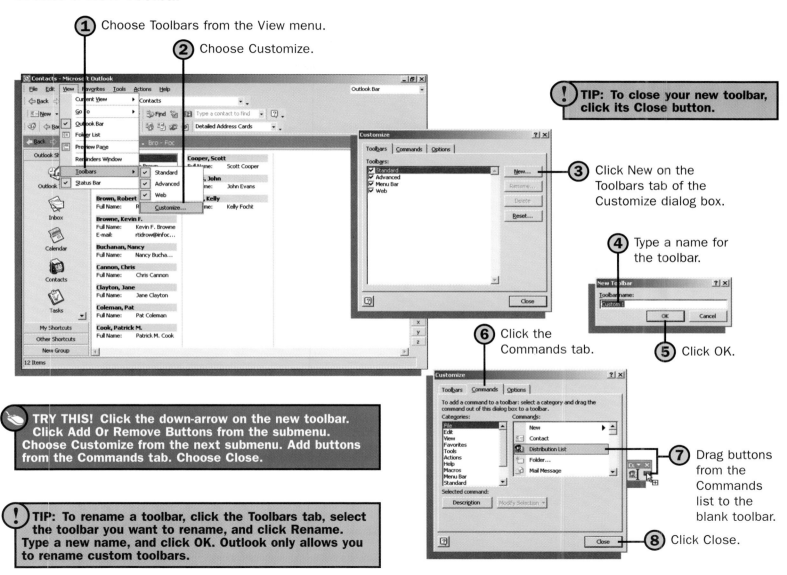

1. Choose Toolbars from the View menu.
2. Choose Customize.

TIP: To close your new toolbar, click its Close button.

3. Click New on the Toolbars tab of the Customize dialog box.

4. Type a name for the toolbar.

5. Click OK.

6. Click the Commands tab.

TRY THIS! Click the down-arrow on the new toolbar. Click Add Or Remove Buttons from the submenu. Choose Customize from the next submenu. Add buttons from the Commands tab. Choose Close.

7. Drag buttons from the Commands list to the blank toolbar.

8. Click Close.

TIP: To rename a toolbar, click the Toolbars tab, select the toolbar you want to rename, and click Rename. Type a new name, and click OK. Outlook only allows you to rename custom toolbars.

Using Office Tools with Outlook

Checking Spelling

Using the Office Clipboard

Using Handwriting Recognition

Using Speech Recognition

As a set of bundled programs, Microsoft Office includes several features that you can use in many or all of the programs. You can use the Office spell checker to check your spelling in Outlook items such as e-mail messages, appointments, and notes. The dictionary in Office lets you add words and customize the dictionary in other ways.

The Office Clipboard expands on the capabilities offered by the Windows Clipboard, allowing you to copy and move data between documents, Outlook items, and even different programs. Unlike the Windows Clipboard that supports only one item at a time, the Office Clipboard can store up to 24 different items at one time. This makes it much easier to move data around between multiple items and documents.

Another area in which Office provides a set of common tools is data input. The speech recognition features in Office make it possible for you to enter text, select commands, and perform other tasks with spoken commands rather than with the mouse or the keyboard. Speech recognition can be a very handy feature for people with physical handicaps, but it can also be useful for those who are simply not very adept at using the keyboard or the mouse. Office's handwriting recognition features allow you to use alternative input devices such as a digitizing tablet.

This section shows you how to use, within Outlook, the most common tools included with Office, including a spelling checker, the Office Clipboard, and speech and handwriting recognition.

Checking Spelling

Incorrect spelling in documents and e-mail messages can have a negative impact on how others perceive you and your work, so checking and correcting your spelling can be particularly important. Microsoft Office includes a spell checker you can use to check your spelling in Outlook. You can also use Office's AutoCorrect feature, which corrects text as you type it and can save you the trouble of performing a separate spelling check.

Customize AutoCorrect

① In Outlook, choose Options from the Tools menu to open the Options dialog box.

> **TRY THIS!** You can use AutoCorrect to speed up entering text that you use often. Rather than type the text, create an AutoCorrect entry for the text. For example, create an AutoCorrect entry that changes "cp" to "Control Panel." Whenever you want to type "Control Panel," just type "cp" instead and AutoCorrect will insert the text for you.

② Click the Spelling tab.

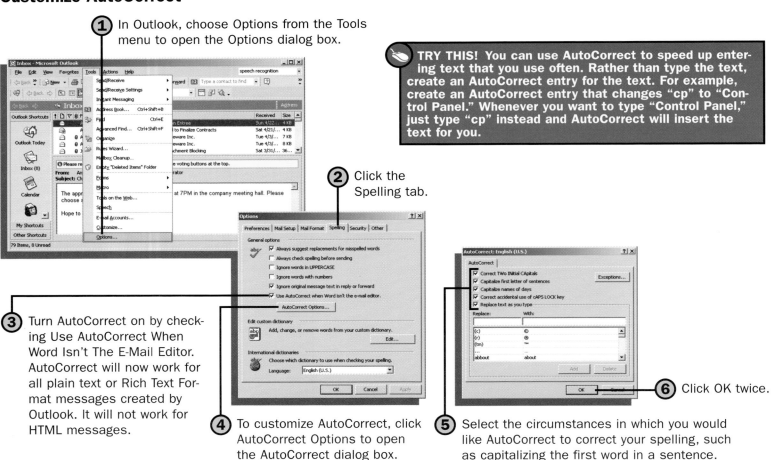

③ Turn AutoCorrect on by checking Use AutoCorrect When Word Isn't The E-Mail Editor. AutoCorrect will now work for all plain text or Rich Text Format messages created by Outlook. It will not work for HTML messages.

④ To customize AutoCorrect, click AutoCorrect Options to open the AutoCorrect dialog box.

⑤ Select the circumstances in which you would like AutoCorrect to correct your spelling, such as capitalizing the first word in a sentence.

⑥ Click OK twice.

Check Your Spelling

(1) In an Outlook item, type some misspelled text.

(2) Choose Spelling from the Tools menu.

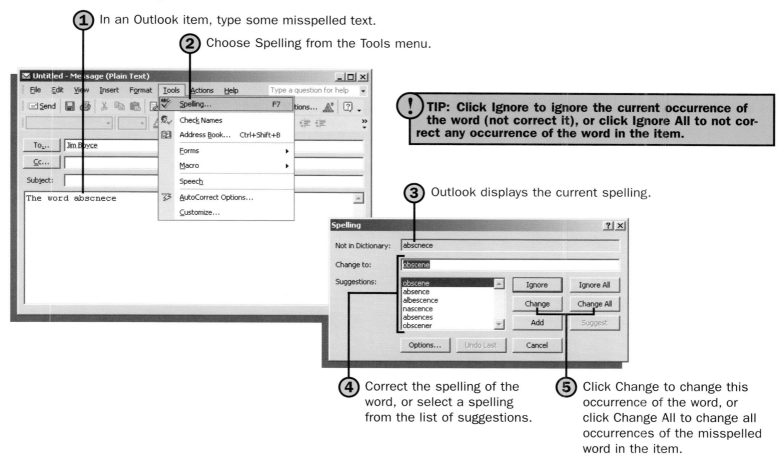

TIP: Click Ignore to ignore the current occurrence of the word (not correct it), or click Ignore All to not correct any occurrence of the word in the item.

(3) Outlook displays the current spelling.

(4) Correct the spelling of the word, or select a spelling from the list of suggestions.

(5) Click Change to change this occurrence of the word, or click Change All to change all occurrences of the misspelled word in the item.

Using the Office Clipboard ⊕ NEW FEATURE

The Office Clipboard allows you to copy or move data from one document to another, even if the documents are created with different Office programs. It supports up to 24 different items at one time. The Office Clipboard works as an extension of the Windows Clipboard, so the same operations (Cut, Copy, and Paste) apply to both clipboards.

Copy and Paste an Item

(1) Open the form from which you want to copy the item.

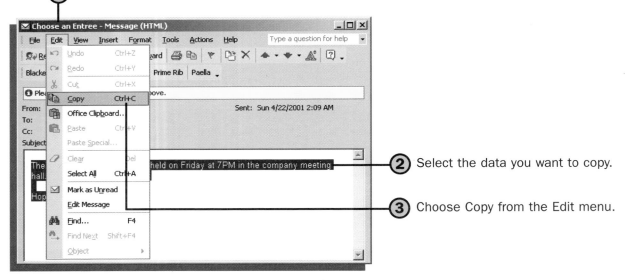

(2) Select the data you want to copy.

(3) Choose Copy from the Edit menu.

> **(!) TIP:** You can also use the Office Clipboard to cut and paste data. Follow the same procedure as when copying data, but choose Cut from the Edit menu. The data selection in the first object will be deleted once it has been copied to the second object.

(4) Open the form or document where you want to paste the data.

TIP: You can right-click an item in the Office Clipboard and then choose Delete to remove the item from the Clipboard.

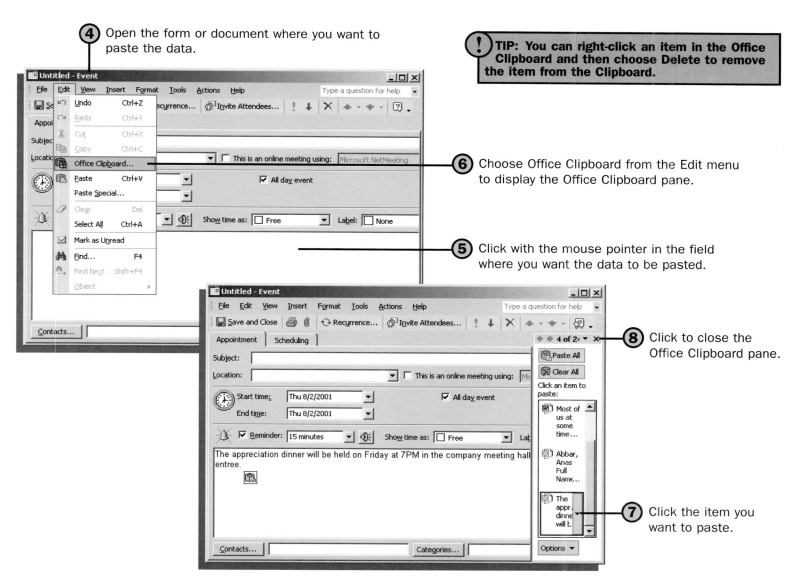

(6) Choose Office Clipboard from the Edit menu to display the Office Clipboard pane.

(5) Click with the mouse pointer in the field where you want the data to be pasted.

(8) Click to close the Office Clipboard pane.

(7) Click the item you want to paste.

Using Handwriting Recognition

Office includes handwriting recognition that lets you use a mouse, electronic stylus, or other pointing or drawing device to enter text instead of using the keyboard. As you write, Office translates the strokes into text.

SEE ALSO: For more information on adding handwriting recognition to Office if it is not currently installed, see "Install Speech Recognition" on page 242.

Write Text by Hand

(1) In an Outlook item, click where you want the text inserted.

(2) Click Handwriting on the Language Bar.

(3) Choose Write Anywhere.

(4) Write anywhere on the screen.

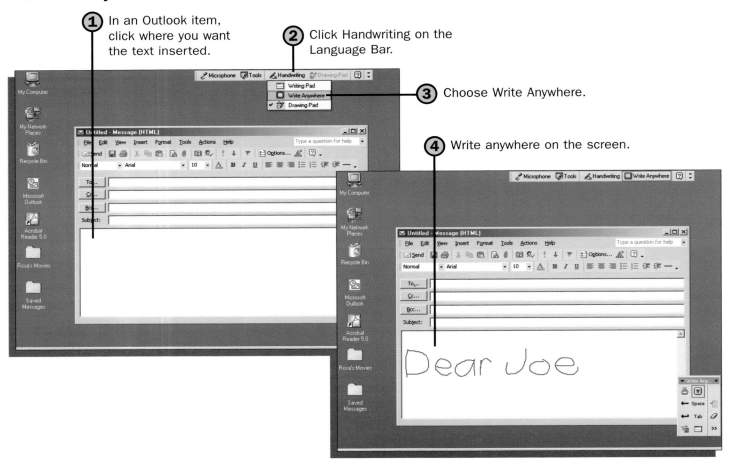

5 Office converts your writing to text at the insertion point.

6 Click Handwriting on the Language Bar.

7 Choose Writing Pad to open the Writing Pad.

Dear Joe

How are you?

8 Write in the Writing Pad.

Dear Joe

How are you?

9 Office converts the writing to text at the insertion point.

Using Speech Recognition

The speech recognition feature in Outlook lets you use a microphone and voice commands to select commands and enter text in Outlook. Before you can begin using speech recognition, however, you need to train the program to your voice for best results. This process includes setting microphone volume, training office to recognize your voice and speech patterns, and turning on the microphone.

Install Speech Recognition

(1) Log on as Administrator, open the Control Panel, and double-click the Add/Remove Programs icon.

(2) In the Currently Installed Programs list, select Microsoft Office XP Standard or Microsoft Office XP Professional (whichever is installed) and click Change.

(3) Select Add Or Remove Features, and then click Next.

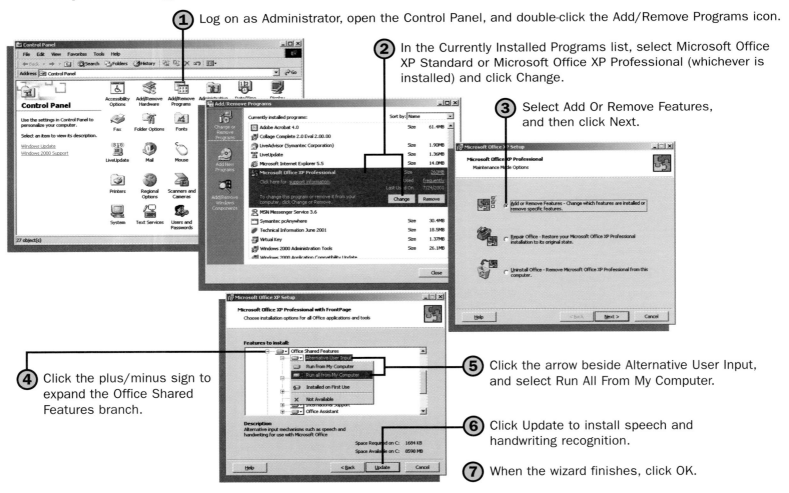

(4) Click the plus/minus sign to expand the Office Shared Features branch.

(5) Click the arrow beside Alternative User Input, and select Run All From My Computer.

(6) Click Update to install speech and handwriting recognition.

(7) When the wizard finishes, click OK.

Show the Language Bar

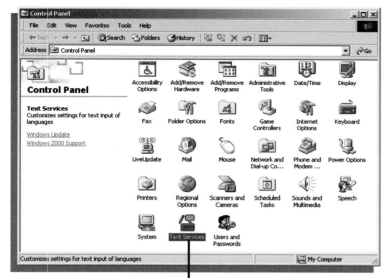

① Open the Control Panel, and double-click the Text Services icon to open the Text Services dialog box.

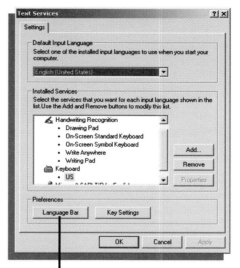

② Click Language Bar to open the Language Bar Settings dialog box.

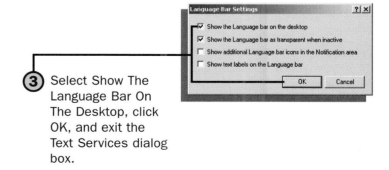

③ Select Show The Language Bar On The Desktop, click OK, and exit the Text Services dialog box.

> **! TIP: Right-click the Language Bar and choose Transparency to make the Language Bar transparent when it is not in use.**

Configure Speech Recognition

(1) In Outlook, click Microphone on the Language Bar, which turns on the microphone and starts the speech recognition training wizard.

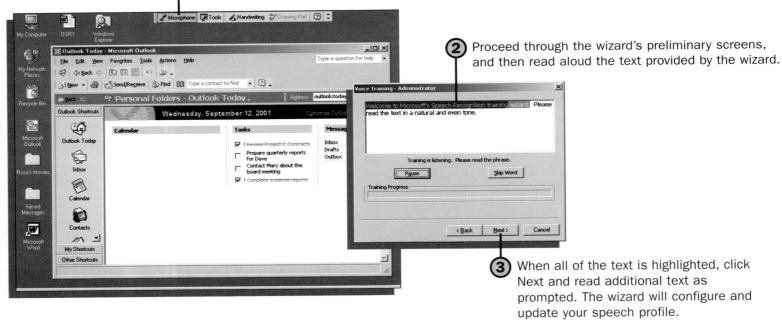

(2) Proceed through the wizard's preliminary screens, and then read aloud the text provided by the wizard.

(3) When all of the text is highlighted, click Next and read additional text as prompted. The wizard will configure and update your speech profile.

CAUTION: Microsoft's speech recognition tool can't distinguish when you're speaking to the computer or to someone in the room or on the phone. You should turn off the microphone when not dictating or issuing commands to avoid inadvertent changes to your documents.

TIP: Office includes several documents you can read to refine the speech recognition engine's ability to recognize your speech. Going through the entire set can take an hour or more, but it's time well spent.

TRY THIS! You can improve Office's speech recognition abilities with additional training. Open the Text Services icon in the Control Panel, select Speech Recognition, and click Properties. Click Train Profile, and follow the prompts provided by the wizard to read additional training text and further train Office to recognize your speech patterns.

Dictate Text

③ If the microphone is not currently turned on, click Microphone on the Language Bar.

① Open the item in which you want to insert the text through dictation.

④ Click Dictation on the Language Bar.

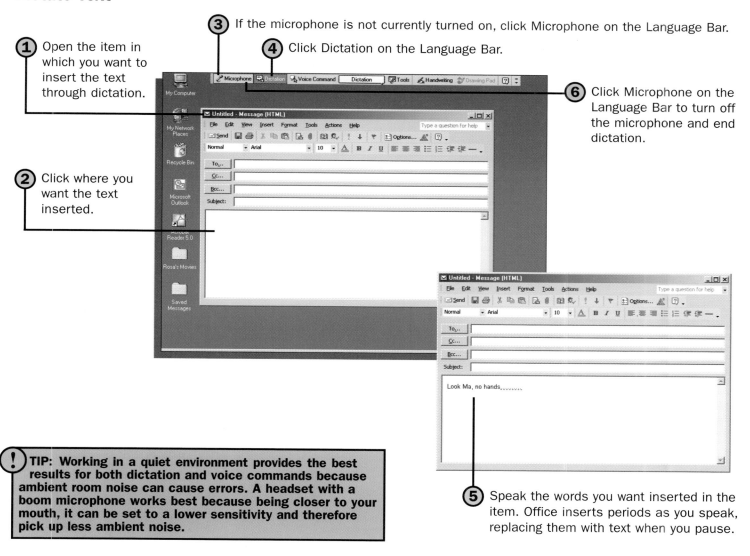

⑥ Click Microphone on the Language Bar to turn off the microphone and end dictation.

② Click where you want the text inserted.

⑤ Speak the words you want inserted in the item. Office inserts periods as you speak, replacing them with text when you pause.

> **! TIP:** Working in a quiet environment provides the best results for both dictation and voice commands because ambient room noise can cause errors. A headset with a boom microphone works best because being closer to your mouth, it can be set to a lower sensitivity and therefore pick up less ambient noise.

Issue Commands

(1) Click Microphone on the Language Bar to turn on the microphone.

(2) Click Voice Command on the Language Bar, or if dictation is currently on, say "Voice Command."

(4) Click Microphone on the Language Bar to turn off the microphone.

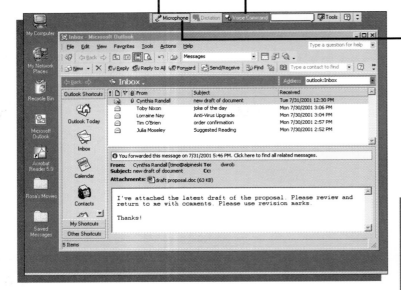

(3) Speak the menu name or command you want Outlook to execute. For example, say "File" to open the File menu, and then say "Print" to open the Print dialog box.

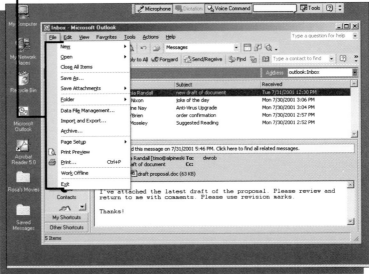

Index

Send feedback about this index to mspindex@microsoft.com.

O

P

priority levels
  of e-mail messages, 220
  of tasks, 154
profiles, 14, 73, 74–75
programs
  supporting attachments, 55
  using Journal to track activity in, 229
program windows, 6. *See also specific*
    windows
PST files. *See* personal folder files (PST files)
push-pin icons, 10

rules, 62–65, 220–21. *See also* filters
Rules Wizard, 62–65

About the Author

Jim Boyce is a former contributing editor and monthly columnist for *Windows Magazine*. Jim has authored and co-authored over 45 books about computer software and hardware and is a frequent contributor to *Winmag.com*, *Techrepublic.com*, and other technical publications. He has been involved with computers since the late seventies as a programmer and systems manager in a variety of capacities. He has a wide range of experience in the MS-DOS, Windows, Windows NT, Windows 2000, and UNIX environments. In addition to a full-time writing career, Jim is a founding partner and vice president of Minnesota Webworks, a Midwest-based Web development firm (*www.mnww.com*).

The manuscript for this book was prepared and submitted to Microsoft Press in electronic form. Text files were prepared using Microsoft Word 2002. Pages were composed by Microsoft Press using Adobe PageMaker 6.52 for Windows, with text set in Times and display type in ITC Franklin Gothic. Composed pages were delivered to the printer as electronic prepress files.

Cover Graphic Designer

Tim Girvin Design

Interior Graphic Designers

Joel Panchot, James D. Kramer

Interior Graphic Artists

Joel Panchot

Principal Compositor

Katherine Erickson, Carl Diltz

Principal Proofreader/Copy Editor

Rebecca Wendling

Indexer

Kari Kells

Your fast-answers, no jargon guides to Windows XP and Office XP

Get the fast facts that make learning the Microsoft® Windows® XP operating system and Microsoft Office XP applications plain and simple! Numbered steps show exactly what to do, and color screen shots keep you on track. *Handy Tips* teach easy techniques and shortcuts, while quick *Try This!* exercises put your learning to work. And *Caution* notes help keep you out of trouble, so you won't get bogged down. No matter what you need to do, you'll find the simplest ways to get it done with PLAIN & SIMPLE!

Microsoft Windows® XP Plain & Simple
ISBN 0-7356-1525-X

Microsoft Office XP Plain & Simple
ISBN 0-7356-1449-0

Microsoft Word Version 2002 Plain & Simple
ISBN 0-7356-1450-4

Microsoft Excel Version 2002 Plain & Simple
ISBN 0-7356-1451-2

Microsoft Outlook® Version 2002 Plain & Simple
ISBN 0-7356-1452-0

Microsoft FrontPage® Version 2002 Plain & Simple
ISBN 0-7356-1453-9

Microsoft Access Version 2002 Plain & Simple
ISBN 0-7356-1454-7

U.S.A.	$19.99
Canada	$28.99

microsoft.com/mspress

Target your problem and
fix it yourself—
fast!

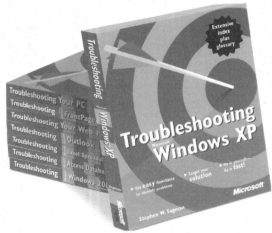

When you're stuck with a computer problem, you need answers right now. *Troubleshooting* books can help. They'll guide you to the source of the problem and show you how to solve it right away. Get ready solutions with clear, step-by-step instructions. Go to quick-access charts with *Top 20 Problems* and *Preventive Medicine* Find even more solutions with handy *Tips* and *Quick Fixes*. Walk through the remedy with plenty of screen shots. Find what you need with the extensive, easy-reference index. Get the answers you need to get back to business fast with *Troubleshooting* books.

Troubleshooting Microsoft® Office XP
ISBN 0-7356-1491-1

Troubleshooting Microsoft® Access Databases
(Covers Access 97 and Access 2000)
ISBN 0-7356-1160-2

Troubleshooting Microsoft® Access Version 2002
ISBN 0-7356-1488-1

Troubleshooting Microsoft Excel Spreadsheets
(Covers Excel 97 and Excel 2000)
ISBN 0-7356-1161-0

Troubleshooting Microsoft Excel Version 2002
ISBN 0-7356-1493-8

Troubleshooting Microsoft® Outlook®
(Covers Microsoft Outlook 2000 and Outlook Express)
ISBN 0-7356-1162-9

Troubleshooting Microsoft Outlook Version 2002
(Covers Microsoft Outlook 2002 and Outlook Express)
ISBN 0-7356-1487-3

Troubleshooting Your Web Page
(Covers Microsoft FrontPage® 2000)
ISBN 0-7356-1164-5

Troubleshooting Microsoft FrontPage Version 2002
ISBN 0-7356-1489-X

Troubleshooting Microsoft Windows®
(Covers Windows Me, Windows 98, and Windows 95)
ISBN 0-7356-1166-1

Troubleshooting Microsoft Windows 2000 Professional
ISBN 0-7356-1165-3

Troubleshooting Microsoft Windows XP
ISBN 0-7356-1492-X

Troubleshooting Your PC
ISBN 0-7356-1163-7

Microsoft
microsoft.com/mspress

Get a **Free**
*e-mail newsletter, updates,
special offers, links to related books,
and more when you*

register on line!

Register your Microsoft Press® title on our Web site and you'll get a FREE subscription to our e-mail newsletter, *Microsoft Press Book Connections.* You'll find out about newly released and upcoming books and learning tools, online events, software downloads, special offers and coupons for Microsoft Press customers, and information about major Microsoft® product releases. You can also read useful additional information about all the titles we publish, such as detailed book descriptions, tables of contents and indexes, sample chapters, links to related books and book series, author biographies, and reviews by other customers.

Registration is easy. Just visit this Web page and fill in your information:

http://www.microsoft.com/mspress/register

Microsoft®

Proof of Purchase

Use this page as proof of purchase if participating in a promotion or rebate offer on this title. Proof of purchase must be used in conjunction with other proof(s) of payment such as your dated sales receipt—see offer details.

Microsoft® Outlook® Version 2002 Plain & Simple
0-7356-1452-0

CUSTOMER NAME

Microsoft Press, PO Box 97017, Redmond, WA 98073-9830